BUILDING
STRUCTURES

BUILDING STRUCTURES

A conceptual approach

MALCOLM MILLAIS

E & FN SPON
An Imprint of Chapman & Hall

London · Weinheim · New York · Tokyo · Melbourne · Madras

Published by E & FN Spon, an imprint of Chapman & Hall, 2–6
Boundary Row, London SE1 8HN, UK

Chapman & Hall, 2–6 Boundary Row, London SE1 8HN, UK

Chapman & Hall GmbH, Pappelallee 3, 69469 Weinheim, Germany

Chapman & Hall USA, 115 Fifth Avenue, New York, NY 10003, USA

Chapman & Hall Japan, ITP-Japan, Kyowa Building, 3F, 2-2-1
Hirakawacho, Chiyoda-ku, Tokyo 102, Japan

Chapman & Hall Australia, 102 Dodds Street, South Melbourne,
Victoria 3205, Australia

Chapman & Hall India, R. Seshadri, 32 Second Main Road, CIT East,
Madras 600 035, India

First edition 1997
Reprinted 1997

© 1997 Malcolm Millais

Printed in Great Britain by the Alden Press, Osney Mead, Oxford

ISBN 0 419 21970 6

A catalogue record for this book is available from the British Library

CONTENTS

Introduction

This book is intended primarily for students of architecture, building and engineering or anyone else who needs to understand how building structures behave under load. This book explains the concepts that are required to achieve this understanding. This is done by developing a **conceptual approach** which enables the structural behaviour of any building to be understood. In developing this approach the complex process of **structural design** becomes clear.

The conceptual approach is presented by description and diagrams without the use of any mathematical ideas. The concepts are introduced by applying them to very simple structures then the understanding is deepened by the gradual introduction of more complex structures. In the penultimate chapter the structural behaviour of a number of existing buildings is explained by applying the conceptual approach.

Although few people give structures or structural design any thought they are surrounded by natural and designed structures. They live in them, travel in them, eat with them, sleep on them, they contribute to almost every aspect of their lives. In pre-historical times humans routinely used structures. Indeed, humans, animals and plants are themselves structures. Many animals build structures, for example birds' nests and spiders' webs. Most groups of pre-historical people regularly used structures in their daily lives. They built forms of housing and constructed boats, bridges, weapons and utensils. Each group tended to produce different designs for their artefacts, how this design process worked is not known, but eventually, **traditional** designs evolved. These traditional designs became fixed and part of the total culture of the group.

When groups of people became **civilisations**, that is an evolving rather than a static culture, new types of buildings were required, temples, storehouse, castles and so on. As the traditional methods no longer applied new technology and design processes were required. These did not always lead to success.

The central requirement for all design processes is to have a method of evaluating the outcome of the proposed design. In the traditional system there are no new problems and the performance of all artefacts is know from experience.

It is clear that early civilised builders thought deeply about their new buildings and often appeared to have clear ideas how their structures behaved. However the acquisition of the technical understanding of structural behaviour was slow and took a long time. It was only during the 19th century that the majority of this knowledge was discovered. This, of course, did not prevent builders constructing the most amazing structures, from pyramids to cathedrals and from catapults to water wheels.

The successful design of any structure requires a satisfactory answer to the following questions:

- **Is the structure strong enough?**
- **Is the structure stiff enough?**

Although this may be stating the obvious the answers may not be readily obtainable. Furthermore, before attempting to answer these questions, two further questions must be answered. These are:

- **What is the structure?**
- **What are the loads?**

The most common answer to the question **what is an (engineering) structure?** would be along the lines **something that carries loads**. Whilst there is truth in this it needs to be extended to the concept of carrying loads from one place to another, that is **transferring loads**. A simple example illustrates this. If people want to cross a stream then a plank could be used as a bridge. Whilst people are on the bridge their weight (**the loads**) are transferred from a point over the water, which cannot directly support them, to points on the banks which can.

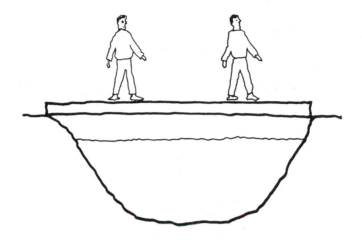

The purpose of the plank is to **transfer** the point of load application to the point of load support. The plank does this by acting as a **structure**. The diagram can be re-drawn showing the **applied loads** (the people), the **structure** (the plank) and the points of **load support** (the banks of the stream). It is more usual to call the load supports the **reactions**.

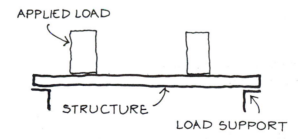

This load transferring function is the main purpose of all structures, whether it is a chair or the Forth railway bridge.

The role of structural design is to choose structures which will transfer the loads satisfactorily. However this is far easier said than done because there is a wide choice of structural forms and a range of structural materials which can be used. Furthermore demonstrating that the chosen structure will perform satisfactorily can often be a major task.

CHAPTER 1 *Loads and load paths*

A structure's main function is to **transfer loads**, but before considering the form of a structure a clear idea of what loads it has to transfer is required. In other words an answer to the question 'what are the loads ?'.

The sources of loads can be divided into **natural, useful** and **accidental** loads. Natural loads occur due to the existence of the structure in the world; useful loads are ones that occur from the purpose of the structure; and accidental loads occur from the misuse of the structure.

1.1   Natural loads

All structures on the surface of the Earth have to resist the force of **gravity**. This force acts through a body in a line joining the body with the centre of the earth (Fig.1.1).

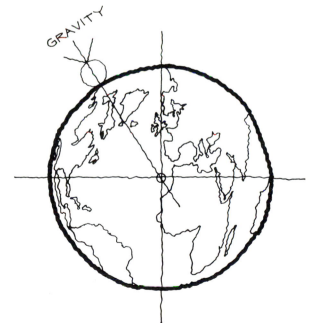

Fig.1.1

However at the local level these forces can be considered vertical (Fig.1.2).

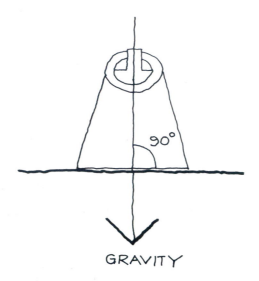

GRAVITY

Fig.1.2

So the first source of **natural** loads is the **gravity load**. Returning to the first example, the plank across the stream, this means that the plank has to transfer its own weight, usually called **self-weight**, to the support points (Fig.1.3).

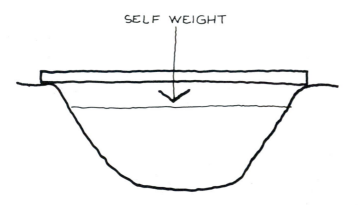

SELF WEIGHT

Fig.1.3

Due to regular and continuous changes in atmospheric pressure from place to place on the Earth's surface air flows across the surface of the Earth, that is wind. All structures built on the Earth's surface have to resist the forces from wind. Near to ground level the wind can be considered to blow along the surface. This not true for the whole of the atmosphere, as any pilot knows.

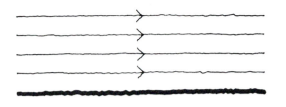

Fig.1.4

If an obstruction is placed in the path of the wind it alters the pattern of the wind flow. Which is why kites and 'planes fly and boats sail. If the object is fixed to the Earth's surface, like a building, the wind must flow around and over it.

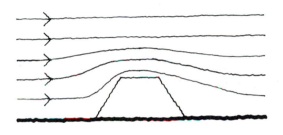

Fig.1.5

How the wind flows around and over an object depends both on the wind speed and the shape of the object. These are the basic questions considered by the complex subject known as **aerodynamics**. But the alteration in wind flow pattern will always cause a **force** on the interrupting object. It is important to notice equating the alteration of the wind flow pattern to a force or **wind load** is an intellectual feat which is intended to clarify the effect of the wind.

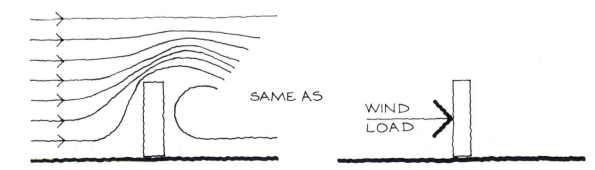

SAME AS

WIND LOAD

Fig.1.6

This can readily be felt by holding a flat object in the flow of a stream. This is why canoes and people can propel themselves through water.

Although the pattern of wind flow around buildings is complex (very!) the resulting loads from the alteration of wind flow are predominately at right angles to the surfaces of the building.

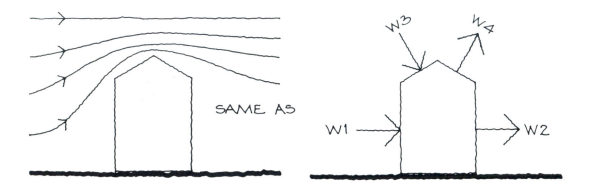

Fig.1.7

So, for the pitched roofed building shown in Fig.1.7, the alteration in wind flow will cause four loads. The loads W1 and W2 are on, and at right angles to the walls, and the loads W3 and W4 are on, and right angles to the roof slopes. These are **wind loads**.

As far as buildings and their supporting structures are concerned **gravity** and **wind** loads are two types of **natural** loads they always have to resist.

There are other natural loads that the structure may have to resist. These are **earth** or **water pressure, earthquakes, temperature,** and **ground movement**.

If the local shape of the Earth's surface is altered to site the building, as it often is, then parts of the building and its structure may be subject to loads from **earth pressure**. This because the natural surface has found a shape that is at rest (not over geological time of course). So, rather like the wind flow, an alteration will cause forces. If dry sand is piled into a heap, there is a maximum slope for the sides.

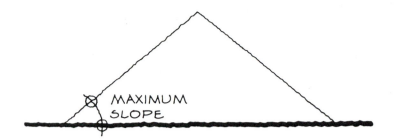

Fig.1.8

What is happening inside the heap is complex, and is further complicated by the addition of water, (which is why sand castles can be made). If, however, a heap with a vertical side is required, forces are needed to keep the heap in the **unnatural** shape.

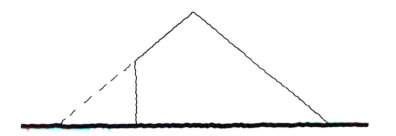

Fig.1.9

This is usually done by building a (retaining) wall. Because the heap wants to return to a natural shape, shown by the dotted line in Fig.1.10, the wall must hold back all the sand above the dotted line.

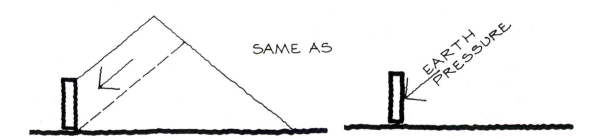

SAME AS

EARTH PRESSURE

Fig.1.10

This causes loads on the wall. In buildings, this occurs when the building has a basement, or is built into a sloping site.

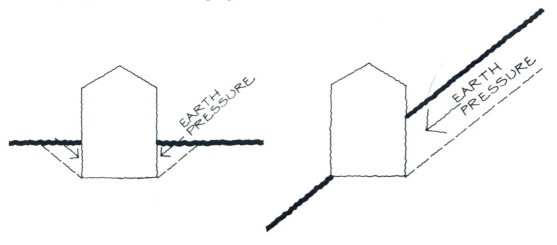

Fig.1.11

In these cases the structure has to resist **natural** loads from **earth pressure**.

Under the surface of the Earth, depending on the local geology and climate, there will be, at some level, water. The top level of this water is called the **water table**. This level may be at the surface, swamps, bogs and beaches, or many metres down in deserts. If the siting of the building interrupts the natural water table an **unnatural water table** is created around and under the building.

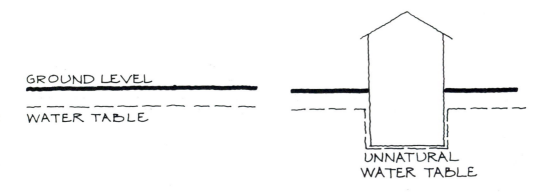

Fig.1.12

Not only are the walls loaded by the water pressure but it also causes **upward** loads on the floor. The building is trying to **float**!

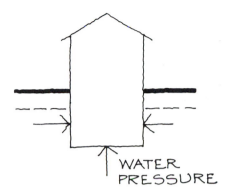

WATER
PRESSURE

Fig.1.13

The structure has to resist natural loads due to **water pressure**.

The general shape of the surface of the Earth is sensibly the same over the life-span of most buildings, but may alter slightly due to climatic or geological changes. As the building is attached to the surface of the Earth, local changes will force a change in the shape of the structure, as the building is hardly likely to prevent the Earth changing shape! In particular, load may be caused if the local shape changes differentially. It is **not obvious** how this causes a load on the structure, if indeed it does. For example, suppose the plank bridge has a support in the stream.

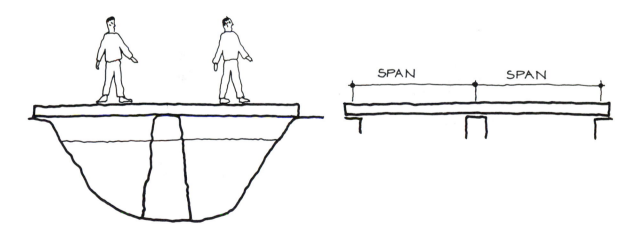

SPAN   SPAN

Fig.1.14

If this central support were to sink into the stream bed, depending on the fixing, it may pull the plank down (load it) or cease to be a support at all!

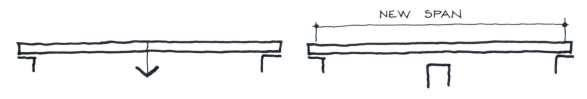

Fig.1.15

So **ground movements** can alter the load-carrying behaviour of a structure, and so be considered, in a rather roundabout way, to load the structure.

Another form of ground movement that can load a structure is an earthquake. Earthquakes are caused by sudden internal movements within the Earth's crust. This causes a shock to the system and results in shaking the crust of the Earth over a certain area. The earth's surface will both bounce up and down and move backwards and forwards.

Fig.1.16

In general the vertical movement is small compared to the horizontal movement. A building, during an earthquake, undergoes an experience similar to a person standing unaided on a cakewalk.

Fig.1.17

Again, it is not obvious where or what the load is but the effect, as far as the building or the person is concerned, is the same as being pushed horizontally to and fro with the foundations (feet) kept still.

Fig.1.18

So earthquakes cause horizontal loads, similar, to some extent, to wind loads.

The last type of natural load is caused by differential dimensional changes in the structure. All structural materials expand when heated and contract when cooled. As structures are often exposed to the ambient climate their **temperature** may vary considerably, from a hot summer day to a cold winter night, and in some case this may cause loads.

An example illustrates how this may happen. Suppose a structure consists of two parts firmly joined by a spanning structure.

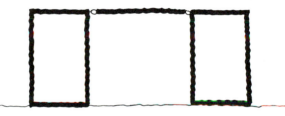

Fig.1.19

As the temperature varies, the spanning structure will expand and contract. As it is firmly joined to the supporting structures, it will push them and pull them causing loads.

Fig.1.20

So, as with ground movements, temperature, in a rather unobvious way, may be a load. To avoid these loads, bridges are often provided with systems of sliding bearings at the tops of the supporting columns. On large bridges these can often be seen.

A successful structure must be able to resist the effects of some or all of these natural loads for the whole of its useful life. On the whole these loads cannot be avoided and are an intergral part of the structure's existence.

1.2 Useful loads

Unlike natural loads, which cannot be avoided and so must be tolerated, **useful loads** are ones that are welcomed. These loads happen because the building and hence the structure have been constructed for a useful purpose.

With the plank bridge, it has been constructed for people to cross the stream. If it couldn't do this it would be of no use, so the previous figures can be re-drawn showing **natural** and **useful loads**.

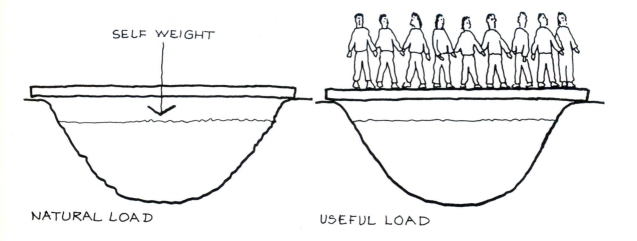

Fig.1.21

The amount of useful load can be altered by how many people are 'allowed' on the bridge at any one time; and whether people are allowed to take their pet elephants on the bridge. It is often practical for the useful load to be the maximum load that is likely to occur. Practically the useful load would be a bridge full of people but no elephants allowed.

NOT ALLOWED

Fig.1.22

So, unlike natural loads, there is a choice for useful loads. Of course if everyone using the bridge had an elephant (or a car!) it would be sensible for the useful load to be a bridge full of people or full of elephants.

As gravity acts on the people and the elephants the effect of this useful load will be towards the centre of the earth, or locally vertical.

GRAVITY

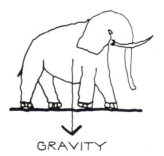

GRAVITY

Fig.1.23

Unlike natural loads, useful loads can vary enormously, depending on the use of the building which may have to carry anything from railway trains to sleeping people.

Whilst the majority of useful loads act vertically, sometimes they act horizontally. It may be useful to store sand, grain or water and these will cause useful earth or water pressure loads.

Fig.1.24

Also, rather like earthquakes, machinery housed in a building may tend to shake a building sideways, causing another type of useful horizontal load.

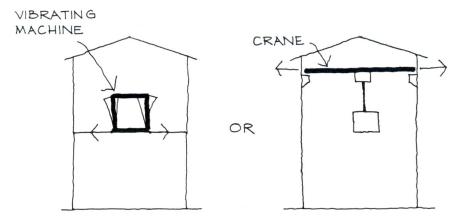

Fig.1.25

Again, industrial processes may increase or reduce the ambient temperature, giving 'useful' temperature loads.

1.3   Accidental loads

The occurrence of **accidental loads** is inextricably bound up with concepts of **safety**. How safe anything is, driving a car or drinking water, is a matter for society to decide, or at least keep under review. If accidents are thought to be likely and unavoidable then the structure should be able to resist loads that these accidents cause.

For instance, in a multi-storey car-park, it is likely and unavoidable that someone will hit the edge barrier whilst parking.

SAME AS

Fig.1.26

The edge barrier should be able to cater for 'run of the mill' collisions but not suicide attempts. Similar situations occur at railway station and ship berthing jetties.

Another unavoidable accident is a minor (!) explosion. Minor explosions in kitchens and bomb factories are of different orders of magnitude, but both should be expected and allowed for. Other unavoidable accidents are crowd panics which require the installation of panic barriers, or tank bursts which require lower structures to carry the extra liquid load.

It is impossible for an individual to decide which accidents, and hence accidental loads, are unavoidable and which aren't and any society is never clear. Compare the numbers of people killed on the roads in 'unavoidable' accidents and the relatively few killed in train 'disasters'.

1.4   Loading summary

The major function of a structure is to transfer loads and the main sources of these loads have now been identified. Whilst each load, or set of loads can be considered to act independently buildings are usually loaded by combinations of the various loads. As the building must carry any combination it is usual to consider a range of combinations called **load cases**.

The only load case that will always be present is the **natural gravity load**. That is the effect of gravity on the building construction and to this load must be added **all other loads**. All the other loads that have been identified may or may not be acting at any particular time. Therefore an almost endless variety of load combinations may act. For example:

Loadcase 1   Natural gravity load + Useful gravity load on all floors
Loadcase 2   Natural gravity load + Wind load in a particular direction
Loadcase 3   Natural gravity load + Useful gravity load on some floors
              + Natural temperature load

However the purpose of considering these different load cases is not to find as many load cases as possible but to ensure that the building structure will safely carry all possible load cases. This apparently contradictory statement means that only the load cases that cause the biggest effect on the structure need to be considered. In other words only the **worst load case** is of interest. This presents two difficulties which are:

1   One load case may cause the biggest effect on one part of the structure whereas another load case may have the biggest effect on another part, so there may be more than one worst load case.
2   How can the worst load case or cases be found without considering **every** possible load case.

Unfortunately there is no automatic process to overcome these difficulties for every situation but guidance is given in technical documents. For buildings it is usual to consider:

1   Natural gravity load + Maximum useful gravity load
2   Natural gravity load + Wind load in direction 1
3   Natural gravity load + Wind load at right angles to direction 1

It is unusual to have to consider loads due to earth or water pressure, ground movement, temperature or accident. But for particular types of building or sites these may have to be considered, and incorporated into the load cases. For example, for a two storey factory building, the following loads would be considered for the structural design.

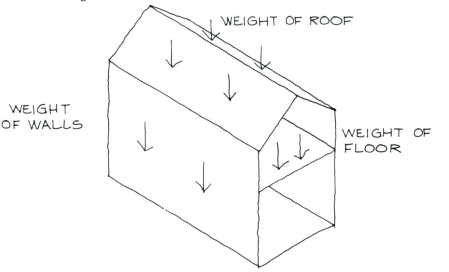

Fig.1.27   Natural gravity loads

The ground floor often bears directly on to the ground and does not load the structure.

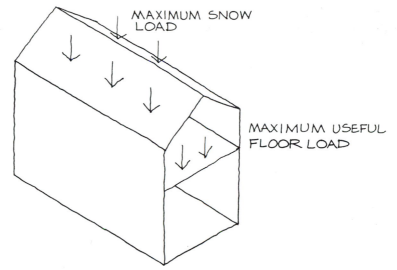

Fig.1.28 Maximum useful gravity load

The natural gravity plus maximum useful gravity loads usually, but not always, gives the **worst vertical load**.

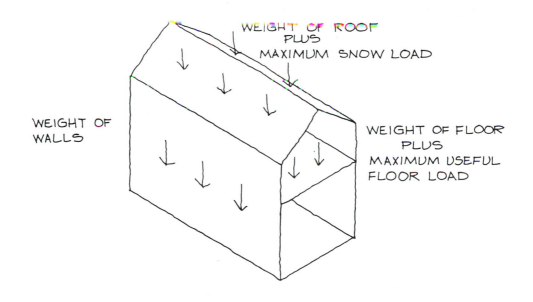

Fig.1.29   Worst vertical load

The combination of natural gravity load and the maximum windloads usually gives the **worst horizontal load**.

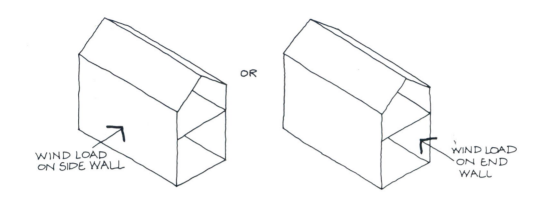

Fig.1.30 Worst horizontal load

It may seem surprising that only two directions are chosen for the wind, because, after all wind blows in any direction. As a maximum wind load has been decided, not by the wind of course, this can act in **any** direction.

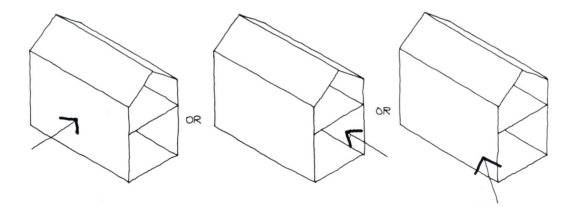

Fig.1.31

But if the building structure is strong enough to carry the maximum wind load separately in two perpendicular directions, then **all** other wind loads can be considered to be smaller proportions of the maximum loads.

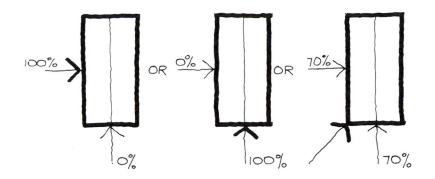

Fig.1.32

The same principle of **load combinations** applies to all buildings.

1.5   Reaction loads

In the same way that people stand on a floor and usually don't fall through, buildings also have to stand on something strong — the foundations.

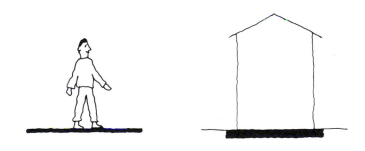

Fig.1.33

But what is the floor doing to stop people from falling through? What it is doing is to provide a **reaction force**, or a **reaction load**. The idea of reactions is due to Issac Newton who, in 1687, stated three fundamental laws, which together with his discovery of gravity, provided the basis of what has come to be known as

Newtonian mechanics. These were used extensively by scientists in their pursuit of knowledge about the natural world. They formed the backbone of physics and still provide the backbone of structural engineering thought.

(It was only at the beginning of the 20th century that Einstein postulated a system of mechanics that were non-Newtonian. This system came to be know as **relativity**, which is used for calculations about the Universe. Fortunately structural engineers can still use Newtonian mechanics for the building structures on the Earth.)

One of Newton's three laws (the third), states:

• **To every action there is always an equal and opposite reaction.**

So when a person stands on a floor, the weight of the person pushes down on the floor with a force equal to their bodyweight. For equilibrium, the floor must push back with an **equal and opposite force!**

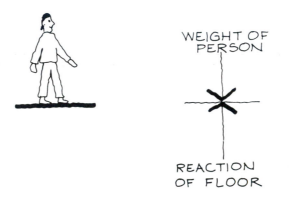

Fig.1.34

An understanding of this statement is fundamental for an understanding of how building structures carry loads.

Whilst it is true that the load and the reaction have to act at the point of the application of the load, a structure transfers the load to another point. Returning to example of the plank bridge.

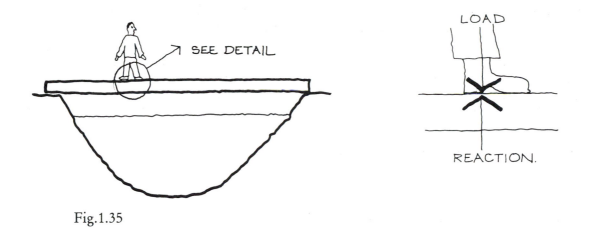

Fig.1.35

The reaction to the person's weight is **in the structure**, and the structure transfers this reaction to the banks.

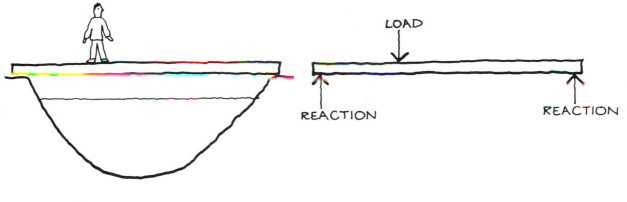

Fig.1.36

Because of Newton's law the numerical sum of the loads and the reactions must be equal.

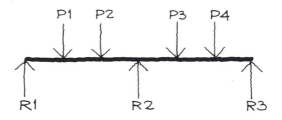

Fig.1.37

For vertical equilibrium of the 2-span beam in Fig.1.37:

● $\quad P1+P2+P3+P4 \;=\; R1+R2+R3$

When loads are acting horizontally a reaction is required for equilibrium. It is to upset this equilibrium that tug-of-war contests are held.

Fig.1.38

Here it unclear which is the load and which is the reaction! Which is why the (applied) load and the reaction (load) should be thought as a **balanced** system of loads.

Fig.1.39

Here the pull of the team is the (applied) load and the tree provides the reaction (load).

Not only are there vertical and horizontal reactions there are also **moment** reactions! What is a moment? A moment is a **force times a distance**. Moments abound in structural engineering but the concept of a moment is often found hard to understand. However, it is because of moments that things can be weighed or people can enjoy see-saws.

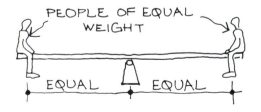

Fig.1.40

The fun in see-sawing can only be enjoyed if the people are of equal weight and sit at an equal distance from the support. This is because they are in moment equilibrium.

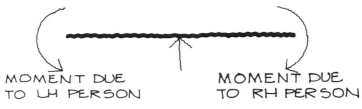

MOMENT DUE TO LH PERSON   MOMENT DUE TO RH PERSON

Fig.1.41

In other words the left-hand person causes an **anti-clockwise** moment and the right-hand person causes a **clockwise** moment about the central support. Because both people are of equal weight and are sitting at equal distances from the support the anti-clockwise and clockwise moments are equal in magnitude but opposite in direction and so are in **moment equilibrium**. By pushing from the ground this equilibrium is upset and the people 'see-saw'.

The same principle can be used for weighing scales. This time to find the unknown weight of some goods.

WEIGHTS   GOODS

MOMENT DUE TO WEIGHTS   MOMENT DUE TO GOODS

Fig.1.42

To balance the scales the moments must be equal. As the distances are equal the weights must equal the weight of the goods.

The idea of **moment reaction** occurs at the support of a **cantilever**.

DISTANCE

FORCE

MOMENT REACTION   MOMENT APPLIED TO SUPPORT

Fig.1.43

The person standing on the end of the cantilevered plank causes a moment at the support (force × distance). The fixing of the plank must balance this moment with a moment reaction, otherwise the plank will rotate away from the wall.

Moment reactions are also required to prevent flag poles, fences and signs from being blown over by the wind.

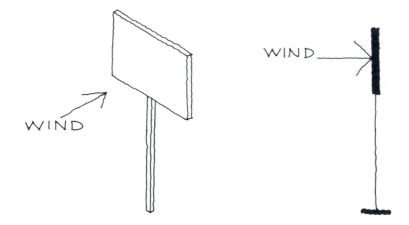

Fig.1.44

In this case the post is acting as a **vertical cantilever** from the ground. The wind force acting on the sign at some height (distance) above the ground causes a moment at ground level, so the post must be dug into the ground to provide a moment reaction.

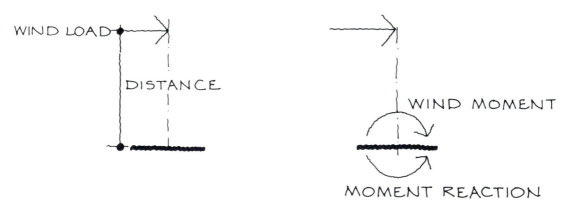

Fig 1.45

Notice that the moment reaction is in the opposite direction to the moment caused by the wind force × height.

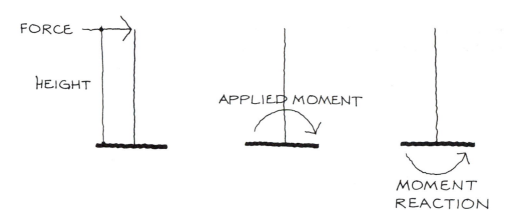

Fig 1.46

Many structures require more than one type of reaction. Using the example of wind blowing on a sign, the support must provide **vertical**, **horizontal** and **moment reactions**. These resist the **weight** of the **sign**, the **wind load** and the **wind moment**.

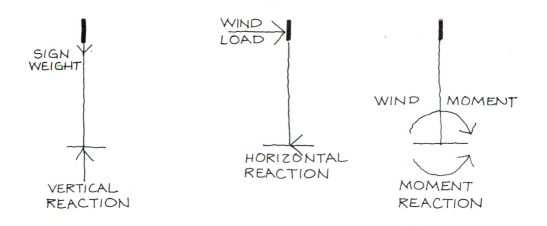

Fig 1.47

The idea of moment equilibrium also plays a part in apportioning vertical reactions for spanning structures. Suppose a weightless (!) plank spans between two weighing scales and a person stands at different points along the plank.

Fig 1.48

The person is the load and the reaction forces occur at the supports on the weighing scales. As the person moves from position A to B and then to C the readings on the scales will vary, giving the values of the reactions for each position. But the fact that the sum of the readings of the scales for each position will equal the weight of the person **does not indicate how they are shared**.

If the person stands in position A, directly over the left-hand weighing scale it is reasonable to expect this scale to give a reading of 100% of the person's weight and the right-hand weighing scale to give a reading of 0% of the person's weight.

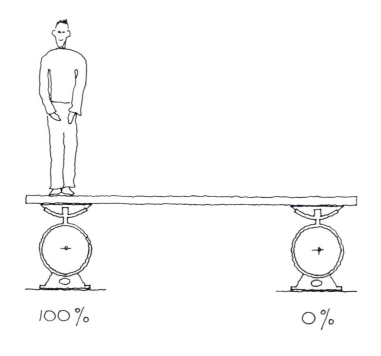

100%   0%

Fig 1.49

28   **Loads and load paths**

But, vertical equilibrium would equally be satisfied by the right-hand scale reading 100% of the person's weight and the left-hand scale reading 0%!

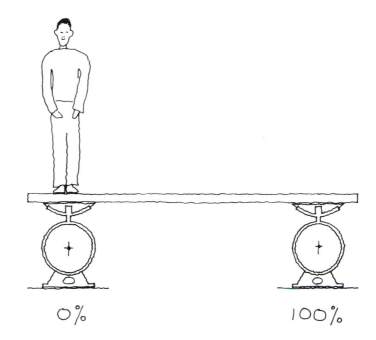

Fig 1.50

This seems unlikely to be true. But why not? The answer is because only Fig 1.49 gives moment equilibrium. But where are the moments? This is far from obvious, but suppose the left-hand weighing scale was removed.

Fig 1.51

Now the person causes an anti-clockwise moment about the right-hand weighing scale and the plank would hinge about the right-hand end. To prevent this the left-hand weighing scale provides a reaction which causes a clockwise moment about the right-hand weighing scale.

Fig 1.52

As these two moments must balance, the left-hand reaction must balance the persons weight, as the distance from the right-hand end is the same for the load and the reaction so:

Person's weight × length of plank = left-hand reaction × length of plank

So Fig 1.49 gives vertical **and** moment equilibrium whereas Fig 1.50 gives vertical equilibrium **but not** moment equilibrium.

- **every time there are loads on structures there must be reactions (vertical, horizontal and moment) and these reactions must balance the loads.**

that is:

- Sum of vertical loads = Sum of vertical reactions
- Sum of horizontal loads = Sum of horizontal reactions
- Moments due to loads = Moments due to reactions

These three statements must be true for all structures and the understanding of these statements unlocks the door to an understanding of structures.

1.6   Load paths

To understand how loads are transferred through complex structures the **concept of load path** is used. This is basically a sequence of loads and reactions between structural elements. The important point here is one element's reaction to the next element's load.

For the simple example of a beam on two walls, the reactions of the beam 'causes' loads on the walls.

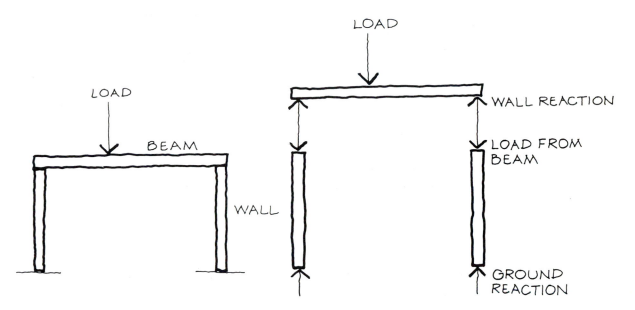

Fig.1.53

The double headed arrow between the beam and the walls represents the reaction and the load. The **upper arrow** represents the wall providing a **reaction** to the beam and the **lower arrow** represents the beam causing a **load** on the wall.

Fig.1.54

Fig.1.55 shows a more complicated situation of two beams, supported by walls, all sitting on a large spanning beam.

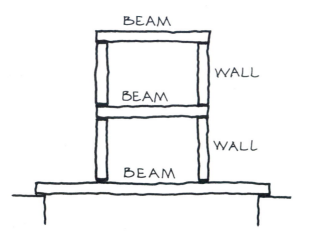

Fig.1.55

First what are the loads? These are natural, the self-weight of the beams and walls, and useful, the loads applied to the beams.

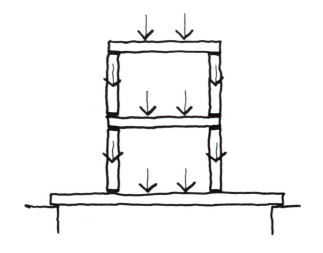

Fig.1.56

Loads P1, P2 and P5 are the self-weight of the beams and P3 and P4 the self-weight of the walls. Loads P6, P7 and P8 are the loads applied to the beams. For vertical equilibrium all the loads P1 to P8 must be balanced by the reactions of the lowest beam.

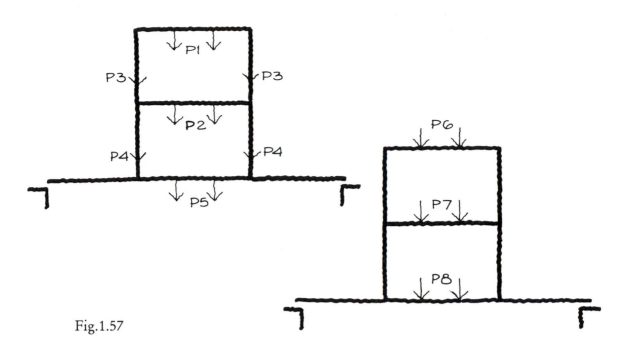

Fig.1.57

For the lowest beam:

The sum of the reactions $= P1+P2+P3+P4+P5+P6+P7+P8$

But how do the loads get to the reactions?

First the upper beam.

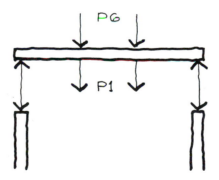

Fig.1.58

Loads to the upper walls $= P1+P6$

The upper walls are loaded by the loads on the upper beam plus their own self-weight.

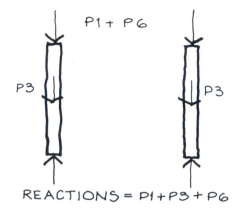

REACTIONS = P1 + P3 + P6

Fig.1.59

The tops of the lower walls are loaded by and provide a reaction to the upper walls and the middle beam.

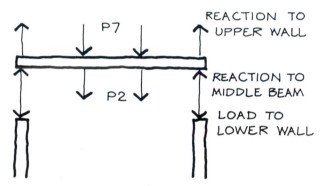

Fig.1.60

So for the lower walls,

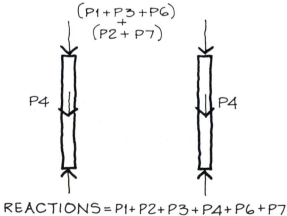

Fig.1.61   REACTIONS = P1 + P2 + P3 + P4 + P6 + P7

And the reactions to the lower walls =   Load from the upper wall
                                      + Load from the middle beam
                                      + Self-weight of the lower wall
                                    =   (P1+P6+P3) + (P2+P7) + P4

The lower beam is not only loaded by its self-weight, P5, and the applied load, P8, but also by providing reactions to the lower walls.

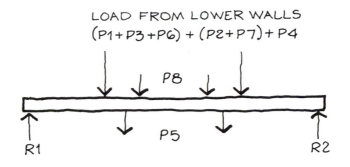

LOAD FROM LOWER WALLS
(P1+P3+P6) + (P2+P7)+ P4

P8

P5

R1   R2

Fig.1.62

So for vertical equilibrium of the lower beam:

The REACTIONS =   Self-weight of the upper beam
                + Self-weight of the middle beam
                + Self-weight of the lower beam
                + Self-weight of the upper walls
                + Self-weight of the lower walls
                + Useful load on the upper beam
                + Useful load on the middle beam
                + Useful load on the lower beam

that is

•   R1+R2 = P1+P2+P3+P4+P5+P6+P7+P8

The load path of load P6 can now be identified. First the upper beam transfers the load to the upper wall, which transfers it to the lower wall, which transfers it to the lower beam, which transfers it to the supports.

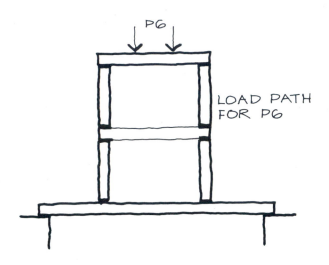

Fig.1.63

And for P2, the self-weight of the middle beam:

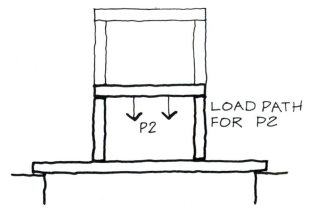

Fig.1.64

The load path joins the load from its **point of application** to the **final support point**. There are two points to be noticed about load paths.

The first point is that **all loads** must and will have a load path from their point of application to the final support. These paths must be identified by the structural designer for **all loads** and **all load cases**.

The second point is, as the function of the structure is to transfer loads, then the **load path is the structure** for each load. So the answer to the question **'what is the structure?'** may vary with each load. For the loads P2 and P6 the structures are different.

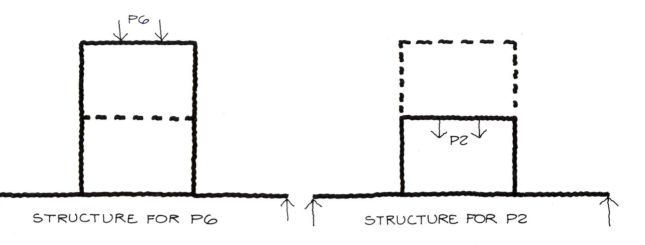

Fig.1.65

The identification of vertical load paths for most buildings is relatively straightforward. Oddly it can be quite complex for 'simple buildings' like houses.

Not only do vertical loads need load paths but so do horizontal loads. These loads are usually caused by wind. How does the sign board shown in Fig.1.66 resist wind forces?

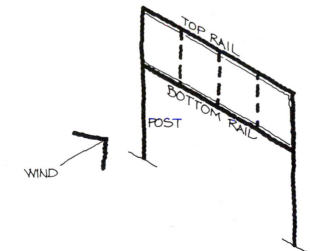

Fig.1.66

The main wind load is caused by the wind blowing on the actual sign, and only the load path for this load is considered. This means the effect of the wind on the rails and posts is ignored.

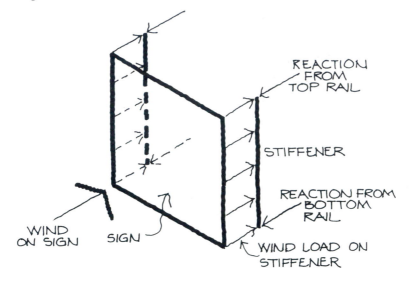

Fig.1.67

The actual signboard spans horizontally between the vertical stiffeners and the stiffeners act as vertically spanning beams supported by the top and bottom rails.

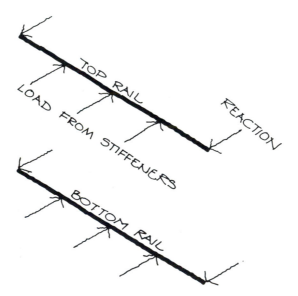

Fig.1.68

The reactions from the stiffeners become horizontal loads on the top and bottom rails. These rails act as horizontally spanning beams supported by the vertical end posts.

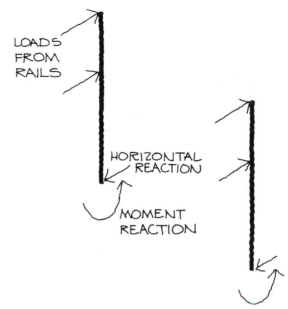

Fig.1.69

The reactions from the top and bottom rails now cause loads on the vertical posts which act as vertical cantilevers from the ground.

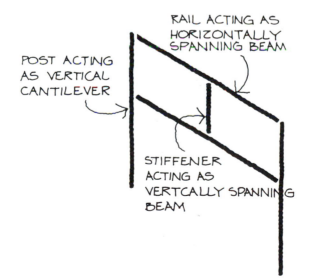

Fig.1.70

Here the wind load path is the whole structure.

Even in simple buildings the load paths for vertical and horizontal loads are rarely the same. As the load path is the structure this means there are usually **different structures** resisting vertical and horizontal loads.

CHAPTER 2 *Internal forces*

So far loads, reactions and load paths have been identified for structures. The parts of the structure that join the load to the reactions is the load path and the structure. But how does the structure transfer the load to the reaction? And what happens to the structure when it transfers loads? The structure transfers loads by **forces** that are '**in the structure**' and these forces cause **stresses** in the structural material. The structure also deforms under the effect of the loads, and the size of the deformation depends on the **stiffness** of the structure.

2.1   Columns and beams

To illustrate the idea of **internal force**, consider a simple column supporting an end load.

Fig.2.1

What happens to a typical 'slice' of the column?

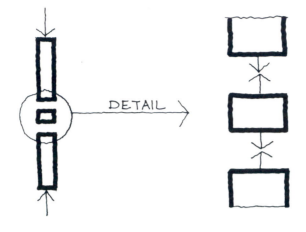

Fig.2.2

The slice is being squashed, or compressed, and furthermore all slices are being squashed.

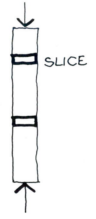

SLICE

Fig.2.3

The column transfers the end load to the reaction by a system of 'squashed slices', or to use the engineering description, the column is **in compression**.

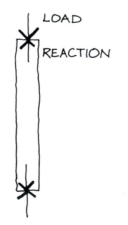

LOAD

REACTION

Fig.2.4

Not only is the column in compression but also deforms by **shortening**. This happens because each slice becomes thinner on being squashed.

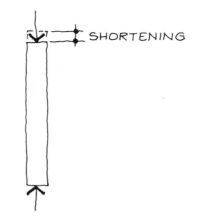

Fig.2.5

If the direction of the load is reversed then each slice is being stretched, and the end load is transferred to the reaction by a system of 'stretched slices'. Or, to use the engineering term, the column is **in tension**.

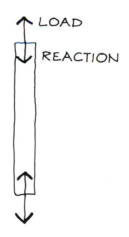

Fig.2.6

Looking again at the load path for load P6, (see Fig.1.63), the walls supporting the upper beam are in compression.

Fig.2.7

But what is happening to the upper and lower beams? These beams are transferring the loads to the supports by a combination of **bending moments** and **shear forces**. Although bending moments and shear forces act together, conceptually they can be considered separately.

To understand what is happening to the beam it helps to see what happens to a slice.

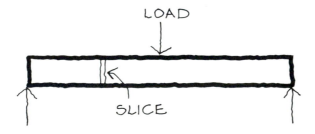

Fig.2.8

Each side of the slice is being bent by a moment.

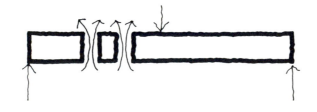

Fig.2.9

The moments at the slice are the forces multiplied by the distances from the slice.

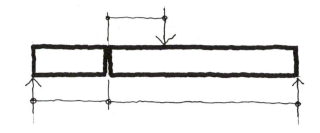

Fig.2.10

So the moments on the slice are:

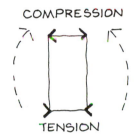

Fig.2.11

This causes the slice to be squashed at the top and stretched at the bottom. In other words the top of the beam is in compression and the bottom in tension, and the slice is being bent by a pair of bending moments.

COMPRESSION

TENSION

Fig.2.12

Because the top is in compression it **shortens**, and because the bottom is in tension it **lengthens**. These effects cause the sides to **rotate**.

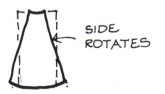

SIDE
ROTATES

Fig.2.13

In general, the size of the bending moment varies from slice to slice. This varying size can be represented by drawing lines at right angles to the beam, with the length of the line indicating the **size of the bending moment**.

Fig.2.14

Because there is a bending moment at every slice and the beam is 'made' of slices, there is a bending moment at every point of the beam. A clearer picture of the bending moments on the beam can be obtained by joining the ends of all the bending moment size lines shown in Fig.2.14. This diagram is called a **bending moment diagram**.

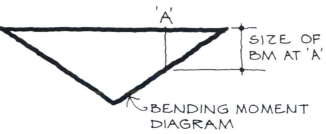

Fig.2.15

And because each slice changes shape, as shown in Fig.2.13, the beam takes up a bent shape.

Fig.2.16

Bending moments in a beam resist the effects of the moments caused by external loads, and reactions acting at different distances from each other. Bending moments **do not** resist the vertical effect of loads on beams, these are resisted by **shear forces**. When a **rectangle** is distorted by an angular change into a **parallelogram**, it is **sheared**.

Fig.2.17

Returning to a slice of a beam, not only does the slice have to transfer the bending moments from one face to the other, it also has to transfer the vertical load from one face to the other.

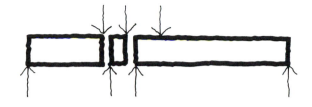

Fig.2.18

The beam either side of the slice has to be in **vertical equilibrium**.

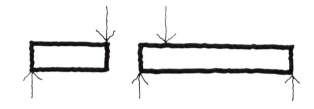

Fig.2.19

And the balancing forces themselves have to be balanced by forces on the face of the slice.

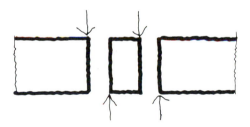

Fig.2.20

It is these pairs of **up and down forces** that are called shear forces, because their effect is to shear the slice.

Fig.2.21

Like bending moments, shear forces will, in general, vary along a beam. So, in a similar way to bending moment diagrams, **shear force diagrams** can be drawn.

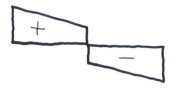

Fig.2.22

To make more sense of bending moment and shear force diagrams the vexed question of the **sign** of a bending moment or shear force must be answered.

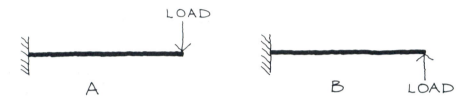

Fig.2.23

The figure shows two cantilevers that are exactly the same except the loads are being applied in **opposite** directions. Some agreement has to be made to distinguish the fact that cantilever A is being bent down, and cantilever B is being bent up! This could be done by deciding that cantilever A deforms in a **negative** way, causing negative bending moments and vice versa for cantilever B.

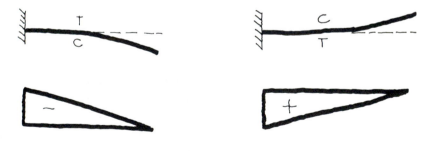

Fig.2.24

In this figure the bending moments have been drawn on the **tension side** of the beam. Although these decisions are supposed to aid clarification, this is not always the case! Especially as the decisions about positive and negative are made by personal whim. However they have to be made and adhered to or the bending moment diagrams become chaotic.

Similar decisions have to be made about shear forces, but here the situation is more incomprehensible. As shear forces are pairs of forces, the sign decisions have to be made about these pairs. A possible sign convention is shown in the following figure.

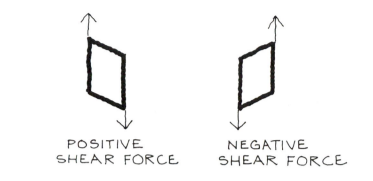

POSITIVE
SHEAR FORCE

NEGATIVE
SHEAR FORCE

Fig.2.25

Again this decision is made by personal whim! Using the stated sign conventions the bending moment and shear force diagrams can be drawn for a simple beam with point load, and these diagrams show the signs of the bending moments and shear forces.

LOAD

BENDING MOMENT
DIAGRAM

SHEAR FORCE
DIAGRAM

Fig.2.26

It is sets of diagrams like this that give engineers pictures of what is happening inside a structure. **The conceptual meaning of sets of bending moment and shear force diagrams is central to the understanding of structural behaviour.** It is far from easy to obtain the correct shapes for these diagrams and even more difficult to calculate numerical values for their size. However a deep understanding of structural behaviour is only obtained when the correct diagrams can be drawn for real or proposed structures. This takes time and persistence but is the only way!

2.2 A simple frame

For the more complicated structure of a goal-post, known as a **portal frame,** diagrams can be drawn showing what is happening inside the structure when it is loaded.

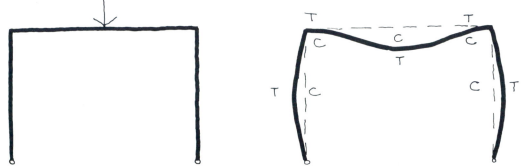

Fig.2.27

Here, although there is only vertical load there are **horizontal reactions.** These exist because otherwise the legs would move apart at their bases.

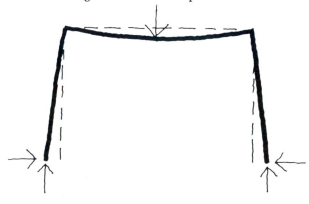

Fig.2.28

The deformed shape (Fig.2.27) shows which sides of the legs and cross-bar are in tension and compression. Using this as a guide the bending moment diagram can be drawn.

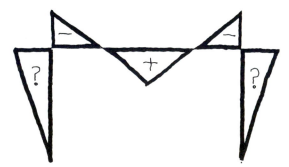

Fig.2.29

The bending moment diagram is drawn on the tension side of the legs and cross-bar. Although the sign convention used for the beam shown in Fig.2.24 can be used for the cross-bar, it is unclear what sign should be given to the bending moments in the legs.

Not only will there be bending moments in the frame but there will also be axial forces and shear forces. There are axial forces in the legs due to the vertical load and an axial force in the cross-bar due to the horizontal reaction.

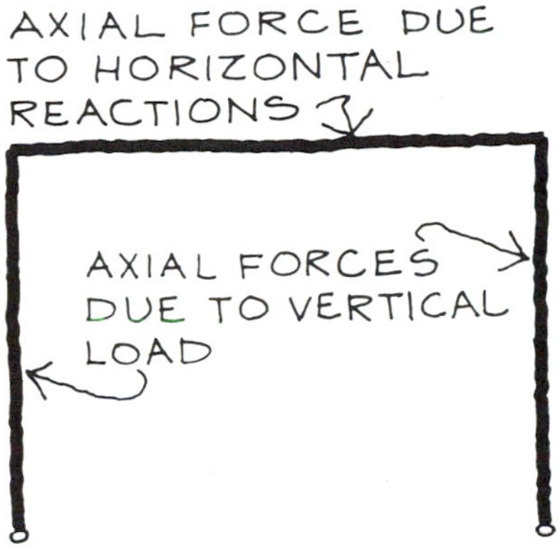

AXIAL FORCE DUE
TO HORIZONTAL
REACTIONS

AXIAL FORCES
DUE TO VERTICAL
LOAD

Fig.2.30

As well as the bending moment diagrams, an axial force diagram can be drawn on the portal frame. For axial forces there is no agreed convention for the sign of axial forces or even the way the diagram should be drawn! In some ways the sign convention for axial forces is simpler than for bending moments and shear forces because compression forces are either positive or negative, and similarly for tension forces. Traditionally, axial force diagrams are drawn with a system of arrows on the structure, with numbers written alongside the member indicating the size of the force. More consistently axial force diagrams should be drawn in the same way as bending moment and shear force diagrams. Both types of diagrams are shown below. The arrow convention is for **arrows pointing away** from the end of a member to indicate compression, and for the diagram compression is assumed to be positive.

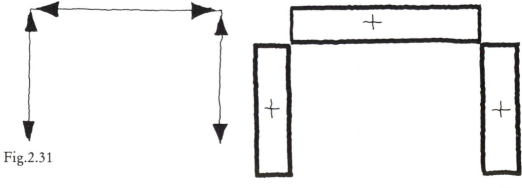

Fig.2.31

A simple frame 51

Also a **shear force diagram** can be drawn, here the beam sign convention shown in Fig.2.26 can be used for the cross-bar but again, as for the case of the bending moment, the sign of the shear force in the legs is unclear.

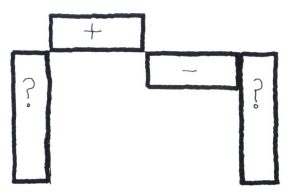

Fig.2.32

It is impossible to have fully consistent sign conventions and diagrams without having agreed local and global axes systems for the whole structure. The importance of this point becomes clear when computer programs are used to find the forces in a structure, and this is commonplace these days.

Further understanding of how the internal forces are acting on a structure can be obtained by considering the parts of a structure as 'free bodies'. In the case of the portal frame the **free bodies** are the beam and the two legs.

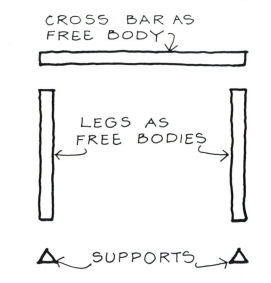

Fig.2.33

The forces acting on these free bodies to keep them in equilibrium are shown in the next diagram.

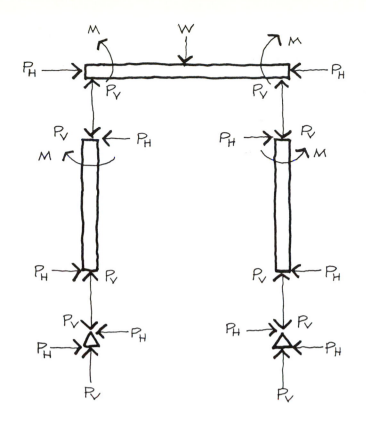

Fig.2.34

The meaning of this bewildering set of forces is easier to understand by considering the forces due to the load and the forces due to the horizontal restraint separately. For the vertical load W, its effect on the beam is balanced by the end forces P_v. These in turn cause forces equal to P_v on the tops of the legs which are balanced by forces, also equal to P_v, at the bottom of the legs. The forces at the bottom of the legs are balanced by forces on the supports which in turn are balanced by the reactions.

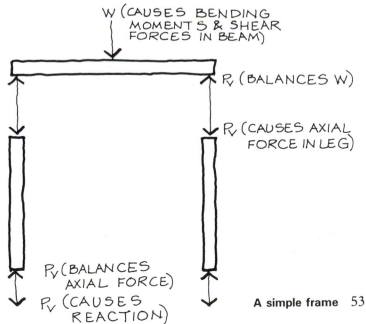

Fig.2.35

The reason for the existence of M and P_h are less clear. They exist because the joints between the legs and cross-bar are **stiff**, that is the joints are **at right-angles before and after loading**. Due to the vertical load W, the cross-bar bends and the ends rotate. To maintain the right-angles at the joints the legs want to move outwards, as is shown in Fig.2.28 (if this did happen M and P_h would not exist). But the connection at the bottom of the legs prevents horizontal movement and this causes the legs to bend.

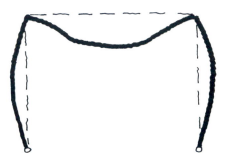

Fig.2.36

And just looking at one leg:

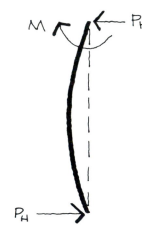

Fig.2.37

This effect can be simulated by holding one end of a flexible stick between two fingers of one hand and rotating the other end with the other hand.

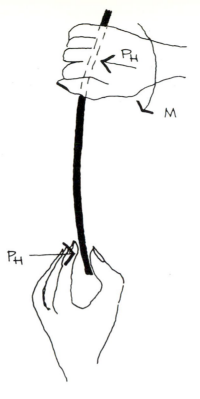

Fig.2.38

So the effect of connection is to cause bending moments in the leg due to M and shear forces due to P_h. A free body diagram can be drawn showing the effect of M and P_h on all the parts of the structure.

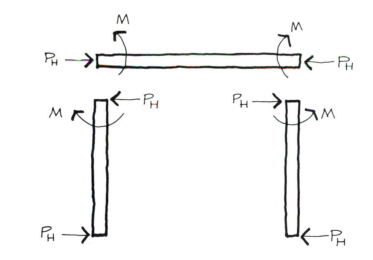

Fig.2.39

The diagrams showing the bending moments, shear and axial forces can also be separated in those caused by the vertical load W, and those caused by the horizontal restraint of the legs. Firstly the effect of the vertical load with no horizontal restraint at the base of the legs.

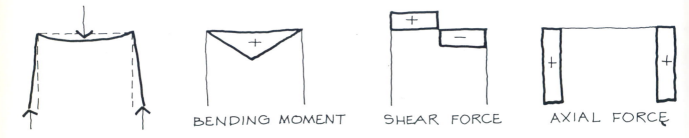

BENDING MOMENT   SHEAR FORCE   AXIAL FORCE

Fig.2.40

And secondly the effect of pushing the bottom of the legs together.

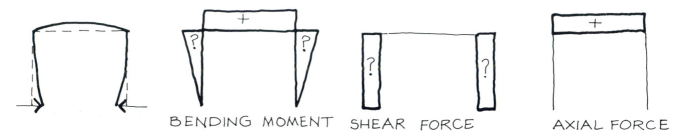

BENDING MOMENT   SHEAR FORCE   AXIAL FORCE

Fig.2.41

As both effects happen together, the diagrams can be combined to give the complete picture.

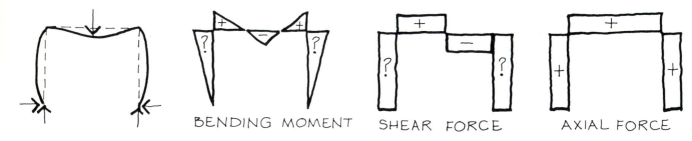

BENDING MOMENT   SHEAR FORCE   AXIAL FORCE

Fig.2.42

It is sets of diagrams like these, together with the magnitude of all the forces, that provided the engineering information on how any structure behaves under any form of loading.

2.3   Slabs

The concepts of bending moments, shear and axial forces are not confined to one dimensional elements, such as beams and columns, they can be applied to all structural forms. For instance a two dimensional element such as a floor slab resists lateral loads by a system of internal bending moments and shear forces.

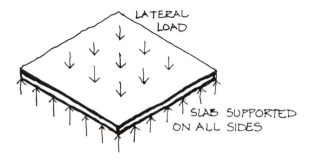

Fig.2.43

Because the slab is two dimensional, bending moments and shear forces can be considered as acting in two separate directions. For example a rectangular slab, supported on all sides and loaded by a central point load, will span in two directions.

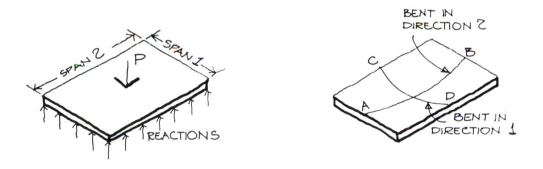

Fig.2.44

A 'strip', AB, of the slab acts rather like a beam spanning from A to B. This strip will have bending moment and shear force distributions which can be represented by bending moment and shear force diagrams.

Fig.2.45

Similarly with strip CD.

Fig.2.46

Because the whole slab is carrying the load P, the amount of load the strips AB and CD carry is less than P. The diagrams drawn for the strips can be compared with those shown in Fig.2.26. These diagrams can be drawn for the two strips.

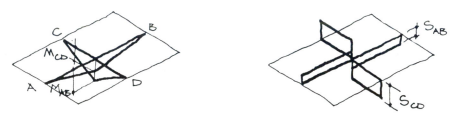

Fig.2.47

Remember that this is for one strip in each direction and the width of the strip is arbitrary. For the real slab these bending moments and shear forces will vary continuously throughout the slab. Unfortunately this is difficult to show as a clear diagram, but an idea can be given by drawing the diagrams for a series of strips. In the next diagram bending moments are drawn for the two directions for a series of strips.

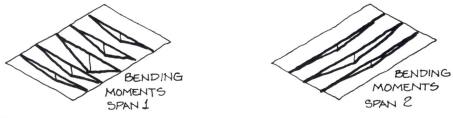

Fig.2.48

Similarly a series of shear force diagrams could be drawn.

2.4 Load paths

Often the edges of floor slabs are supported by beams and the beams are supported by columns. The slab spans two ways on to the beams and the beams, together with the columns, forms a series of portal frames.

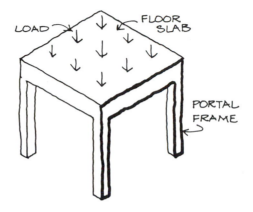

Fig.2.49

The slab carries the load to the beams by a system of bending moments and shear forces acting in two directions. At the edges of the slab there are vertical reactions which balance the load on the slab. In turn, these reactions cause loads on the portal frames.

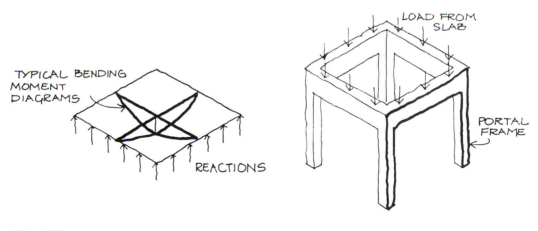

Fig.2.50

The portal frames resist these loads by internal bending moments, shear and axial forces. These internal forces are distributed throughout the portal frames and are summarised by diagrams like those shown in Fig.2.42. The columns are now part of two portal frames!

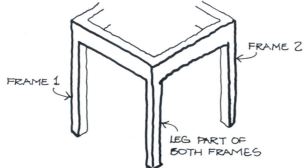

Fig.2.51

The bending moments and shear forces from the action of portal frame 1 are in the plane of frame 1 and those from frame 2 in the plane of frame 2.

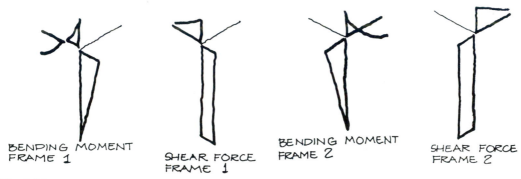

Fig.2.52

As the column can't bend in two different directions at the same time it actually bends in a third direction which is not in the plane of frame 1 or frame 2.

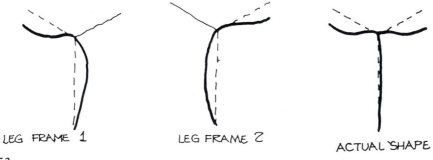

Fig.2.53

This illustrates the fact that whilst it may be conceptually convenient to view the slab supports as a series of portal frames the structure acts in a way that is most structurally 'convenient'.

The example of the slab supported by beams and columns, shown in Fig.2.49 has a simple load path. With the new concepts of structural actions it can be seen that this load path carries the loads by a sequence of these structural actions.

Now two essential skills required for the understanding of structures have been presented and these are:

- **Identifying the load path for each load — this is what carries the load**

- **Identifying the sequence of structural actions in the load path — this is how the load is carried.**

To see how the concept of structural actions shows how the load path carries the load the earlier example of the wind loaded signboard, see Fig.1.66, is re-examined using these concepts.

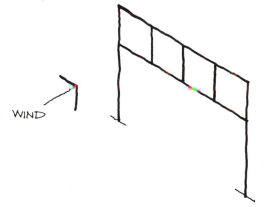

Fig.2.54

The sign itself is a two dimensional structural element which is supported by three stiffeners and the posts. As these lines of support are parallel the element acts like a one dimensional element.

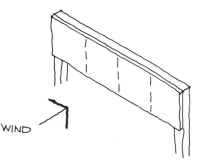

Fig.2.55

The bending moments and shear forces caused by the wind vary along the sign but are constant across it.

Fig.2.56

It may be clearer to draw as a view from above.

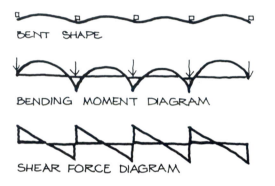

Fig.2.57

The reactions from the sign load the stiffeners, and these act as beams spanning between the rails. Bending moment and shear force diagrams can be drawn for a typical stiffener.

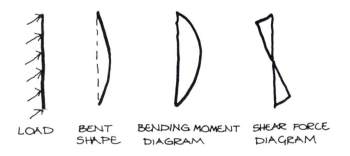

Fig.2.58

The reactions from the ends of the stiffeners act as three point loads on the top and bottom rails. These act as beams spanning between the posts so bending moment and shear force diagrams can be drawn for the rails.

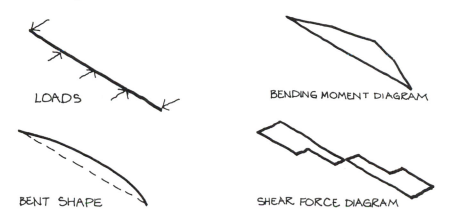

Fig.2.59

The posts act as cantilevers carrying the loads from the ends of the rails plus the load from the sign. The bending moment and shear force diagrams are drawn for the posts.

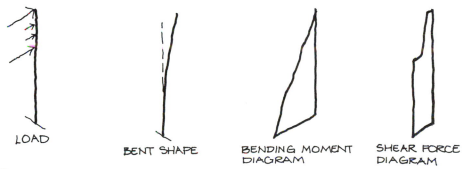

Fig.2.60

So each part of the loads path transfers the load by some form of structural action, these may be bending moments and shear forces or axial forces or some combination of these. Not only is the load path the structure but as a sequence of internal structural actions the **load path acts as a structure**.

It is the prediction of the structural behaviour of the load path that is the major skill required for successful structural engineering design. When structures are proposed the structural action of each load path must be predicted as part of the proposal. The more complex the proposed structure the more difficult it is to predict the structural behaviour of the load paths. In very complex structures it may even be difficult to identify the load paths! Severe problems can arise in the design process when complex structures with unpredictable structural behaviour are proposed. A prime example of this was the structural design of the Sydney Opera House for which thirteen different structural schemes were proposed before a suitable structural design was found, this took six years and an undisclosed and probably unknown amount of money. Often it is wise to propose simple and therefore easily predictable structures unless there is ample time during the design process for the inevitable modifications to be made.

CHAPTER 3 *Structural element behaviour*

In this chapter the behaviour of the structure that is part of a load path is examined in detail. The understanding that is obtained from this examination makes it clear how parts of structures resist the internal forces. It also gives guidance on the best shape or **structural form** for any particular part of the load path. The choice of overall structural form for any particular structure is one of the basic tasks of the structural designer but before the behaviour of whole structural forms can be understood the behaviour of very simple structures must be clear. To do this it is helpful to think of structures being **assemblies of elements**.

3.1   Structural elements

For structural engineering 'convenience' elements are considered to be one-dimensional, two-dimensional or three-dimensional! The basic element can be thought of as a rectangular block, with sides of dimensions A, B and C.

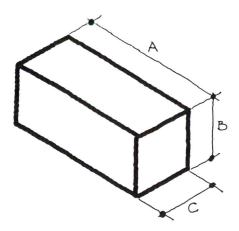

Fig.3.1

If the three dimensions are very approximately equal then such an element is a **three-dimensional element**. Examples of three-dimensional elements are rare in modern building structures but often occur in older buildings, such as wall buttresses or thick stone domes.

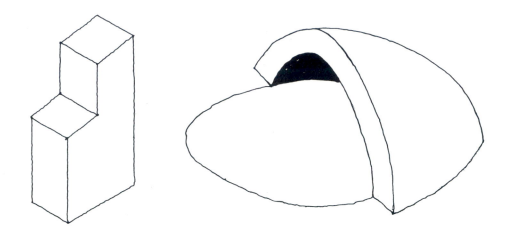

Fig.3.2

If one of the dimensions, say dimension C, is small compared to dimensions A and B, then the element is a **two-dimensional element**.

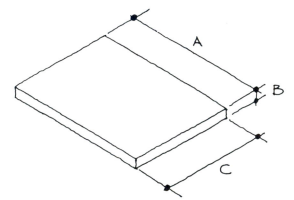

Fig.3.3

Many parts of modern building structures are two-dimensional elements such as floor slabs, walls or shell roofs.

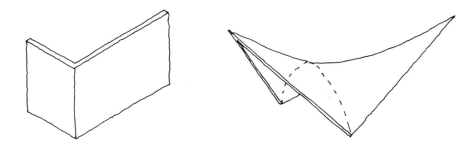

Fig.3.4

If two of the dimensions of the basic element, say B and C, are small compared to dimension A, then the element is a **one-dimensional element**.

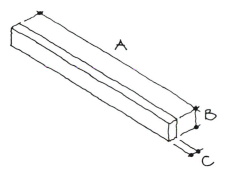

Fig.3.5

One-dimensional elements are used abundantly in nearly all buildings, examples are beams, bars, cables and columns. Using the concept of elements, structures can be conceived as assemblies of elements. Examples can be found both in traditional and modern structures.

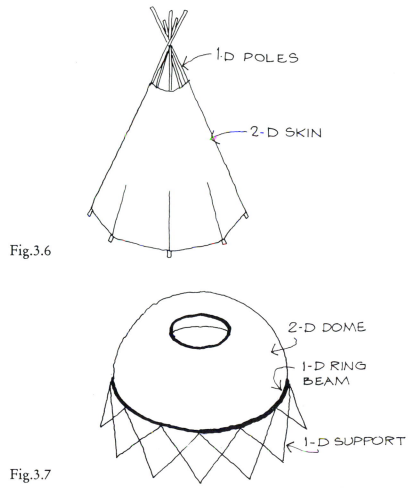

Fig.3.6

Fig.3.7

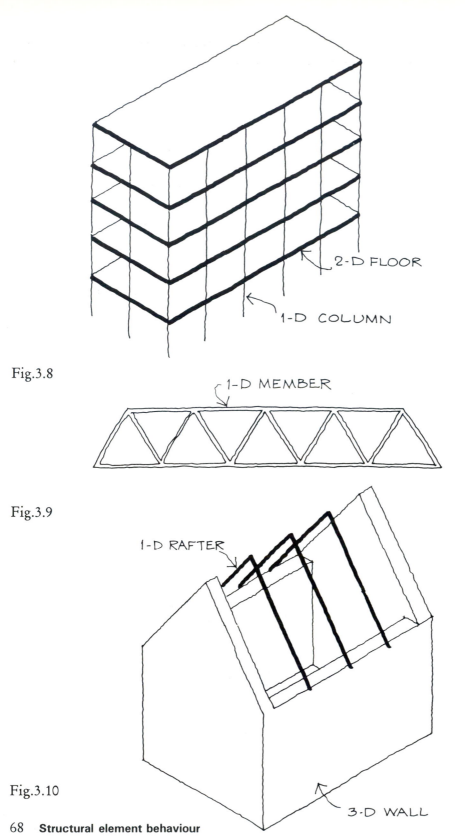

2-D FLOOR

1-D COLUMN

Fig.3.8

1-D MEMBER

Fig.3.9

1-D RAFTER

3-D WALL

Fig.3.10

Nowadays structures are usually conceived and designed as assemblies of structural elements. This means the structural behaviour can be quantified by considering the behaviour of each **structural element** in each load path.

3.2   Concepts of stress and stress distribution

For any structure all the elements that make up each load path must be strong enough to resist the internal structural actions caused by the loads. This means detailed information is required about the structural behaviour of different materials and of the structural elements.

To obtain this knowledge a new concept has to be introduced, this is the concept of **stress** and the related idea of **stress distribution**. Stress is a word in common usage but for engineering it has a particular meaning and that is **force per unit area**. Stress distribution describes how the size of stresses vary from unit area to unit area.

To begin to understand these ideas it is helpful to look at the slice of a column shown in Fig.2.2

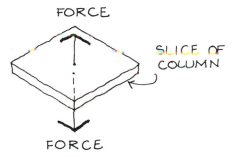

Fig.3.11

Suppose the cross-section of the slice is gridded into squares of the same size (unit squares), then a force can be attached to each square.

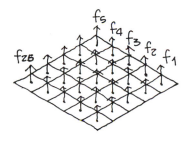

Fig.3.12

The slice is divided into 25 unit squares so the force shown in Fig.3.10 is divided into 25 forces per unit area, f_1 to f_{25}. For equilibrium the numerical sum of the sizes of the twenty five forces per unit area must equal the total force on the cross-section. So far there is no requirement that any of the forces per unit area, f_1 to f_{25}, are numerically equal.

Fig.3.12 is redrawn as Fig.3.13 showing a possible **pattern of variation** for f_1 to f_{25}.

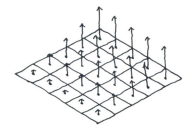

Fig.3.13

The length of each force arrow indicates the size of the force in each unit square and it can be seen that these forces (stresses) vary in a pattern. Suppose, for clarity, just one strip of squares is drawn and the tops of the arrows are joined with a line.

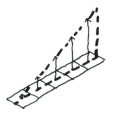

Fig.3.14

As can be seen the resulting shape is a triangle, so along this strip there is a **triangular stress distribution**. Fig.3.13 shows the stresses varying in both directions across the cross-section so the tops of all the arrows can be joined with lines.

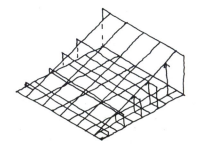

Fig.3.15

70   **Structural element behaviour**

These lines show a triangular shapes in one direction and rectangular ones in the other direction.

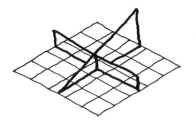

Fig.3.16

It usual to simplify these diagrams of stress distribution by just drawing the outline along the edges.

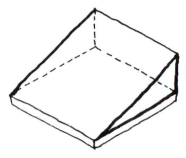

Fig.3.17

Notice that the stress distribution is drawn right across the section. The stress distribution shown in Fig.3.17 is **triangular** in one direction and **uniform** in the other direction. Uniform, or constant, stress distributions mean that the size of the stresses do not vary in that direction.

In general there is no restriction on how stresses vary across any cross-section of any structure except that the sum of the stresses must be equal to the internal force acting at the section and the internal force acts at the **centre of gravity** of the stresses. This new concept of centre of gravity has been used, in a different way for the see-saw (see Fig.2.40). Suppose a see-saw has people of different weights all along its length, their weights are indicated by their sizes.

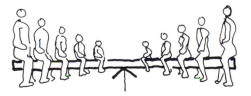

Fig.3.18

In this figure the see-saw is divided into ten equal spaces and to balance, pairs of people of equal weight sit at equal distances from the balance point.

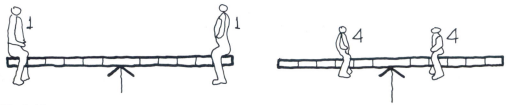

Fig.3.19

Two such pairs are shown. Provided the equal pairs sit at equal distances from the balance point the order of the pairs does not matter. Fig.3.20 shows two different seating arrangements both of which balance and that is because the centre of gravity of the ten people is at the balance point of the see-saw.

Fig.3.20

As the seated height of the people relate directly to their weight these diagrams are conceptually similar to the diagrams of stress distributions. For instance the left-hand seating arrangement shown in Fig.3.20 relates to a triangular stress distribution.

Fig.3.21

If the seating arrangement was altered to have all the heaviest people at one end, Fig.3.22, then the balance point will have to be moved.

Fig.3.22   NEW BALANCE POINT

The new balance point will be nearer the end of the heavier people than the lighter. This is because the centre of gravity of this new seating arrangement is no longer in the centre of the see-saw. In the same way the internal force at any point of any structural element must act at the centre of gravity of the stress distribution. Where stresses vary in two directions across the section the centre of gravity will also vary in two directions.

This new concept of stress allows checks to be made along each load path to ensure that it is strong enough to resist the internal forces caused by the loads. This is checked by making sure that the stresses in the structural elements that are in the load path are less than the **maximum stress** allowed for the structural material being used. In other words the structure must not be **over-stressed**. How a maximum stress is decided is far from straightforward and is discussed later.

Using the concepts of load path, structural action and maximum stress the main parts of the **process of structural design** can be outlined. Once the reason for the existence for the structure has been identified, building, water tank, bridge, then the process can be used.

Step 1 Choose a structural form and material or materials.

Step 2 Identify the loads that the structure has to carry.

Step 3 Find the structural actions in the load path for each loadcase.

Step 4 Check that each load path is not over stressed.

The details of the process of structural design are examined later but now the concept of stress has been explained the main steps of the process can be stated. This gives the basic framework which allows the overall behaviour of structures to be understood or designed.

The main point about the size of stresses is that they can be varied without altering the force. Carrying out step 4 of the design process may indicate that some part of a load path is overstressed. If this is the case then it may be convenient to alter the structure locally, by altering the geometry, so that the stress is reduced below the maximum stress that is allowed.

This idea is used widely in everyday life, stresses are increased or reduced purposely. For example, the weight of a person may be constant, but the stress under the person's feet will vary with the area of the shoe in contact with the ground. This variation may have good or bad effects. Fig.3.23 shows three types of shoes, normal shoes, high-heeled shoes and snow shoes.

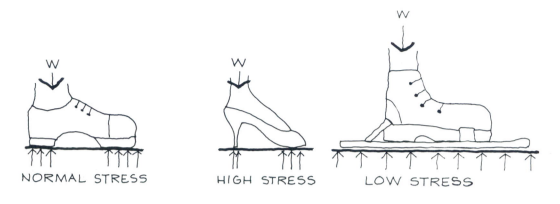

NORMAL STRESS   HIGH STRESS   LOW STRESS

Fig.3.23

Normal shoes cause normal stresses and can be used on surfaces that can resist these stresses. High-heeled shoes however, as they provide a much smaller area to carry the same weight, cause higher stresses under the shoe, particularly under the heel. With very slender (stiletto) heels the stresses can be high enough to permanently damage some types of normal floor surfaces. Where stresses must be kept low, for walking on snow for instance, the area under the foot must be increased. This is why snow shoes prevent people from sinking into snow.

The meaning of 'comfortable' shoes, beds and chairs etc. are party based on limiting the stresses on the human body to 'comfortable' ones. Padded chairs with large seat areas are more comfortable than hard chairs with small seat areas.

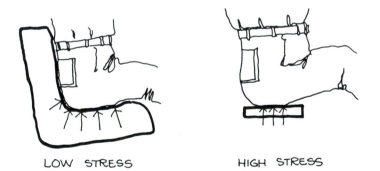

LOW STRESS   HIGH STRESS

Fig.3.24

The idea of deliberately **altering** stress sizes by geometric methods is also widely used in many other objects used by humans. For example drawing pins are provided with large heads, to allow comfortable stresses on the thumb, and pointed shafts to cause high stresses under the point. The point stress is so high that the base surface fails and allows the drawing pin to be driven in.

LOW STRESS

HIGH STRESS

Fig.3.25

The important idea is that for equilibrium, the force on the head must equal the force on the point, but the stresses vary. The stresses are varied by varying the geometry (of the drawing pin). The provision of handles, points, sharp edges and wide shoulder straps are all familiar devices for deliberately raising or lowering stresses.

Returning to engineering structures, the task is to provide a structure which will carry the prescribed loads down the loadpath with 'comfortable' stresses everywhere. Depending on the material used the size of the comfortable stress will vary. For instance as steel is stronger than timber the allowable (comfortable) stress for steel is higher than for timber. So, in a general sort of way, timber structures will have larger structural elements than steel structures if they are to carry the same load.

As it is usually impractical to arrive at satisfactory structures by guesswork or by testing whole structures the modern approach is to calculate the size of the stresses on each loadpath and to check that all the stresses are within set limits. For this to be a practical proposition rather than a research project many simplifying assumptions have to be made. These assumptions allow what is usually known as **Engineer's theory** to be used for stress calculations. Some of these assumptions are concerned with the nature of the material from which the structure is made. These are:

That the material is **isotropic**. This means that the mechanical behaviour of the material is the same in all directions.

That the material is **linear elastic**. An elastic material is one which after deforming under load returns to exactly the same state when the load is removed. If an elastic material deforms as an exact proportion of the load then it is linear elastic. This is discussed further in Chapter 6.

Concepts of stress and stress distribution   75

There are also assumptions about the geometry of the structure. These are:

That the structure is **homogeneous**. This means that is there are no cracks, splits or holes or other discontinuities in the structure.

That the **deflections of the loaded structure are small**. This means that using the shape of the unloaded structure for calculations to determine structural behaviour will not lead to any significant errors. This does not apply to very flexible structures, think for example of a washing line.

That **plane sections remain plane**. This rather cryptic statement means that certain parts of a structure that are flat before loading are still flat after loading. This is explained more fully in this chapter.

The Engineer's theory is used for most structural design because it leads to simple stress distributions in structural elements when they are subjected to internal forces of bending moments, shear and axial forces.

3.3 Axial stresses

An axially loaded structural element has axial internal forces and these cause axial stresses across the element (see Figs.3.11 and 3.12). Using the Engineer's theory leads to a very simple stress distribution.

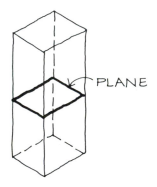

Fig.3.26

This plane cross-section remains plane after the column is axially loaded. This is visually implied in Fig.2.2 where a slice of a loaded column is shown. What the 'plane sections remain plane' assumption means in this case is that the flat faces of the unloaded slice are flat after the slice is loaded.

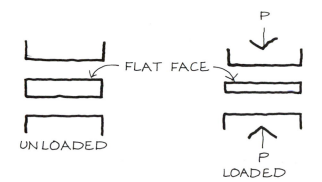

Fig.3.27

This assumption gives a very simple stress distribution for an axially loaded column. Because the loaded faces remain flat all parts of the column cross-section deflect by the same amount.

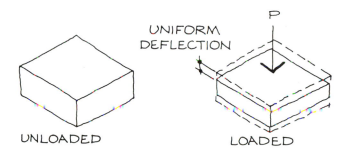

Fig.3.28

Because the deflections are equal over the cross-section the stress (load/unit area) is the same everywhere, in other words there is a constant (or uniform) stress distribution.

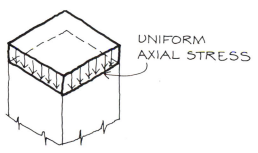

Fig.3.29

The constant stress over the cross-section of an axially loaded column gives a very simple relationship between force and stress and this is:

•   **Axial stress = Axial force divided by the cross-sectional area**

This means that for a given force the size of the stress can be varied by increasing or decreasing the cross-sectional area of the column.

The assumption that plane sections remain plane also gives guidance as to when a structural element should be regarded as a one, two or three dimensional (see Figs.3.1, 3.3 and 3.5).

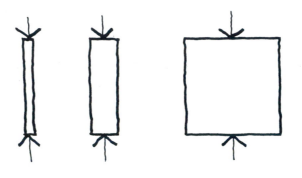

Fig.3.30

The assumption implies that the whole cross-section is equally stressed. Fig.3.30 shows three columns each subjected to a local load. For the widest column it does not seem reasonable to assume that the whole cross-section is equally stressed or even that the whole cross-section is stressed.

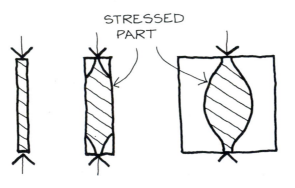

Fig.3.31

This figure shows the stressed part of the three columns. Very approximately the stress 'spreads out' at about 60 degrees. This means that for the widest column plane sections do not remain plane. The faces of the loaded slice of the widest column **do not remain plane**.

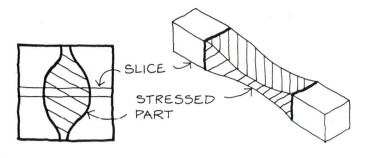

Fig.3.32

From an engineering point of view this gives guidance as to whether structural elements are one, two or three dimensional. Where simple stress distributions are reasonable then elements can be regarded as one dimensional but where the stress distributions are no longer simple the elements are two or three dimensional. In Fig.3.32 the widest column has to be regarded as a two dimensional element. This effect can be seen by pulling on progressively wider and wider sheets of paper. The stressed part of the paper will become taut, the unstressed areas will remain floppy.

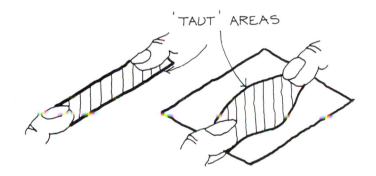

Fig.3.33

3.4   Bending stresses

Where parts of the load path are spanning elements, beams and slabs, the elements will have internal bending forces (moments). The top and bottom surfaces of these elements become curved however plane cross-sections still remain plane.

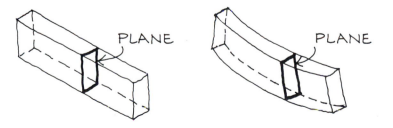

Fig.3.34

Again looking at unloaded and loaded slices (see pages 45 to 46) the plane sections can be identified.

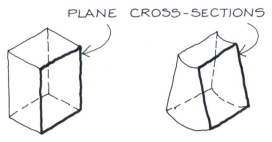

Fig.3.35

By viewing the slice from the side it can be seen that the plane sections rotate.

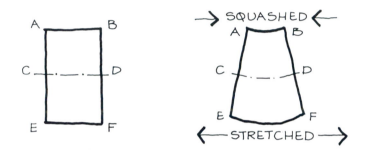

Fig.3.36

When the slice is bent by an internal bending moment, AB is squashed, EF is stretched and CD remains the same. Because the cross-sections remain plane the amount each part of the slice is squashed or stretched varies directly with the distance it is from CD.

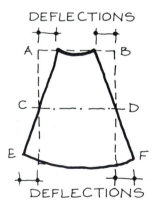

Fig.3.37

As the structural material is linear elastic the force is directly proportional to the deflection so the maximum compression is at AB and the amount of compression decreases constantly from AB to CD. Similarly the maximum tension is at EF and the tension decreases constantly from EF to CD. The maximum compression is at the top of the slice and the maximum tension is at the bottom of the slice and at CD, the change point there is neither compression nor tension. Using this information a stress distribution diagram can be drawn for the side view of the slice.

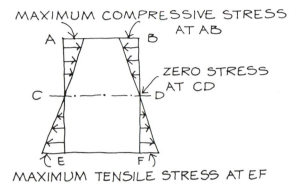

Fig.3.38

If it is also assumed that these stresses that are caused by an internal bending moment do not vary **across** the beam a three dimensional diagram of the stress distribution of the compressive and tensile stresses can be drawn.

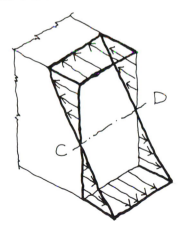

Fig.3.39

This stress distribution, which is based on the assumptions of linear elasticity and plane sections remaining plane is widely (but not exclusively) used in structural engineering. It can be viewed as being in two parts, a triangular distribution of compressive stress and a triangular distribution of tensile stress. Figs.3.8 to 3.12 explained how a stress distribution balanced a force at the centre of gravity of the stress distribution. The two parts of the stress distribution gives a new concept which is the **moment as a pair of forces**. In Figs.2.9 to 2.12 a bending moment is shown as a rotating force. Now the bending moment acting on a slice of a beam can be thought of in three alternative ways. As a rotating force, as a double triangular distribution of compressive and tensile stresses or as a pair of forces.

Fig.3.40

This figure illustrates a **key concept** in the understanding of structural behaviour. This concept applies, often disguised, to almost all structures. These three alternative views are logically connected by the various concepts that have been introduced, really **three steps** have been made.

Step 1   Connects the idea of a moment bending a beam, with plane sections remaining plane, and the sides of a slice of the beam rotating.

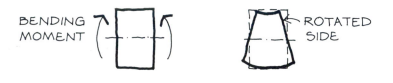

Fig.3.41

Step 2   Connects the deflection of the slice caused by the rotation of the sides to the ideas of linear elasticity and stress distribution.

Fig.3.42

Step 3   This uses the idea that if a force causes a stress distribution, then, where there is a stress distribution there must be a force! And this force must act at the centre of gravity of the stress distribution.

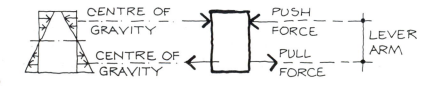

Fig.3.43

82   **Structural element behaviour**

In this figure the **distance** between the 'push forces', which are the effect of the compressive stresses, and the 'pull forces', which are the effect of the tensile stresses is called the **lever arm**. Remembering that any moment is **a force times a distance**, the push and pull forces 'give back' the bending moment. Here, rather confusingly, the force can be the push or the pull force and the distance is the lever arm.

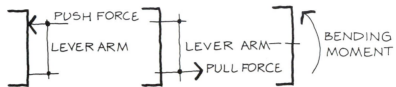

Fig.3.44

The push and pull forces and the lever arm show how by altering the local geometry of the beam the **size** of the stresses can be altered for any bending moment. From Fig.3.44 two statements can be made about the sizes of the forces from the requirements of equilibrium.

Firstly the forces on each face must be in horizontal equilibrium.

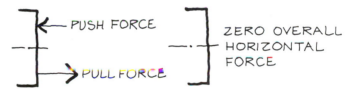

Fig.3.45

So the first statement is:

• **The size of the push force must equal the size of the pull force.**

Secondly, from moment equilibrium the bending moment must equal a force times the lever arm.

So the second statement is:

• **the size of the push force times the lever arm must equal the size of the pull force times the lever arm must equal the size of the bending moment.**

The size of the bending moment is 'fixed' by the position of the element in the load path and the size of the loads the load path has to carry. So, from the second statement, if the lever arm is made bigger the push (or pull) force is smaller and vice versa.

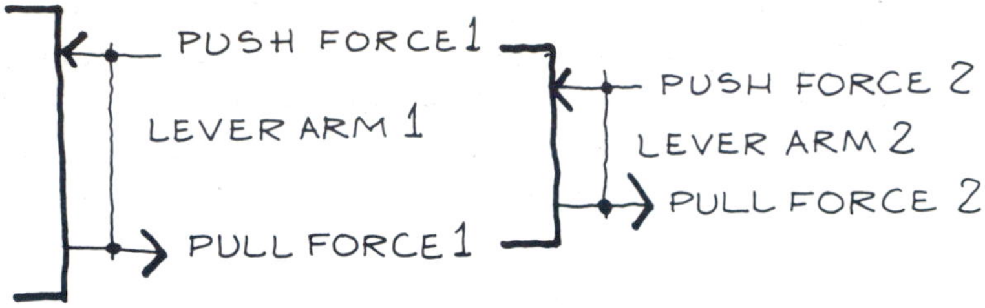

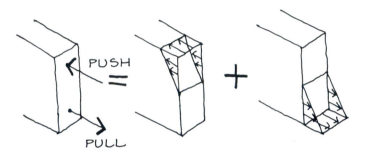

Fig.3.46

Because of statement two, the size of push force 1 times lever arm 1 must equal push force 2 times lever arm 2. As lever arm 1 is bigger than lever arm 2 then push force 1 will be smaller than push force 2. The relationship between the size of stresses and forces is dependent, for any force, on the area and the shape of the distribution. For bending stresses the distribution shown in Fig.3.39 has been used.

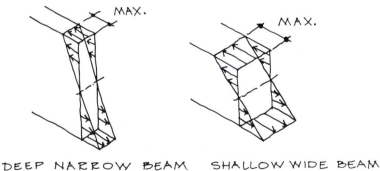

Fig.3.47

All the compressive stresses (force per unit area) on the upper part of the beam must add up to the push force, and all the tensile stresses on the lower part of the beam must add up to the pull force. By varying the **depth** and therefore the lever arm the size of the push and pull forces can be altered, which means the sizes of the stresses can be altered. This is only true if the width of the beam is not altered. The size of the stresses can also be altered by varying the **width** because this alters the area. Or the size of the stresses can be altered by varying both the depth and the width.

DEEP NARROW BEAM   SHALLOW WIDE BEAM

Fig.3.48

84   **Structural element behaviour**

Unlike axially loaded elements which are equally stressed over the whole cross-section (Fig.3.29) beams bent by moments have varying stresses which are at a maximum at the top and bottom. As all structural materials have a maximum usable stress rectangular solid beams like those shown in Fig.3.48 are 'understressed' for all of the cross-section except for the top and bottom faces.

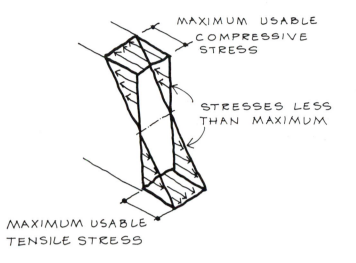

MAXIMUM USABLE
COMPRESSIVE
STRESS

STRESSES LESS
THAN MAXIMUM

MAXIMUM USABLE
TENSILE STRESS

Fig.3.49

It is one ambition of structural design to try and stress all parts of a structure to the maximum usable stress of the structural material being used. In this way no structural material is 'wasted'. This is a sensible ambition provided it does not lead to geometrically complex structures that are expensive to build.

Not only can material be wasted within the depth of a beam but it can also be wasted along its length. Suppose a beam of constant depth and rectangular cross-section is used to carry a load over a simple span. The size of the bending moment will vary along the length of the beam.

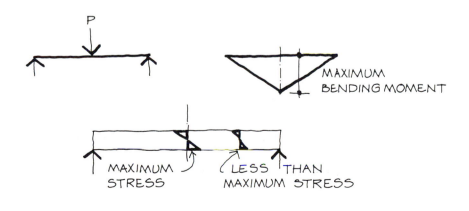

MAXIMUM
BENDING MOMENT

MAXIMUM
STRESS

LESS THAN
MAXIMUM STRESS

Fig.3.50

Bending stresses 85

For this simple structure the maximum stress only occurs at one place where the bending moment is at its maximum. Almost the whole the beam has bending stresses less than the maximum. This contrasts sharply with a column with end loads. Here the whole of the cross-section and the whole of the length of the column can be at the maximum stress and so none of the structural material is wasted.

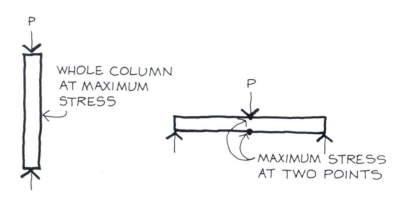

Fig.3.51

To try and make beams more 'stress effective' non-rectangular shapes have been evolved. Although there is some visual evidence that ancient builders were aware of the effect of cross-sectional shapes on the bending performance of beams the pioneers of modern engineering in the early 19th century took some time to evolve efficient shapes. As the maximum stresses for bending are at the top and bottom of a beam more efficient beam sections have more structural material here. These efficient sections are I, channel or box sections.

Fig.3.52

The exact details of these shapes depend on the structural material used as methods of construction are different. Furthermore where bending efficiency is not of paramount importance or for a variety of other reasons, cost, speed of construction, for example other shapes such as tubes, rods, angles may be used.

To understand why the shapes shown in Fig.3.52 are 'bending efficient' it is helpful to compare an 'I' shaped section with a '+' shaped section. Both have the same depth and the same cross-sectional area.

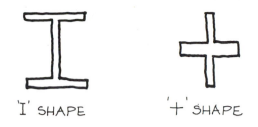

'I' SHAPE   '+' SHAPE

Fig.3.53

As plane sections are assumed to remain plane and both section are assumed to have the same maximum usable stress the side view of the stress distribution is the same as Fig.3.38 for both the sections.

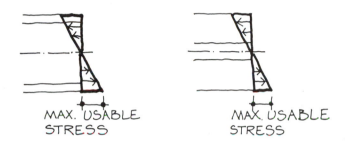

MAX. USABLE STRESS   MAX. USABLE STRESS

Fig.3.54

However if the three dimensional stress diagrams are drawn, similar to Fig.3.39, dramatic differences appear.

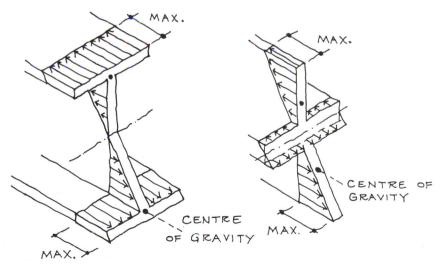

Fig.3.55

The I section has large areas of the cross-section with stresses near to the maximum but the + section has large areas with stresses near to zero. This means that the push and pull forces of Fig.3.43 are much bigger for the I section than for the + section. Also the positions of the centres of gravity of these stresses are different and this gives the I section a larger lever arm than the + section.

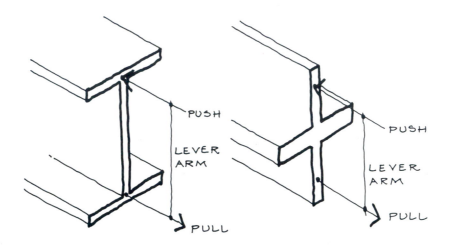

Fig.3.56

The maximum bending moment a beam with any particular cross-section can carry is given by the second statement stated on page 83 and this moment is:

• **The push force, with the maximum usable stress, times the lever arm**

which is the same as:

• **The pull force, with the maximum usable stress, times the lever arm**

Both the lever arm and the push force (or pull force) are greater for the I section than for the + section. Because of this if beams have the same depth, the same cross-sectional area and the same maximum usable stress then those with I sections will be able to resist larger bending moments than those with + sections. Although I beams, as they are called, can be made from timber or reinforced concrete they are readily made from steel. Due to the bending efficiency of I beams they are very widely used in steel construction as any visit to a steel construction site will show.

By adopting more efficient cross-sections more structural material is used at, or near to, the maximum usable stress. But as the size of the bending moment usually varies along a beam higher stresses can be achieved away from the position of maximum bending moment by reducing the width or the depth of the beam.

BENDING MOMENT DIAGRAM   BEAM   DEPTH REDUCED

Fig.3.57

By reducing the depth the lever arm is reduced so that the push and pull forces are higher for the smaller bending moment. Reducing the width has the effect of reducing the stress area for the push and pull forces and so increasing the stresses.

Building a beam with an I section and varying the depth or width to keep the bending stresses high where the size of the bending moment reduces is an efficient use of structural material compared to using a solid rectangular section of constant depth and width. Whether it is worthwhile using the more complex bending efficient beam depends on cost, both of the material and cost of construction. It is common to see beams of varying depth used for road bridges but unusual in building structures. It is also common to see steel I beams but timber structures, particularly in houses, nearly always use timber beams of rectangular cross-section of constant width and depth.

As with columns (see pages 77—78), the assumption that plane sections remain plane is not always valid. There are two situations where it may not apply. The first is when the span of the beam is not more than about five times the depth of the beam. As the plane sections are no longer plane the bending stress distribution is not the one shown in Figs.3.28 and 3.29.

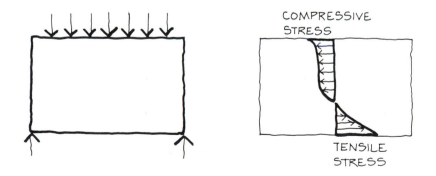

COMPRESSIVE STRESS

TENSILE STRESS

Fig.3.58

These so-called deep beams cannot be regarded as one-dimensional elements but are two-dimensional elements (see page 66).

If a beam is not deep but is made from an I or similar section again plane sections may not remain plane. If the width of the top and bottom parts of the section are increased eventually they will become 'too wide' and not all of the section will be stressed by the bending moment.

NORMAL I BEAM   'TOO WIDE' I BEAM

Fig.3.59

For a normal I beam the bending stresses are assumed to be constant across the top and bottom parts but for wide beams only part of the beam may be stressed and the stress is not constant across the beam.

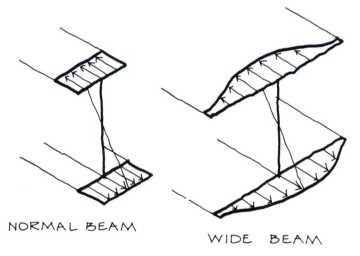

NORMAL BEAM   WIDE BEAM

Fig.3.60

The effect which causes this varying stress across wide beams is called **shear lag** and the part of the beam that is stressed is often called the **effective width**.

3.5   Shear stresses

Axial forces cause axial stresses (see page 77) and bending moments cause bending stresses (see pages 79—82) so it is not unreasonable to expect shear forces to cause **shear stresses**. Shear stresses resist vertical loads so it is to be expected that shear stresses act vertically. For the vertical shear force acting on the face of the slice of the beam ideas similar to those shown in Fig.3.12 can be used. Here, unlike the column, the shear stresses (force per unit area) act in line with the face of the slice.

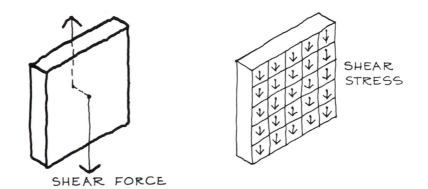

Fig.3.61

Unfortunately the distribution of shear stress cannot be deduced from the straightforward assumptions that were used for axial and bending stress. At the top and the bottom the shear stress must be zero otherwise there would be vertical shear stresses on the surface of the beam which is impossible! So what shape is the distribution of shear stress? Mathematical analysis shows that for a rectangular beam the shear stress distribution has a curved shape, accurately described as parabolic. The maximum is at the middle of the beam and it is zero at the top and bottom and it is constant across the width of the beam.

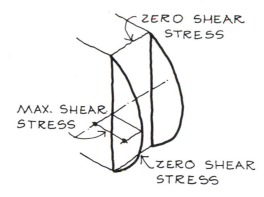

Fig.3.62

It is common to assume for 'practical' structural engineering design that the shear stress distribution is rectangular rather than curved. This means that this shear stress is 50% less than the maximum shear stress and that there are vertical shear stresses at the top and bottom faces! In spite of these inaccuracies this assumption is thought to be worthwhile as it simplifies the numerical calculation of shear stresses.

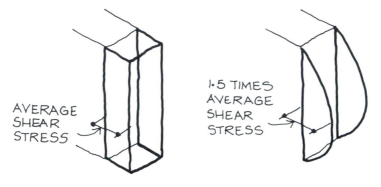

Fig.3.63

With this assumption there is a similar relationship between shear force and shear stress as that used for the axial forces and stresses (see page 78) and this is:

- **Shear stress = Shear force divided by the shear area**

The term **shear area** is introduced because for non-rectangular cross-sectional shapes the 'vertical' area is used rather than the total area.

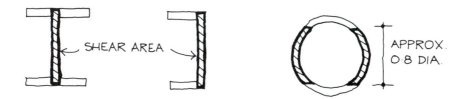

Fig.3.64

This figure shows typical shear areas for a few common structural cross-sections and illustrates the general idea of vertical shear areas.

3.6   Combined stresses

When a one-dimensional element is part of a load path it will have internal forces and these may be axial forces, bending moments or shear forces. These internal forces can be thought of as distributions of axial stress, bending stress and shear stress. With the simplifying assumptions that have been made these stresses have very simple **stress distributions**.

For axial forces and axial stresses:

Fig.3.65

for bending moments and bending stresses:

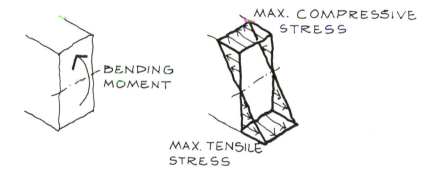

Fig.3.66

and for shear forces and shear stresses:

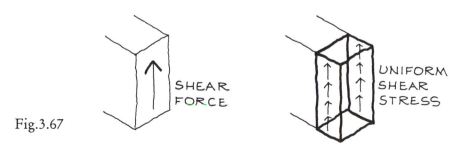

Fig.3.67

On page 56, Fig.2.42 shows how axial forces, bending moments and shear forces vary around a portal frame when it is loaded with a point load. Each part of the portal frame has an axial force and a bending moment and a shear force. These means that at each part of the structure there are distributions of axial stresses **and** bending stresses and shear stresses. Can, and if so how can these stresses be combined to give the total stress distribution? One way is to combine the stresses on the face of a slice, and this type of combination is frequently used in engineering.

This way of combining stresses is relatively straightforward as it 'just adds' stresses that are in the same direction on the face of the slice. Both axial stresses and bending stresses act at right angles to the face of the beam, that is along the beam, so they are combined by adding the stress distributions together.

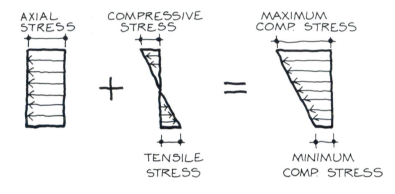

Fig.3.68

In this figure because the size of the axial compressive stress is bigger than the maximum tensile bending stress the whole of the cross-section is in compression. The effect of combining the stresses gives a combined **maximum stress** and a combined **mimimum stress**. The sizes of these stresses are:

- Maximum stress = Axial compressive stress plus Maximum compressive bending stress

- Minimum stress = Axial compressive stress minus Maximum tensile bending stress

Because the shear stress is at right angles to the face of the slice it is not added to the axial and bending stresses but is kept separate. Depending on the relative sizes of the axial and bending stresses and whether the axial stress is tensile or compressive the combined stress distribution is all tensile, tensile and compressive or all compressive.

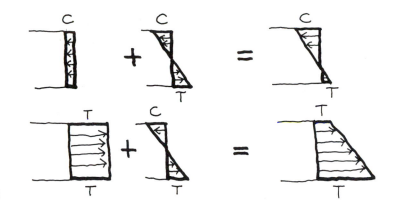

Fig.3.69

The axial stress distribution can be thought of as an axial force acting at the centre of gravity of the axial stress distribution and the bending stress distribution can be thought of as a pair of push-pull forces acting at the centres of gravity of the tensile and compressive parts of the bending stress distribution.

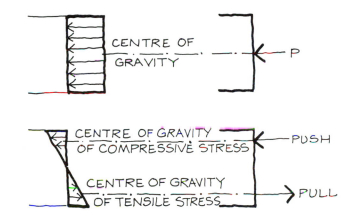

Fig.3.70

As the stress distributions have been combined to give one stress distribution can the forces be combined to give one force, if so what is this force and where does it act? As Fig.3.45 showed the push equals the pull so the combined force can only be the axial force. But this force must act at the centre of gravity of the combined stress distribution.

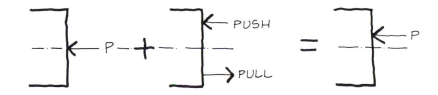

Fig.3.71

And this centre of gravity is not at the centre of gravity of the axial stress

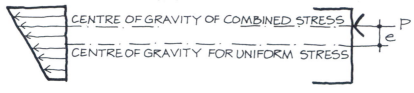

Fig.3.72

The effect of the moment is to 'move' the axial force by a distance **e** from the centre of gravity for uniform axial stress. This distance **e** is called the **eccentricity** and with this new concept many common engineering situations can be better understood.

Before combining the forces there was an axial force P and a bending moment M now there is an axial force P that has 'moved' by a distance, the eccentricity e. What has happened to M, the bending moment? The bending moment still exists but now as P times e. This is the by now familiar force P, times distance e.

Fig.3.73

This idea of the axial force acting at an eccentricity can be used for both internal forces and external forces. If a structural element has an internal axial force and a bending moment then this can be viewed as being the same as the axial force being applied at a point eccentric from the centre of gravity for uniform stress. Alternatively if an external axial load is applied to a structural element at a point eccentric from the centre of gravity for uniform axial stress then this can be viewed as being the same as applying an **axial load plus a moment**. This gives a very simple relationship between axial force, bending moment and eccentricity, which is:

- **Bending moment = axial force times the eccentricity**

or

- **Eccentricity = bending moment divided by the axial force**

Suppose a beam is supported on a wall as in Fig.1.53. Then, for the wall only to have uniform axial stress from the reaction of the beam the beam must be supported exactly at the position of the centre of gravity for this uniform stress distribution.

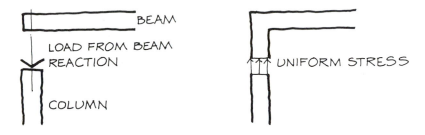

Fig.3.74

This is usually impossible in any real structure unless very precise precautions are taken. This means the reaction from the beam that the wall is supporting will be applied to the wall at an eccentricity. So the wall is loaded by an axial load plus a bending moment.

SAME AS

$M = P \times e$

Fig.3.75

In this figure the eccentricity is within the width of the wall but this will not always be the case. What happens at the base of a garden wall or any other free-standing wall, when the wind blows? The axial force is caused by the weight of the wall itself and the bending moment is caused by the wind blowing horizontally on the wall.

$M = WIND\ MOMENT$

Fig.3.76

Here the eccentricity could be of any size depending on the relative sizes of the axial force caused by the weight of the wall and the moment caused by the wind. The top diagrams in Fig.3.69 shows a cross-section with only compression stresses and a cross-section with compressive and tensile stresses. This means that the eccentricity is greater in the second diagram.

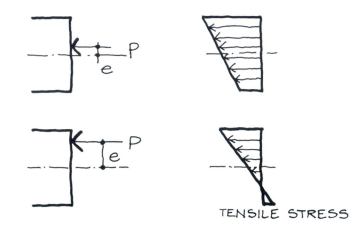

Fig.3.77.   TENSILE STRESS

For rectangular sections the eccentricity must be kept within the middle third of the cross-section if there is to be no tensile stress.

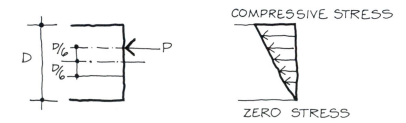

Fig.3.78

This has very important consequences for structures made from structural materials such as masonry or mass concrete which cannot carry significant tensile stresses. For structures made from these materials axial forces must be 'kept' within the central part of the cross-section or the structure will crack or collapse. This is why brick chimneys and walls sometimes blow over in high winds.

This way of combining stresses makes it easy to check that the stresses in a structure are with the limits of the usable stress for the material. This means that all parts of a load path can be checked to see if the elements are strong enough, which is a very important part of structural design.

CHAPTER 4 *Advanced concepts of stress*

In the last chapter the concept of stress was introduced and it was shown how axial forces, bending moments and shear forces could be related to stress distributions in a structural member. By making simplifying assumptions, the Engineer's theory, particularly simple stress distributions were obtained. At the end of the chapter the idea of combining stresses was used to show how axial loads and moments are related. Most engineering design is carried out just using these concepts however the idea of stress can be used to understand more complicated structural behaviour.

This chapter could be omitted on first reading but the concepts used in this chapter give a deeper understanding of structural behaviour. These concepts can be used to understand more complicated structures than those made of simple beam and column elements but they also give deeper insights into how simple structures behave.

4.1   Principal stresses

Section 3.5 of the last chapter gave one way of combining stresses but there is another way of combining stresses at points in a structure by using the idea of **principal stress**. The idea of principal stress is both conceptually and mathematically more difficult than just adding the axial and bending stresses and keeping the shear stresses separate, but it does give much more information on how a structure acts.

To try and understand how a structure acts slices of the structure have been examined and the idea of stresses has been presented as the effect of forces acting on the face of a slice. The structure does not 'know' that the human brain has decided that it is stressed by axial, bending and shear stresses nor does it 'think' that it is made up from a series of slices! When a structural element is loaded by being part of a load path it deforms. Some parts squash and others stretch and internal forces do exist. However the idea that three types of stress exist on the face of a slice cut at right angles to the length of the element is simplistic.

To get a better idea of what is happening inside a structure a 'small part' of the structure is examined. This is similar to the approach used for slices cut at right angles to a one-dimensional structural element only this time there is no restriction on the position of the part examined. This approach can apply to one, two or three dimensional elements.

What is meant by a small part is usually taken as a small cube. How small is small is never stated explicitly but it is larger than molecular size but small enough for stresses not to vary across the faces of the cube! Because the stresses do not vary a stress on a face can be represented by a single **force arrow**.

As before, if a beam is subjected to lateral loads it resists these by internal forces called bending moments and shear forces. Using simplifying assumptions these cause constant shear stress and linearly varying bending stresses on a face cut at right angles to the length of the beam.

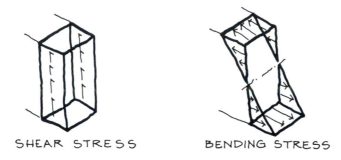

SHEAR STRESS   BENDING STRESS

Fig.4.1

If two small cubes are cut from the beam, one near the top and one near the bottom, then these cubes would be subjected to axial stresses from the bending moment and shear stresses from the shear force.

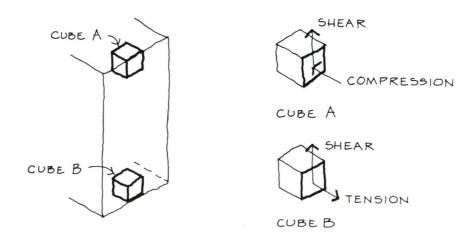

Fig.4.2

100 **Advanced concepts of stress**

Because the cubes have been cut from a beam rather than a more general structure and because they have been cut at right angles to the length of the beam it seems that only two of the six faces of the cube have been stressed. Each of the two faces are stressed with a shear stress and an axial stress.

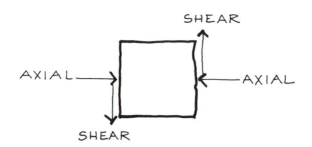

Fig.4.3

The cube is in horizontal equilibrium and vertical equilibrium as the stresses balance but the cube is not in moment equilibrium as the shear stresses are tending to rotate the cube.

Fig.4.4

As this cannot happen there must be other stresses to balance the rotation. These 'new' stresses are shear stresses on the top and bottom faces of the cube.

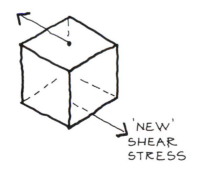

Fig.4.5

So the small cubes when cut from the beam in the positions shown are stressed by axial stresses, vertical shear stresses and the new **horizontal shear stresses**. For moment equilibrium the horizontal shear stresses must be numerically equal to the vertical shear stresses. Because there are no forces across the beam there are no further stresses.

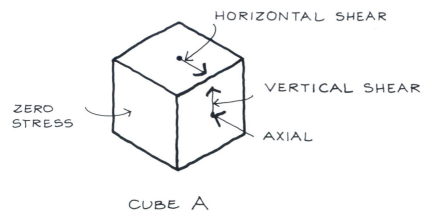

Fig.4.6

Before exploring these ideas further the effects of 'rotating cubes' must be clear. If a square flexible sheet is pulled on two opposite sides it will stretch and if pushed it will squash.

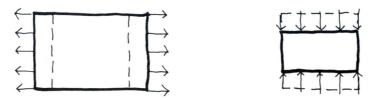

Fig.4.7

If the sides of the sheet are subjected to shear forces the sheet will take up a lozenge (or parallelogram) shape.

Fig.4.8

Draw a square on the sheet at 45 degrees to the sides. If the sheet is pulled on one pair of opposite sides and pushed on the other pair then the square sheet becomes a rectangle but the square drawn on the sheet becomes lozenge shaped.

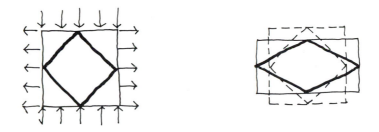

Fig.4.9

And if the sheet is subjected to shear forces the square sheet becomes lozenge shaped and the square drawn on the sheet becomes a rectangle.

Fig.4.10

This shows that for push and pull forces the sheet 'thinks' it is in tension and compression but the drawn sheet 'thinks' it is in shear! When the sheet has shear forces on the sides the situation is reversed and the drawn sheet 'thinks' it is in tension and compression. So, depending on how the element is cut from the structure, the type and the sizes of the stresses depend on the angle at which it is cut. The sheet example illustrates the two-dimensional case (as in the beam). In general the element is a cube and the stresses are in three directions, the concept of rotating is the same but the diagrams would be distorted cubes.

When shear stresses are absent, that is there are **only axial stresses**, then these stresses are called **principal stresses**. At some point in a structure a small cube positioned in some particular direction will, in general, have axial and shear stresses acting on the faces of the cube. To find the principal stresses at this point the cube must be rotated so that the shear stresses are zero. For the previous examples push and pull are principal stresses so no rotation is needed but for shear the element must be rotated by 45 degrees.

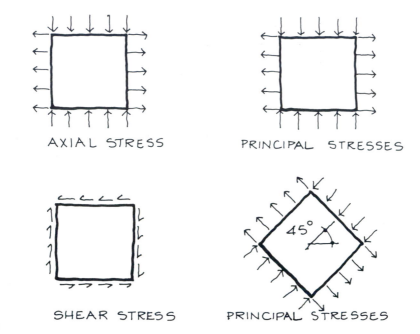

Fig.4.11

AXIAL STRESS   PRINCIPAL STRESSES

SHEAR STRESS   PRINCIPAL STRESSES

Generally at any point in a structure axial and shear stresses will exist. Depending on the numerical size of these stresses the cube will have to be rotated a specific amount for the shear stresses to be zero. The stresses on the rotated cube will be principal stresses.

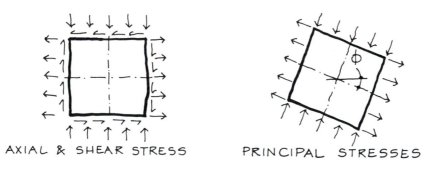

AXIAL & SHEAR STRESS   PRINCIPAL STRESSES

Fig.4.12

As the stresses vary in type and size from point to point of a structure under load the principal stresses will vary in size and direction from point to point. To see what information principal stresses give it is helpful to look at a simple beam loaded with a constant lateral load.

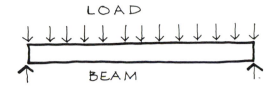

LOAD

BEAM

Fig.4.13

The beam transfers the lateral load to the supports by a system of internal forces which in this case are bending moments and shear forces. As before, the variation in the size of these forces are shown on bending moment and shear force diagrams.

MAX. MOMENT AT MID-SPAN

BENDING MOMENT DIAGRAM

MAX. SHEAR AT SUPPORT

SHEAR FORCE DIAGRAM

Fig.4.14

If the beam has a rectangular cross-section the stresses on a face at right angles to the length of the beam are those shown in Figs.3.49 and 3.62. That is linearly varying for bending and curved (parabolic) for shear.

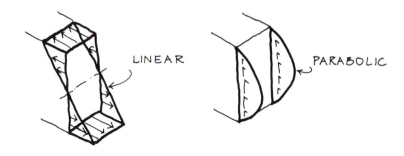

LINEAR

PARABOLIC

Fig.4.15

The size of the bending moment and shear force vary along the length of the beam so the size of the stresses vary both across the depth and along the length of the beam. For bending stresses the maximum is at the top and bottom faces in the centre of the beam and the shear stress is at a maximum at mid-depth at the ends of the beam.

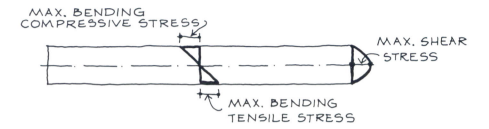

Fig.4.16

For the top and bottom faces the shear stress is always zero and at the centre of the beam the bending stress is always zero. For these points on the beam the principal stresses are horizontal or at 45 degrees, see Fig.4.11.

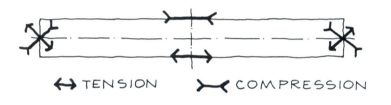

Fig.4.17

For other points on the beam the size and direction of the principal stresses can be calculated and these can be plotted. To indicate how the directions of these stresses change lines can be drawn connecting the stresses at each point.

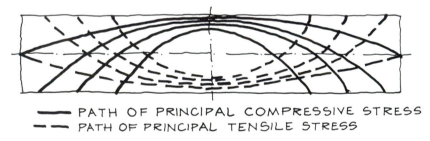

Fig.4.18

The paths of stress (sometimes called stress trajectories) show that for this load case near the middle of the beam the principal stresses are nearly horizontal whilst near the supports the influence of the shear forces causes the stress paths to curve. The size of the stress varies along each path. Fig.4.18 shows that for the beam shown in Fig.4.12 the two sets of principal stresses act in a series of 'arch like' curves. Each curve crossing at right angles with every other curve.

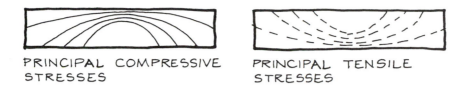

PRINCIPAL COMPRESSIVE
STRESSES

PRINCIPAL TENSILE
STRESSES

Fig.4.19

These diagrams give a far clearer picture of what is happening to the beam than do a series of bending moment and shear force diagrams. Pictures of the paths of principal stress can be drawn for any structure including those for which bending moment and shear force diagrams do not apply. Suppose a plate (a two-dimensional element) has a hole in it and the plate is stretched in one direction. The principal stress paths give a clear picture of how the plate behaves under this loading.

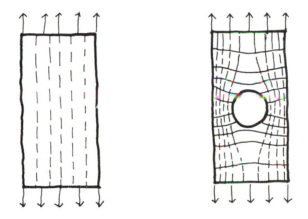

Fig.4.20

For the plate without a hole the lines of tensile stress are parallel but for the plate with the hole these lines have to curve around the hole. Because the line of principal tensile stress curve there are curved lines of principal compressive stress near the hole.

Diagrams can be drawn of principal stresses to show how a column changes into a beam.

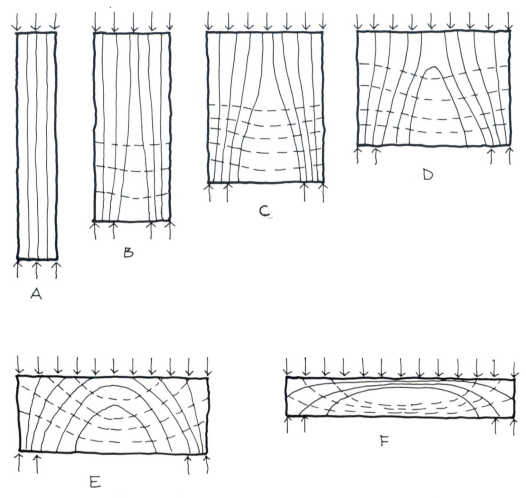

Fig.4.21

Fig.4.21A shows the stresses for a column, a one-dimensional element, and Fig.4.21F shows the stresses for a beam, also a one-dimensional element. Figs.4.21B to E show the stresses for various intermediate stages, and all these are two-dimensional elements. Whilst bending moment, axial and shear force diagrams make sense for the column and beam they cannot usefully be drawn for the intermediate structures.

Principal stresses can also be drawn for curved elements like a shell. If a curved shell is spanning between end supports and loaded laterally the pattern of principal stresses will be similar to those for the beam shown in Fig.4.18 but the stresses will be curved across the shell.

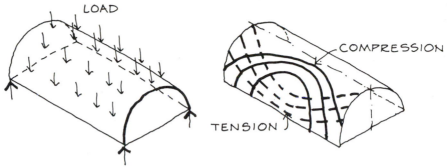

Fig.4.22

As with the beam the two sets of tensile and compressive stresses act as 'arch-like' curves. The compressive stresses move together at the top of the centre of the shell whereas the tensile stresses move apart to the bottom of the shell at the centre.

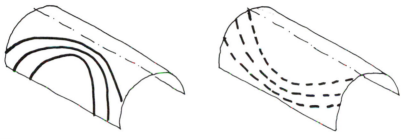

Fig.4.23

It is often quite difficult to calculate the size and direction of the principal stresses for structures in general however if the pattern of the paths of the principal stresses can be visualised this gives a clear picture of how the structure is acting. With materials such as concrete or masonry, which cannot resist significant tensile forces, principal stress paths show where problems may occur or tensile reinforcement is needed.

4.2   The role of shear stresses in beams

When beams do not have simple rectangular cross-sections, as is often the case, the actual behaviour can be quite complex. Fig.3.52 shows a number of common non-rectangular shapes used for beams and Fig.3.55 show the distribution of the bending stresses for an I beam. Fig.3.64 illustrates the idea of shear area used in the simple design of non-rectangular cross-sectional shapes.

The idea of the new shear stress shown in Fig.4.5 is crucial to the understanding of the complex behaviour of beams with non-rectangular cross sections. Although this shear stress is required for the equilibrium of a small cube cut from a beam what does it contribute to the behaviour of a beam with a rectangular cross section? Suppose there are two beams of equal depth, one on top of the other and separated by a perfectly slippery surface.

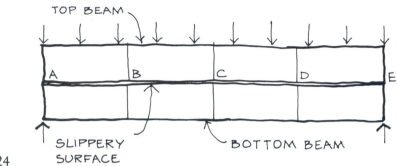

Fig.4.24

The bent shape of the two beams will be the same, with the top of each beam shortening and the bottom lengthening (see Fig.2.13). This means ABCDE of the top beam gets longer and ABCDE of the bottom beam gets shorter. Note that point C is at midspan.

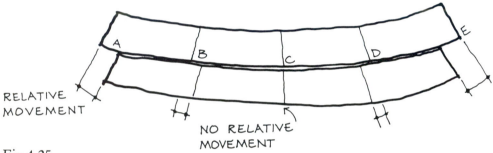

Fig.4.25

Along the slippery surface ABCDE there will be a relative movement between the top and bottom beams. At midspan the movement is zero and the relative movement increases to become a maximum at the ends A and E. If the two beams are to act as one beam there would no relative movement along ABCDE. If this movement is to be zero there must be a force to stop the movement and the force will be proportional to the relative movement. So the force will be zero at midspan and a maximum at the ends.

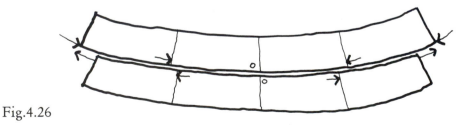

Fig.4.26

It is the existence of these forces that cause the new shear stress. Because it is acting along the beam it is often called **horizontal shear** (or in timber design rolling shear). It is this horizontal shear stress that alters the bending stress distribution from a 'two beam' to a 'single beam' one.

ZERO HORIZONTAL
SHEAR STRESS

HORIZONTAL
SHEAR STRESS

Fig.4.27

Not only does the size of the horizontal shear stress vary along the beam but it also varies within the depth of the beam. The size of the stress at any point within the depth of the beam is related to the size of the horizontal force being transferred. This force is due to the change in size of the bending stress across a slice. The difference in the size of the bending stresses has an out of balance horizontal force on any horizontal cut and this force is balanced by the horizontal shear stresses at the cut.

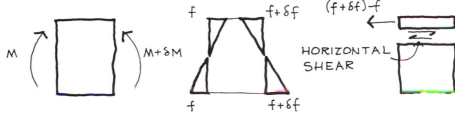

Fig.4.28

By taking a series of horizontal cuts across the slice the size of the horizontal shear stresses can be found. At the top and bottom faces of the beam this stress is zero whilst at mid-depth it is at a maximum. The actual shape of the distribution is parabolic, the same shape as the distribution of the vertical shear stress (see Fig.3.62).

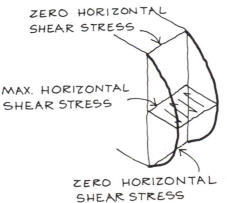

ZERO HORIZONTAL
SHEAR STRESS

MAX. HORIZONTAL
SHEAR STRESS

Fig.4.29

ZERO HORIZONTAL
SHEAR STRESS

The role of shear stresses in beams   111

If an I section is used for a beam the horizontal shear stress still exists but the distribution is rather different. Because of the changed distribution of bending stresses the largest part of the bending stress is in the top and bottom flanges (see Fig.3.55). The maximum horizontal shear stress is still at mid-depth but because the section is 'made up' of flanges and a web the horizontal shear force has to be transmitted from one part of the beam to another. If the section is 'exploded' it can be seen how the horizontal shear forces 'join' it together.

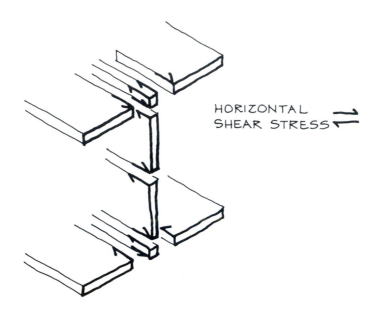

Fig.4.30

What is happening is that the change in push force in each half of the top flange is being transmitted to the top of the web by a horizontal shear force.

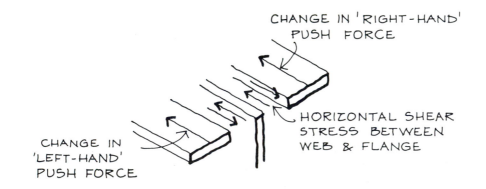

Fig.4.31

112   **Advanced concepts of stress**

The total change in flange force is then transmitted by a horizontal shear force to the web underneath the flange.

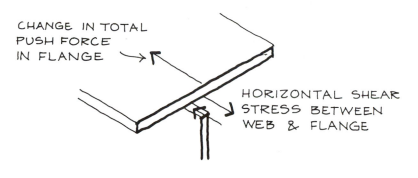

CHANGE IN TOTAL PUSH FORCE IN FLANGE

HORIZONTAL SHEAR STRESS BETWEEN WEB & FLANGE

Fig.4.32

At the mid-depth of the beam the total change in web and flange force is being transmitted by a horizontal shear force.

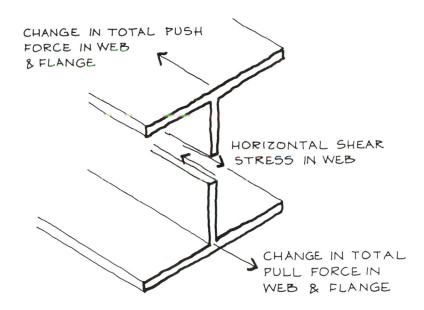

CHANGE IN TOTAL PUSH FORCE IN WEB & FLANGE

HORIZONTAL SHEAR STRESS IN WEB

CHANGE IN TOTAL PULL FORCE IN WEB & FLANGE

Fig.4.33

Similarly for the change in bending tensile forces. Note that the word force has been used rather than stress because the stress will depend on the relative thickness of the flanges and the web. The horizontal shear stress in the web is balanced by the vertical shear stresses but the horizontal shear stresses in the flange are acting in the plane of the flange and have to be balanced by shear stresses acting **across** the flange.

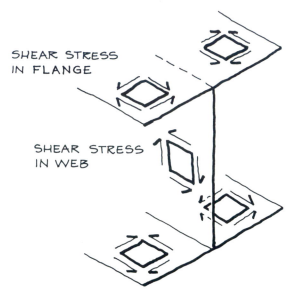

SHEAR STRESS
IN FLANGE

SHEAR STRESS
IN WEB

Fig.4.34

The cross flange shear stress is zero at the outer edges and increases linearly towards the web. Because the web shear under the flange is the sum of the change of both the left and right-hand push forces there is an increase at this point. The stress in the web then varies parabolically with a maximum at mid-depth.

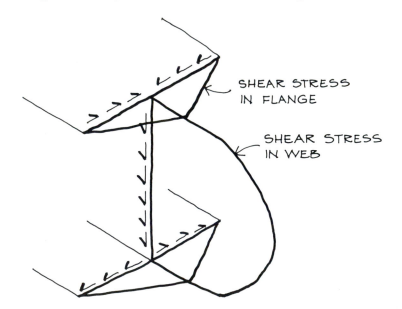

SHEAR STRESS
IN FLANGE

SHEAR STRESS
IN WEB

Fig.4.35

These shear stresses can be plotted on the cross-section. These shear stresses in built up sections are often called the **shear flow**. Strictly the shear flow is a force as it is the shear stress times the thickness.

Fig.4.36

The horizontal forces in each flange are in horizontal equilibrium and the vertical shear stresses are in vertical equilibrium with the shear force. However if a channel section is used for a beam the shear flow can be obtained from the diagram for the I beam.

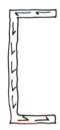

Fig.4.37

Here although the horizontal forces in each web are in overall equilibrium these forces are some distance apart which means there is a moment.

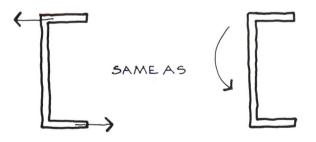

SAME AS

Fig.4.38

This moment is trying to twist the channel rather than bend it. This example of the channel has been introduced to show how structural actions can become complicated even for a 'simple' beam and a 'simple' section like a channel.

4.3   Effect of beam cross-section

The reason the channel wants to twist and the I beam does not is because the I beam is symmetric about a vertical line and the channel is not.

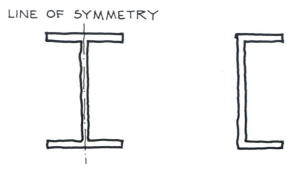

Fig.4.39

More generally the effect of the cross-sectional shape of a structural element interacts with the type of loading to produce different types of structural behaviour. This structural behaviour can become extremely complicated for general shaped elements. The important point is to appreciate what causes simple or complex behaviour.

For axially loaded elements, if all parts are to be equally stressed, i.e. uniform stress distribution (see Fig.3.29), then the load has to be applied to the element at a particular point. This point is confusingly called the centre of gravity of the cross-section, a better term is **centre of area**. This point is the same point that balances a uniform stress distribution. To illustrate this concept imagine a tee shaped platform carrying people of equal weight equally spaced on the platform.

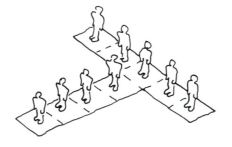

Fig.4.40

These people are supposed to represent a uniform stress distribution. But where is the balance point? Unlike the see-saw the balance point has to be found in two dimensions. Two pictures can be drawn, one along the tee and one across it.

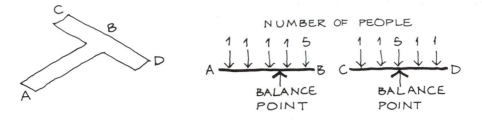

Fig.4.41

In the AB direction the balance point will be nearer B than A, but for the CD direction the loading is symmetrical so the balance point is midway between C and D. The balance points are really lines and where these lines intersect is the centre of area.

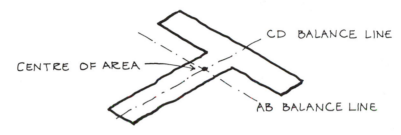

Fig.4.42

So if the axial loads are applied through the centre of area a uniform stress distribution will be caused. If another shaped cross-section (or platform) is used then the centre of area will move. The balance lines will always be along any axes of symmetry so for shapes with two axes of symmetry the centre of area will be at the intersection of the axes.

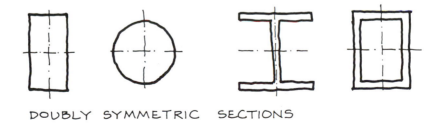

DOUBLY SYMMETRIC SECTIONS

Fig.4.43

Notice that for the box section the centre of area is not actually within the cross-section! Where there is only one axis of symmetry the unsymmetrical balance line will vary with the geometrical dimensions of the cross-section.

Effect of beam cross-section 117

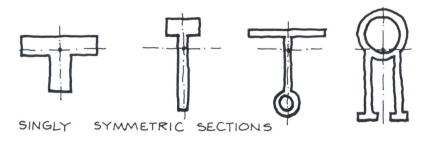

SINGLY SYMMETRIC SECTIONS

Fig.4.44

And where there is no axis of symmetry the centre of area can only be found by calculation.

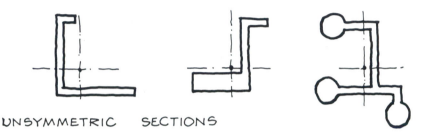

UNSYMMETRIC SECTIONS

Fig.4.45

For each cross-sectional shape there is only one position for the centre of area and the position depends on the shape, and if the section is not doubly symmetric, the dimensions of the cross-section. In other words the centre of area is a **section property**. In actual structures it is not easy to ensure that axial loads are always applied through the centre of area.

As well as affecting the behaviour of elements when axially loaded the cross-sectional shape also affects the way they behave when they bend as beams. When a beam bends part of the cross-section is in compression and part is in tension (see Fig.3.38). Where the stress changes from compression to tension the stress is zero. The question is where is this point? And the answer is where it needs to be to satisfy horizontal equilibrium (see Fig.3.46). This is not a helpful answer but if no simplifying assumptions are made the position of zero stress in not easy to find. If the Engineer's theory (see page 75) is used the position can be found. With this theory plane sections are expected to remain plane and the structural material to be linear elastic. This results in the points of zero stress due to bending to be in a straight line. Because this is a line of zero stress it is often called the **neutral axis**.

For a rectangular beam loaded laterally there has been a tacit assumption (see pages 80 to 82) that the neutral axis is across the beam at mid-depth.

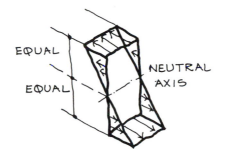

Fig.4.46

Because the horizontal (push/pull — see Fig.3.44) forces must balance, then, for cross-sections that are symmetric about a horizontal axis that are being loaded vertically, the neutral axis will be at mid-depth.

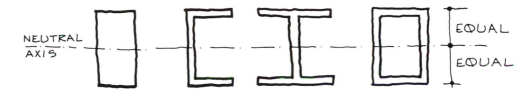

Fig.4.47

Because of this symmetry the stress due to bending at the top of the section will be equal to the stress at the bottom of the section.

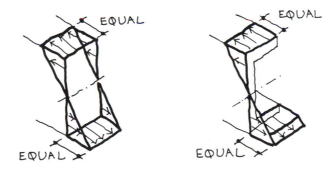

Fig.4.48

For sections that are not symmetrical about a horizontal axis the neutral axis will not be at mid-depth, but where will it be? Surprisingly and very fortunately it passes through the centre of area!

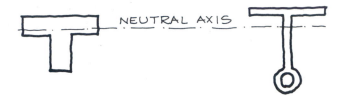

Fig.4.49

As the Engineer's theory is being used the bending stresses vary linearly with the depth of the beam (see pages 80 and 82). Where the neutral axis is not at mid-depth this linear variation means that the stresses at the top and the bottom will no longer be equal.

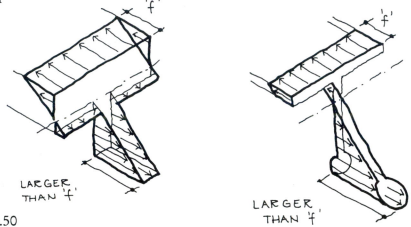

Fig.4.50

That the neutral axis passes through the centre of area may seem fortuitous but this is not so. To see why consider a cross-section in two parts, one double the area of the other. The centre of area is the balance point for constant stress over the whole area of the cross-section. In this case it means the stress **f** is constant over the two parts of the section.

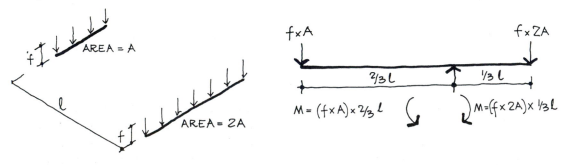

Fig.4.51

The force in each part of the cross-section is the area multiplied by the constant stress f. The moments about the balance point (see Fig.1.41) will be equal if the position is as shown in Fig.4.51. For bending, plane sections remain plane and due to linear elasticity the stress is directly proportional to the movement. For this section, if it is rotated about the balance point (centre of area — see Fig.3.37) the movement of one part will be twice that of the other. This means where the movement is double the stress will be double.

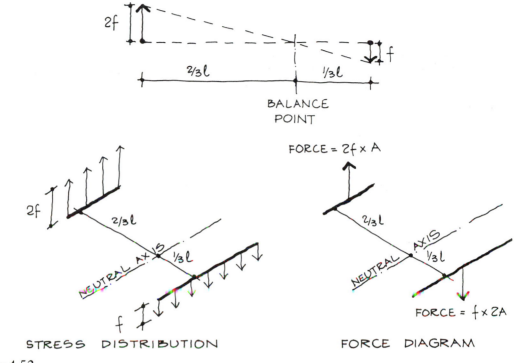

Fig.4.52

This diagram shows that for the part of the section with area **A** the stress is 2f giving a force of 2fA in one direction. For the part of the section with an area of 2A the stress is f giving a force of 2Af in the opposite direction. Therefore the push/pull forces are equal and opposite as required for horizontal equilibrium (see Fig.3.45). This in principle is why the neutral axis goes through the centre of area and this principle applies to a cross-section of any shape or any number of 'parts'.

4.4 Biaxial bending

Whilst the neutral axis goes through the centre of area its position rotates depending on the loading. For a rectangular beam loaded 'vertically' the neutral axis is 'horizontal', that is at right-angles to the load direction. The same is true for the beam if it is loaded 'horizontally'. The associated stress diagrams due to bending are drawn as before.

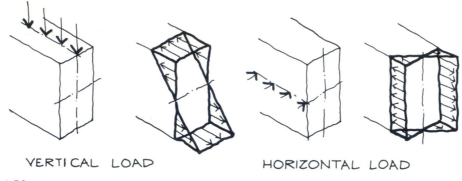

VERTICAL LOAD   HORIZONTAL LOAD

Fig.4.53

If both the vertical and horizontal loads (not necessarily of the same size) are applied to the beam simultaneously the beam will have a 'new' neutral axis. The position of this neutral axis can be found by adding together the two bending stress diagrams. This addition is similar to the addition of stresses shown in Fig.3.68.

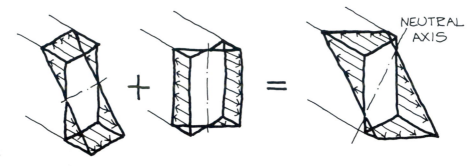

Fig.4.54

Whilst this is relatively straightforward what is not obvious is that now, except for a few special cases, the new neutral axis is not at right-angles to the axis of loading. Why is this? The answer is the beam has 'provided' push/pull forces at the centres of gravity of the now rather odd shaped stress distributions. These forces are also on the line of the load axis. This neutral axis is no longer at right-angles to the load axis which means that the beam does deflect in the direction of the load!

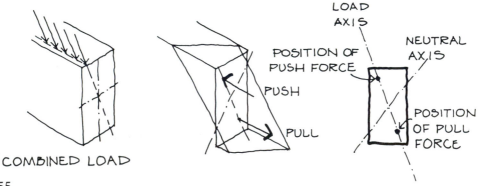

COMBINED LOAD

Fig.4.55

The reason for this is that any cross-section will have axes of bending called **principal axes**, and these are another section property. When the load is applied through a principle axis the neutral axis will be at right-angles to the load axis but for loads in other directions this will not be true. To predict the bending behaviour of beams of different cross-sections the positions of the principal axes need to be known. They intersect at the centre of area but in what direction do they go? They will go through an axis of symmetry so for sections with an axis of the symmetry the directions of the principal axes are clear.

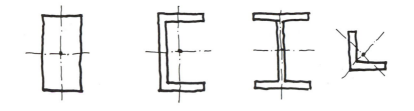

Fig.4.56

For sections with no axis of symmetry the direction can only be calculated.

Fig.4.57

When a beam bends there will be bending stresses and, except for very special cases, there will also be shear stresses. The effect of shear stresses on beams has been described (pages 109 to 115). Fig.4.38 shows that shear stresses may also cause twisting even when only vertical loads are present. This is because of another section property called the **shear centre**. The shear centre is the point through which the load axis must pass to avoid any twisting caused by the shear stress distribution. (Conversely the shear centre is the point about which the section will twist if loaded with twisting loads.) For doubly symmetric or skew symmetric cross-sections the shear centre will coincide with the centre of area. For cross-sections with only one axis of symmetry the shear centre will be on this axis of symmetry but will not in general coincide with the centre of area.

Biaxial bending 123

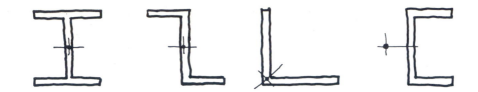

SHEAR CENTRES

Fig.4.58

Three important **section properties** of cross-sectional shapes have been identified and these are:

• **Position of the centre of area**

• **Directions of the principal axes**

• **Position of the shear centre**

For doubly symmetric cross-sections these properties are readily found but for general cross-sectional shapes these properties can only be found by calculation.

Knowing these section properties the distributions of axial, bending and shear stress can be drawn provided the assumptions of the Engineer's theory are used. Even when the Engineer's theory is used, for structural elements of general cross-sectional shape the structural behaviour is quite complex. If the element itself is curved or varies in cross-sectional shape along its length engineering analysis, both conceptual and mathematical, rapidly becomes extremely difficult. This analysis is the subject matter of advanced texts or even research papers.

4.5   Composite elements and pre-stressing

Often structural elements are made from more than one type of structural material to form composite structural elements. These combinations are made to exploit the different qualities of the materials to produce an element that performs better than one made from only one of materials. The usual combination is of a relatively cheap material such as concrete or masonry with a relatively expensive material such as steel. In these elements the concrete or masonry carry the compressive stresses and the steel carries the tensile stress.

By far the most common form of composite construction for building structures is **reinforced concrete**. Reinforced concrete, together with structural steelwork, is widely used throughout the world for a great variety of structures both large and small. Because concrete has no useful engineering tensile strength the steel, usually called reinforcement or re-bar, is placed in areas of the structural element where calculations predict tensile stresses. This is where diagrams like Fig.4.18 are useful. This shows that there are tensile stresses along the bottom of the beam near the centre and these slope near the ends of the beam. So, to make a reinforced concrete beam, there would be longitudinal reinforcement in the bottom of the beam and sloping reinforcement towards the ends.

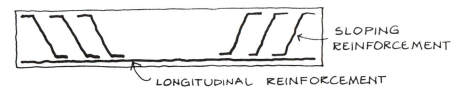

Fig.4.59

Historically the sloping bars shown in Fig.4.59 were used but it is now more usual to resist the sloping tensile stresses by vertical reinforcement. This vertical reinforcement is bent into rectangles called links. The reinforcement is made into a cage by tying the bars together with wire.

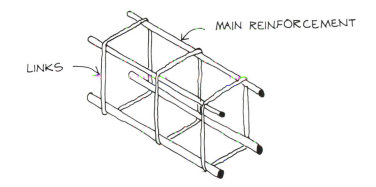

Fig.4.60

The cage is placed into a mould or form and the wet concrete is poured around the reinforcement thus forming a composite element. As the concrete dries it shrinks and 'grips' the reinforcement. To aid this grip the reinforcing bars are often made with a rough pattern.

Fig.4.61

When the composite beam is bent by a moment the principle of push/pull forces (see Fig.3.43) still applies but because concrete cannot resist tensile stresses the pull force is resisted by tensile stresses in the reinforcement.

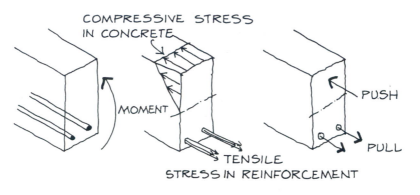

Fig.4.62

For the steel and concrete to act compositely the steel must not slip relatively to the concrete. This is the same effect as that shown in Fig.4.27 for horizontal shear stresses. The relative slip is resisted by horizontal shear stresses on the face of the reinforcement, these stresses are often called **bond stresses**.

Fig.4.63

The behaviour of reinforced concrete when subjected to shear forces is very complex but, as can be seen from the principal stress diagram (Fig.4.18) in areas of high shear there are diagonal tensile stresses. In unreinforced concrete these would cause cracks at right angles to the lines of tensile stresses.

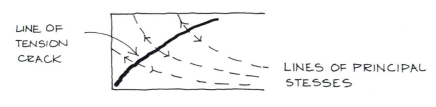

Fig.4.64

The role of the diagonal reinforcing bars or links is to provide tensile strength across these lines of tensile force.

TENSILE FORCES IN REINFORCEMENT
PROVIDING TENSILE STRENGTH
ACROSS TENSION CRACK

Fig.4.65

Although in theory concrete only needs reinforcement in areas of tensile stress, except for very minor elements, it is usual to provide a complete cage of reinforcement. The reinforcement that resists the tensile stresses is called the **main reinforcement** and the other reinforcement is called **nominal reinforcement**. For a portal frame shown in Fig.2.27 loaded on the cross-beam the bending moments cause tensile bending stresses in both the cross-beam and the columns.

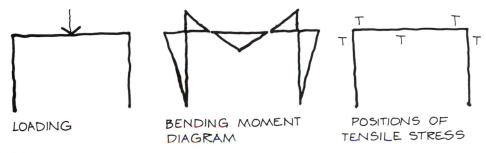

LOADING   BENDING MOMENT   POSITIONS OF
           DIAGRAM   TENSILE STRESS

Fig.4.66

Here the main reinforcement is placed in areas of tensile stress, but for practical reasons whole cages of reinforcement would be used for the cross-beam and the columns.

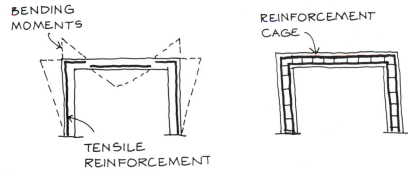

BENDING
MOMENTS

REINFORCEMENT
CAGE

TENSILE
REINFORCEMENT

Fig.4.67

It is not always possible to provide continuous reinforcement in areas of tensile stress so reinforcing bars are 'joined' by lapping. The bars are laid next to each other in the mould and the concrete is poured around both bars. The force is transmitted from one bar to other by bond (shear) stresses in the surrounding concrete.

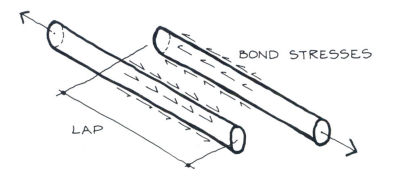

Fig.4.68

By lapping bars parts of the reinforced concrete structure can be cast in a preferred sequence. In the case of the portal frame the sequence would be foundations, columns and then the cross-beam. Bars would be left projecting from each part to be lapped with the reinforcement of the next part.

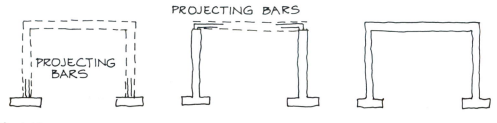

Fig.4.69

Whilst reinforced concrete is the most common form of composite construction structural steelwork and reinforced concrete can also be combined to form structural elements. This form is frequently used in spanning structures where the floor structure, a two-dimensional reinforced concrete element, is also used as part of the main beams, one-dimensional structural steel elements.

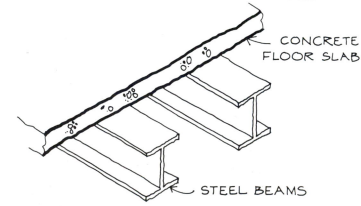

Fig.4.70

To achieve composite action the slab is joined to the top of the floor beams by what are known as **shear connectors**. These are pieces of steel, usually in the form of studs, welded to the top of the beam.

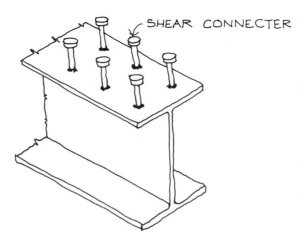

SHEAR CONNECTER

Fig.4.71

The concrete slab is cast around the shear connectors and these prevent the slab and the top of the steel beam moving relatively to each other. This allows horizontal shear stresses to develop between the slab and the steel beam as is explained on pages 110 and 111.

SLAB

SLIP

BEAM

HORIZONTAL SHEAR STRESS BETWEEN SLAB & BEAM

Fig.4.72

Now the floor beam is the steel beam and the concrete slab. By the addition of the shear connectors the concrete slab becomes part of the compression flange.

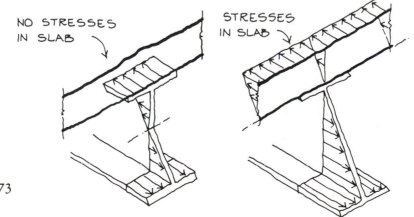

NO STRESSES IN SLAB

STRESSES IN SLAB

Fig.4.73

Another form of composite construction is to **pre-stress** materials such as concrete (or less often masonry). This is a technique which causes stress in structural elements **before** they are loaded. Like the addition of reinforcement, the purpose of pre-stressing is to add tensile strength to elements made of materials which can only resist compressive stresses. The principle can be illustrated by stressing together some match boxes with an elastic band. This pre-stressed element can now act as a beam.

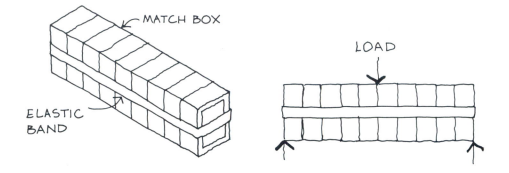

Fig.4.74

Here the stretched elastic band causes compressive stresses between the match boxes before is acts as a beam. When the lateral load is applied it is resisted by internal push/pull forces which cause tensile and compressive bending stresses (see Fig.3.40). Provided the numerical size of the pre-stressed compressive stress is equal or greater than the bending tensile stress the match boxes, with the pre-stress, will act as a beam. The stresses due to pre-stress and bending can be combined as shown in Fig.3.69.

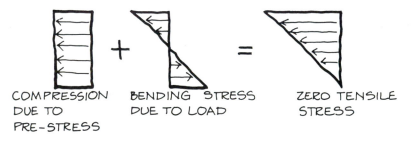

Fig.4.75

Exactly the same principle is used to make pre-stressed concrete elements. The pre-stress is caused by tensioning the steel reinforcement and this can be done in two ways called **pre-tensioning** and **post-tensioning**. For pre-tensioning the steel reinforcement is tensioned by jacking against strong points fixed to the ground, then the concrete is poured around the tensioned reinforcement. When the concrete has hardened the jacks are released.

130   **Advanced concepts of stress**

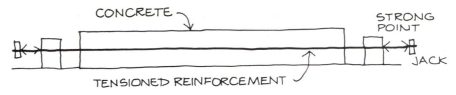

Fig.4.76

When the jacks are released the stretched reinforcement tries to shorten. But, because the hardened concrete has shrunk around tensioned reinforcement (see Fig.4.61), it prevents the reinforcement shortening and by doing this goes into compression. So in the case of pre-tensioned pre-stressed concrete there are bond (shear) stresses between the (tensioned) reinforcement and the concrete before any load is applied.

Fig.4.77

Concrete can also be pre-stressed after it has hardened, this is called post-tensioning. The concrete element is made with a hole through it, this hole is usually called a duct. The reinforcement to be stressed it then threaded through the duct, in many cases the reinforcement is put in the duct before the concrete is cast. When the concrete is hard enough the reinforcement is tensioned by jacking it against the end of the concrete element. This causes tension in the reinforcement and compression in the concrete. When the required tension force has been obtained the reinforcement is 'locked off' and the jacks removed. There are several methods of locking off and these depend on the proprietary method being used.

In the pre-tensioned method the force in the tensioned reinforcement is transferred to the concrete along the whole length of the element but in the post tensioned method the force is transferred at the jacking points. This can sometimes require special end details to make sure the concrete is not over-stressed locally.

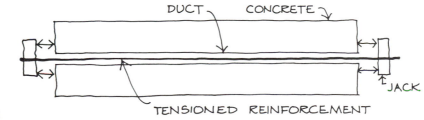

Fig.4.78

In the same way as eccentric applied loads cause axial stresses and bending stresses (see Fig.3.75), if the tensioned reinforcement does not go through the centre of area of the section then the pre-stress will not be a constant axial stress. This can be an advantage as it can increase the size of the compressive stress in the part of the element that will have tensile stresses due to the applied load.

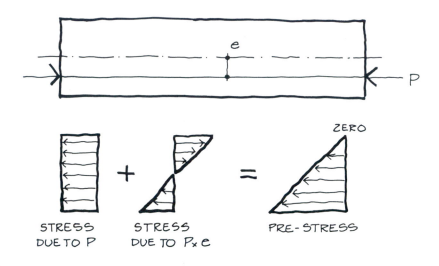

STRESS DUE TO P + STRESS DUE TO $P_x e$ = PRE-STRESS

Fig.4.79

The idea is that the stress distribution due to pre-stress is completely reversed under maximum applied lateral load. This means that, for a simple beam element, the stress at the top is zero due to pre-stress and the stress at the bottom due to pre-stress and applied load is zero.

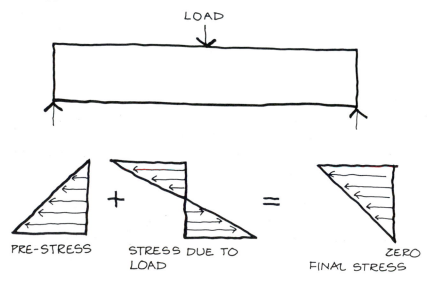

PRE-STRESS + STRESS DUE TO LOAD = FINAL STRESS

Fig.4.80

The effect of the eccentrically applied pre-stress is to apply a moment to the element and this moment can be used to counteract the effect of the bending moment caused by the self-weight of element. For concrete elements the self-weight is a significant part of the total load. By careful adjustment of the pre-stress force and its position the stress distribution due to pre-stress and self-weight can be made triangular, with zero stress at the top face.

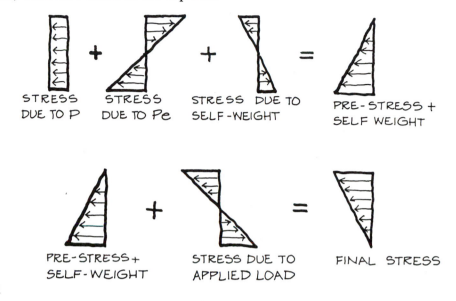

Fig.4.81

When the maximum live load is applied the stress diagram is reversed as before. It is usual for the maximum compressive stresses to be the maximum allowable for the concrete. By using pre-stress in this way the concrete member can be used more effectively than a reinforced element because the maximum stress in a reinforced element has to include both self-weight and live load. Because of this the pre-stressed element can carry higher loads or alternatively be shallower for the same load than a reinforced element.

The pre-tensioning method means that the pre-stressing reinforcement has to be straight but there is no restriction on the shape duct that can be cast into a concrete element. This means that the post-tensioning method allows the position of the pre-stressing force to be varied along the element. As the lines of the principal tensile are rarely straight the ducts can be cast into the concrete along these lines.

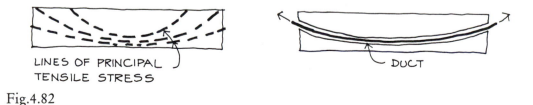

Fig.4.82

This has the advantage of putting compressive stresses into the element which directly counteract the tensile stresses caused by the applied load.

The method of pre-tensioning is ideally suited to the production of **standard** pre-stressed elements made in pre-casting yards. These types of elements are used extensively as floor spanning members or beams, usually called lintels, over openings in masonry walls. The method of post-tensioning is relatively slow so its use in building structures is relatively rare and is limited to unusually large elements in major buildings. It is used extensively for large bridges. Often these are made from a number of pre-cast units which are stressed together exactly like the matchboxes (see Fig.4.74).

Composite action can also be used to increase the 'size' of a beam in a masonry wall. This is done by making the masonry that is built on top of the concrete beam act with the beam.

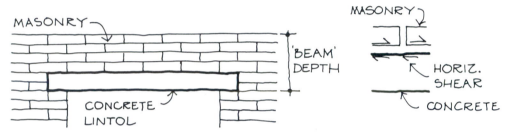

Fig.4.83

This is similar in principle to the action between the concrete slab and the steel beam shown in Fig.4.71. Here the horizontal shear stresses that are essential for the composite action are resisted by the mortar joints, the beam and the masonry units (bricks or blocks).

Many other examples of composite action could be given but the essential point is to understand the role played in the total structural action of the element by the different materials. This is done by understanding how each part of the element is stressed when it acts as part of a load path.

As buildings are constructed by joining together a variety of elements, walls, floors, windows, stairs etc. it is important to be sure that loads do go down the chosen load paths and not into non-loadbearing elements that are not capable of carrying the loads. This is really composite action in reverse ! For example the portal frame when loaded, will deflect. If the portal frame is glazed as part of the building design the glazing would try and prevent the portal frame from deflecting. This means that the glazing is acting compositely with the portal frame to 'make' a two-dimensional wall element.

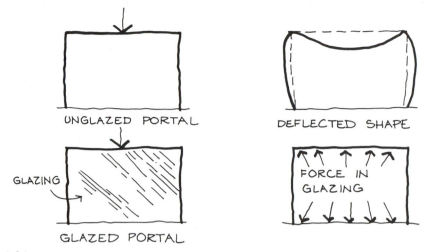

Fig.4.84

Unless the glazing is designed to be part of the load path it may fail as it tries to carry a share of the load due to composite action. In these cases special 'soft' joints, or other devices must be introduced to prevent the composite action. These are exactly opposite to the idea of the shear connectors shown in Fig.4.71. In this case the joint between the glazing and the portal frame must be designed so that the portal frame can deflect without loading the glazing.

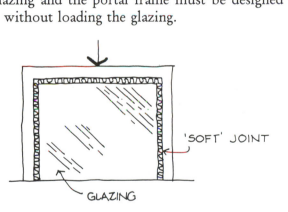

Fig.4.85

4.6 Summary

This section shows how structural elements act when they are loaded as part of a load path. This behaviour has been characterised by the stress distribution at each point of the element. These stresses are caused by the structural actions, axial bending and shear forces described in Chapter 3. The stress distributions in this section have been obtained by using the Engineer's theory. These assumptions have been used by several generations of structural designers. Whilst the Engineer's theory is still widely used non-elastic theories are now also used. These theories are outlined in Chapter 6.

Part of the skill of designing structures is the prediction of the stress distribution in each element as it acts as part of a load path (or paths!). The accuracy of prediction will vary depending on the stage of the design process. For instance the exact size of elements may not need to be calculated at preliminary stages. However it should be clear to the structural designers that the proposed types of elements, shells, slabs, I beams etc., will act effectively as their part of the load path. This is clarified if the stress distribution is know in principle. For instance if load-bearing walls are used at different levels and they cross at angles then the whole wall will not be effective (see Fig.3.31).

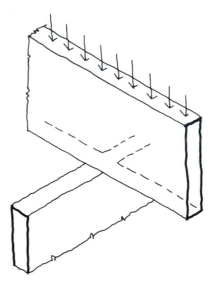

Fig.4.86

Or again if an element is acting as a beam then an I section is better than a + section (see page 89) and it might be worthwhile to vary the depth (see Fig.3.57).

The important point to understand is that structural design is not the result of a logical process but the result of an imaginative concept. For this concept to be successful it must be informed by a conceptual understanding of how the imagined structure will behave.

CHAPTER 5 *Structural materials*

To build any structure, whether it is a chair or the Forth bridge, it has to be constructed of a suitable material. That is a material that at least has the necessary structural properties. The two basic properties that are required are:

• **Strength and stiffness**

Because the structure has to transfer forces is has to be **strong enough**, and because, on the whole the structure is expected to maintain its shape, it has to be **stiff enough**.

Strangely, strength and stiffness of material are unrelated. The reason for this is that the molecular structure varies from material to material. However structural designers usually consider the macroscopic rather than molecular level of behaviour. The behaviour of materials at the molecular level is the concern of material scientists and is beyond the scope of this book.

5.1 Types of material behaviour

Engineering materials are classified by comparing the relationship between strength and stiffness or 'stretchiness'. Everyone is familiar with stretching rubber bands or pulling pieces of Plasticine. After being stretched the rubber band and the piece of Plasticine behave quite differently. The rubber band returns to its original size whereas the piece of Plasticine stays stretched!

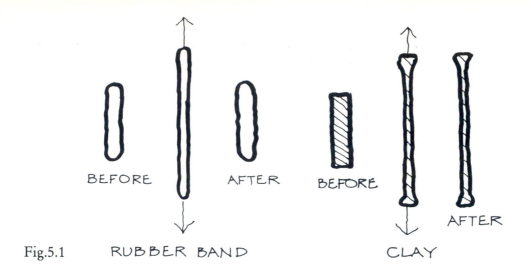

Fig.5.1   RUBBER BAND   CLAY

This is because the rubber is **elastic**, hence elastic band, and Plasticine is **plastic**. Elastic and plastic are technical engineering terms. The elastic and plastic behaviour are best described by drawing graphs of the **load/deflection** behaviour.

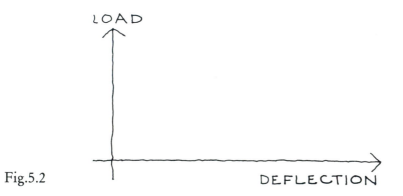

Fig.5.2

It is usual to plot the load on the vertical axis and to plot the deflection on the horizontal axis. If the load/deflection graph is plotted for an elastic band, the deflection will increase with load.

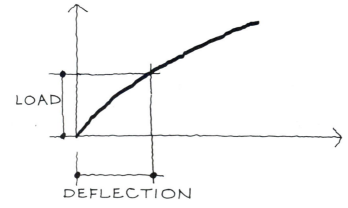

Fig.5.3

However once a piece of Plasticine starts to stretch it can be continuously stretched with a constant load. So the load/deflection graph is more or less a horizontal line.

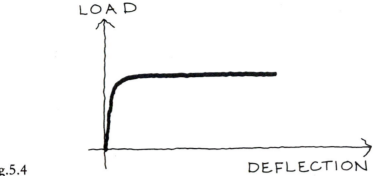

Fig.5.4

Naturally it is preferable for structures to act elastically rather than plastically when loaded, otherwise the structure would be permanently deformed.

Some materials can be both elastic and plastic, steel for example. This can readily be demonstrated with an ordinary paper clip. When being used to hold papers together the clip acts **elastically**, returning to its former shape when the papers are removed. But the clip can easily be permanently deformed by being bent out of shape. To achieve this the steel acts **plastically**. The load/deflection graph has two parts, an **elastic part** and a **plastic part**.

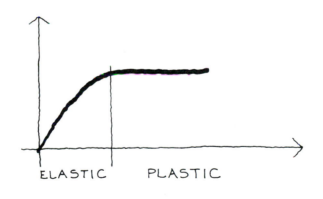

Fig.5.5

Some materials will act elastically and then, on further loading, suddenly break. Glass and plaster are examples of these materials. These materials are called **brittle** materials. This type of material is unsuitable for important structural elements as accidental overloading may cause sudden, and therefore catastrophic, failure.

To aid the process of numerical structural design structural materials are idealised, where possible, as **linear elastic/perfectly plastic** materials.

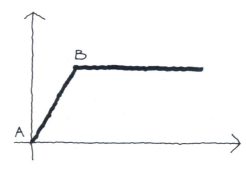

Fig.5.6

For this **idealised** structural material the load/deflection graph consists of two **straight** lines. A sloping line AB, which is the linear elastic part, and a horizontal line, starting at B, which is the perfectly plastic part. The fact that AB is straight means the **load is directly proportional to the deflection**. So if the load doubles then the deflection doubles. The fact that AB is straight means that any load is some constant proportion (in other words a number) of the deflection. This number varies from material to material and indicates how 'stretchy' it is. This number is named after Thomas Young (1773-1829) and is known as **Young's modulus of elasticity** and is often denoted by E. A low number, or low E indicates a material is 'stretchy' and a high number, or high E indicates a material is 'stiff'. For example the number for timber is low and the number for steel is high.

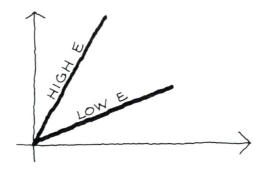

Fig.5.7

At point B, on Fig.5.6, the material's behaviour changes from linear elastic to perfectly plastic, this point is called the **yield point**. From point B the material deflects (forever!) under constant load. The vast majority of building structures are expecting to spend their entire useful lives within the elastic part of their behaviour. Otherwise the structure would change shape permanently after every loading and this would be rather inconvenient.

5.2   Actual structural materials

Every stiff physical object is a structure, the choice of suitable materials is immense. A slice of toast, a pair of shoes, flowers, aeroplanes and bicycles are all structures. However for a **building structure** the choice of suitable materials is very limited. This is because the materials must be strong, stiff, durable and cheap. These are relative terms but building structures must be strong and stiff enough to carry the required loads without deflecting excessively, to be sufficiently durable to last for the structure's useful life and to be cheap enough to make the structure affordable. Because building structures consume considerable amounts of material they, unlike materials for musical instruments and racing cars, must be cheap which means plentiful.

Few materials comply with these requirements in any culture at any historical time. The original traditional buildings were constructed from **natural** materials. These were vegetation (trees, grass, leaves etc), animals (skins and less commonly bones), rocks and stones (including caves) and, in the case of the Inuit people, ice and snow! Slowly **man-made** materials were evolved so mud-dried bricks and woven cloth were used and stones were shaped rather than used as found. Later kiln-dried bricks and lime-based mortar and concrete were used. Even though bronze, first smelted about 4500BC and iron first smelted about 2500BC, are strong, stiff and durable they were far too expensive for use in building structures. Even as late as 1750AD the use of iron nails was rare. Thus, for thousands of years building structures were constructed of timber, brick and stone.

This was changed by what is wrongly called the **Industrial Revolution**, a better word would be evolution (because it took about 150 years). In 1709, Abraham Darby, discovered a method of smelting iron ore using coal (actually using coke, a product of coal). Previously iron ore, which is plentiful, was smelted using charcoal which was not cheap, and as the supply of trees ran out, nor plentiful. This crucial discovery meant that iron became a plentiful and so a cheap material. Now iron, or more correctly cast iron, could be used for building structures. This was dramatically demonstrated by the erection, in 1779, of the **Ironbridge** at Coalbrookedale in Shropshire. What is revolutionary about this bridge, which still stands, was not its size or method of construction but the fact that it was **wholly constructed of iron.**

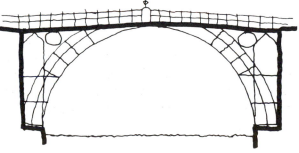

Fig.5.8

The evolving manufacturing and transport industries required a variety of new types of buildings and structures. These included mills, bridges, workshops, chimneys and railway buildings.

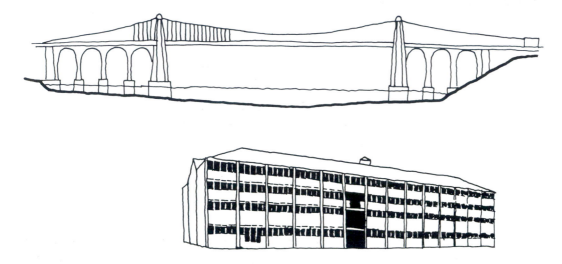

Fig.5.9 Menai Straits Bridge and The Boat Store at Sheerness

Because the size of these structures and the magnitude of the loads were much greater than traditional buildings there was pressure to produce both new types of structure and new structural materials. After the availability of cast iron, **wrought iron**, due to Henry Cort in 1784 and later **steel**, due to the Bessemer process (1850) became cheap enough for building structures. About 1811 Joseph Aspdin invented artificial **cement** made from Portland stone which allowed strong mortars and mass concrete to be made. In France Hennebique began to use concrete reinforced with iron and steel, patented in 1892 and now known as **reinforced concrete**. Thus by about 1900 all the 'modern' building structural materials were available.

Nowadays, building structures are constructed using concrete, both mass and reinforced, timber, brick or block masonry and steel. So a combination of new materials, steel and concrete, and traditional materials, brick and timber are used. Cast iron, wrought iron and stone are now rarely used for building structures. Although there are constant efforts being made to find 'new' materials for building structures none have been found mainly due to lack of cheapness. Many developments have taken place since 1900 but these have mainly been either new uses or methods of design and construction.

On the whole the behaviour of structures in the real world is too complicated to be modelled by structural theory. So theories are derived which are based on various simplifying assumptions. This provides theories which are simple enough (but not necessarily simple!) to be used for structural design.

Although structural theory exists which can predict behaviour of structures built of non-linear elastic materials, computations are enormously simplified if **linear elasticity** is assumed. But is this a valid assumption for the limited range of materials used in building structures?

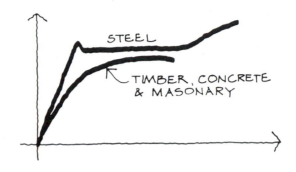

Fig.5.10

The figure shows that only steel, and mild steel at that, closely approximates the idealised linear elastic/perfectly plastic behaviour. However all exhibit some type of elastic behaviour at the beginning of the load/deflection graph. Therefore, for design rather that research purposes, **steel, concrete, timber and masonry are assumed to be linear elastic**. This means that 'ordinary' structural theory can be used for the structural design of all the commonly used materials. (It should be noted that Fig.5.10 only shows the relative shape of the load/deflection graphs rather than the relative numerical values.)

The most important concept to grasp for an engineering understanding of structural materials is the **load/deflection behaviour**. For designing structures it is also necessary to know the **strength** of the materials. Of the four common structural materials steel is the strongest with concrete, masonry and timber very roughly the same strength. All the materials can vary considerably in strength depending on the process of manufacture, or in the case of timber, the species. Again the steel is the stiffest material with concrete about one tenth, masonry about on twentieth and timber about one thirtieth as stiff as steel. Again these values, apart from steel, vary considerably.

Not all the materials are equally strong is tension and compression, that is pulled or squashed. Steel and timber are equally strong in tension but masonry and concrete although strong in compression are very weak in tension. So weak in fact that their tensile strength is usually ignored in structural design. This difference in material behaviour has a great influence on the choice of structural form because if the loaded structure has to carry tensile forces then steel or timber must be used.

Another influential characteristic is the **strength to weight ratio**. The self-weight of structures constructed from steel or timber is usually not more than 15% of the total load carried whereas the self-weight of masonry and concrete structures can be 40% of the total load carried. This is because steel and timber have high strength to weight ratios and masonry and concrete have low strength to weight ratios, so **timber and steel are lightweight materials and masonry and concrete are heavyweight materials**.

5.3   Soil as a structural material

All building structures rest on the surface of the earth and the foundations are the final part of the structure. Loads imposed on the planet Earth by buildings are trivial but locally the behaviour of the surface of the earth matters. The purpose of the foundations is to ensure that the stress on the local surface is within the safe bearing stress of the soil. The concept of foundations is the same as using snowshoes (Fig.3.23).

If a hole is dug in the surface of the earth rock will eventually be found. This rock may be many metres below the ground level so the foundations are usually placed on the soil that lies above the underlying rock. This layer of soil may be very compressible under load so the foundations will move downwards causing them to settle. This means that the building may move downwards as a rigid body or it may settle differentially causing the building to tilt and distort! So not only strength but foundation movement have to be considered by the engineering designer. Unfortunately for engineering designers the behaviour of soils under load is complex. Due to this complexity a specialist subject has come into existence called **soil mechanics**.

The first stage in understanding the engineering behaviour of soils is to identify the types of soil that are found. These are broadly classified as **rocks, granular soils and clayey soils**. These are often found in layers or **strata**, so immediately under a building site there usually several different types of soil.

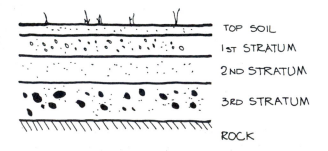

Fig.5.11

Examples of rocks are granite, sandstone and chalk, granular soils are sands and gravels and clayey soils are various types of clay. Foundations on rock are rarely a problem for buildings as they are strong and stiff but foundations on granular or cohesive soil need careful consideration.

There are two basic differences between the behaviour of structural elements and the structural behaviour of the soil. The first is that the part of soil loaded by the foundations of a structure soil cannot act in isolation as a column can. The loaded part of the ground is affected by adjacent 'unloaded' parts of the ground.

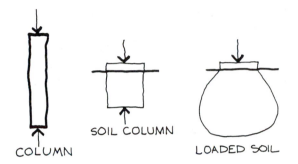

Fig.5.12

How much of the adjacent soil is affected by the load is hard to determine but it can be significant. To see why this happens look at two simplified models of soil. One is of unlinked elastic coil springs and the other of elastic spheres. Both are in pits with completely rigid sides.

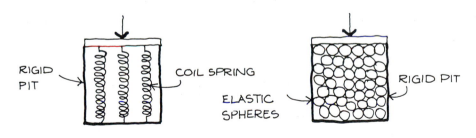

Fig.5.13

For the first model the behaviour is quite simple. As the load is applied through the rigid foundation each coil spring deflects vertically under its share of the load. As the load increases so does the deflection. The bottom and sides of the pit do not move.

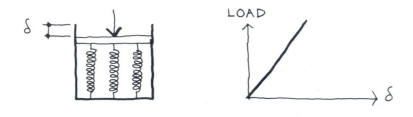

Fig.5.14

This model assumes that the soil under the foundation **does** act as an isolated structure; the springs. This is the same as assuming there is a finite column of elastic soil under the foundation and that soil outside the 'rigid box' is unaffected.

Fig.5.15

The second model using elastic spheres is more complex as there are three phases of behaviour. The pit of elastic spheres will not be tightly packed so the load causes compaction of the spheres. This compaction can be seen by shaking a jar of rice or sugar and noting the depth before and after shaking.

Fig.5.16

The second effect is the restriction on the shape into which the spheres can deform. Because the spheres are touching each other and the sides of the pit, each sphere cannot deform freely.

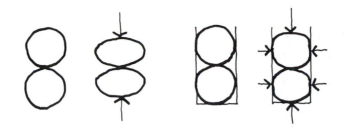

Fig.5.17

As the confined spheres are compressed the restriction on their lateral deformation causes horizontal loads on the rigid pit walls. As the spheres deform the foundation moves down into the pit, this reduces the overall volume of the pit and the size of the voids between the spheres.

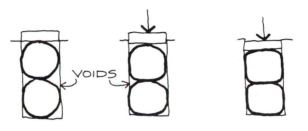

Fig.5.18

When all the voids are filled the pit will be completely filled with the elastic material. This is quite a different structure from the pit filled with barely touching spheres. This means that the pit filled with elastic spheres will have three phases of behaviour.

Phase 1   Reduction of voids by compaction.
Phase 2   Deformation of spheres until the voids are filled.
Phase 3   Deformation of pit filled with elastic material.

This gives a three part load/deflection diagram.

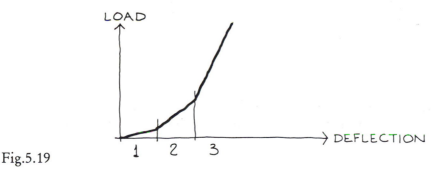

Fig.5.19

It is possible to find single sized spherical stones occurring naturally, these can be seen on some shingle beaches. For this 'soil' the model of elastic spheres is reasonable but the rigid pit restriction is not. A new model of this soil would be an 'infinitely wide' layer of elastic spheres with finite thickness. This layer rests on a rigid base.

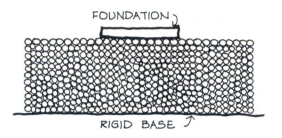

Fig.5.20

As the foundation is loaded the spheres compact locally. Then the touching spheres begin to deform. With no rigid pit walls the adjacent, 'unloaded' spheres have to provide lateral forces.

Fig.5.21

The lower spheres will provide the lateral force if they are heavy enough. Each layer of spheres transfers its load to a lower layer and each lower layer will have more spheres.

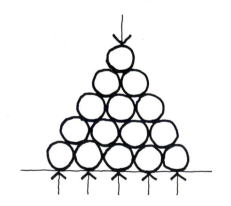

Fig.5.22

148   **Structural materials**

In this way the area of loaded spheres increases with depth and the level of load in the spheres reduces.

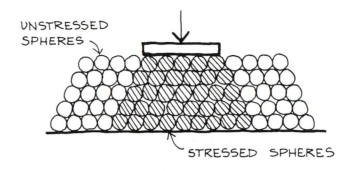

Fig.5.23

As soil is not usually made from elastic spheres and there is not a rigid base the stressed volume under a single foundation becomes bulb shaped.

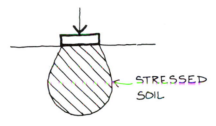

Fig.5.24

For an elastic sphere to deform into an elastic cube, thus filling all the voids the material has to be very elastic. A stone sphere could not deform into a cube as it would split first. If the foundation load is increased the highly stressed spheres will fail or the lateral forces required will become too high for the 'unloaded' spheres and these will heave upwards.

Fig.5.25

The load/deformation curve can be drawn for this model and again this has three phases.

Phase 1   Reduction of voids by compaction.
Phase 2   Deformation of spheres.
Phase 3   Failure by crushing or heaving.

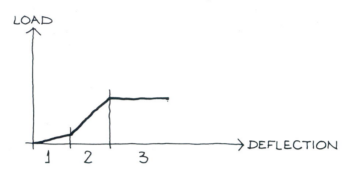

Fig.5.26

So far the models have been used to understand the behaviour of the **soil skeleton**. If, as is often the case, there is water in the soil the behaviour of the soil skeleton **plus water** has to be modelled. The behaviour of this composite structure can be quite different from the behaviour of the soil skeleton. Fill the pits of the first two models with water and assume that the foundations fit into the pits in a watertight manner.

Fig.5.27

Water is almost incompressible so the load from the foundations is carried by water pressure in both of the models with almost no deformation.

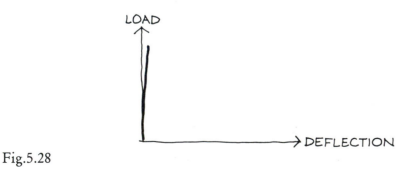

Fig.5.28

The behaviour will be altered if holes are made in the foundation which relieve the water pressure and allow some water to escape.

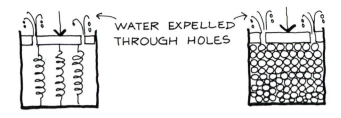

Fig.5.29

Now the water that is filling the voids in the soil skeleton has a drainage path. As the water is expelled from the voids the soil skeleton carries the load as before. If the holes are large then the water will be expelled immediately, but if the holes are very small the water will only seep through the foundation slowly.

For the coil spring model with no water the deflection will double if the load is doubled. This because the model is linear.

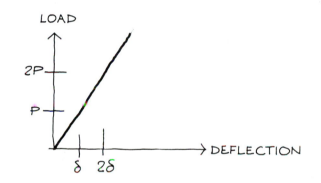

Fig.5.30

If the pit is filled with water and only very small holes are made in the foundation the water will take time to seep through. Initially the water will carry all the load but as the water pressure is gradually reduced by seepage the load is transferred to the coil springs. Now the deformation is **time dependent**, and under a constant load will deform in a non-linear way until the springs are carrying all the load.

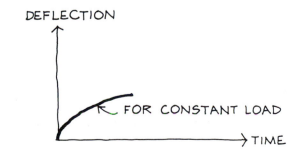

Fig.5.31

If further load is applied the process will repeat.

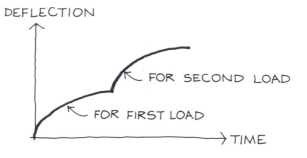

Fig.5.32

In the water filled soil skeleton the pressure of the water in the voids is called the **pore water pressure**. Before loading the pore water pressure is just the hydrostatic head, but the loads cause an increase in the pore water pressure. This increase is relieved by the drainage until the pressure returns to the hydrostatic pressure. How long this takes is called the **seepage rate**. The smaller the drainage holes the longer it takes. In a real soil there is no rigid pit so the water drains away laterally as well as vertically.

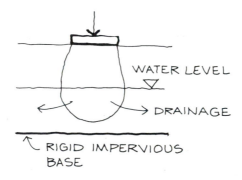

Fig.5.33

Even with the first model the presence of water and a low seepage rate dramatically alters the soil structure behaviour. With all the variations of underlying strata, particle size and shape and rate of loading if water is present the soil structure behaviour of a real soil can be complex.

Just to complicate matters further, if the particle size is very small (less than 0.002mm) and the particles are made from certain chemically complex minerals, then the presence of water is always a consideration. If water is poured over a heap of large stones, apart from a small part that wets the surfaces of the stones, all the water will drain away.

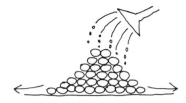

Fig.5.34

However with a heap of very small particles this will not happen as the wetted area of the particle is enormous compared to its volume.

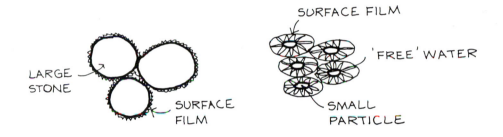

Fig.5.35

The water does not drain away but is adsorbed on to the surfaces of the particles. Complex electro-chemical actions between the wetted particles now cause them to cohere together to form a **clayey soil**. In soil mechanics soils are divided into freely **draining soils — non-cohesive or granular soils** and **non-draining soils — clayey soils**. Examples of granular soils are sands and gravels and examples of clayey soils are clays and marls. The difference can be physically experienced by squeezing handfuls of wet sand and clay. The water is readily squeezed from the sand but cannot be squeezed from a clayey soil. This is because the proportion of 'free' water in clayey soil is small and diameter of the drainage paths are also small which causes very low permeability.

For non-cohesive soils water may or may not be present but in clayey soils water is **always** present. If a clayey soil is loaded by a foundation the load is initially carried by an **increase** in pore water pressure. As with granular soils the pore water pressure in cohesive soils reduces by draining laterally to unstressed areas. But due to the extremely low seepage rate in cohesive soils this may take years!

In summary three broad statements can be made about the soil as a structural material and these are:

- **The engineering behaviour of many real soils is difficult to formulate analytically. Many aspects are not fully understood and these are subjects for research by specialists.**

- **For the majority of building structures the foundations can be designed using simplified processes. This is not true for embankments, tunnels, dams or large underground structures.**

- **It is much more common to have problems with foundations than the superstructure.**

5.4   Non-structural effects

Structural materials also have 'non-structural' characteristics which influence their use in structures. These include behaviour due to temperature change, exposure to fire, exposure to climatic changes and dimensional change due to moisture variation. The common structural materials behave quite differently under these influences. Because these material characteristics are non-structural they do not directly affect the structural performance of the materials, but they strongly influence their use for structures.

Temperature change and moisture variation both cause a change of size of a structure. This would not matter if the structure could just grow or shrink but usually there is a **differential change** in size between different members of the structure.

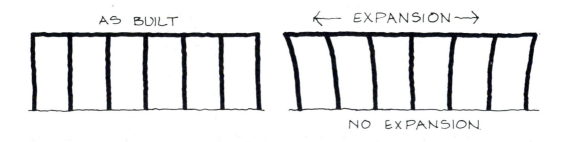

Fig.5.36

To avoid these effects structures are jointed which means a change in structural form.

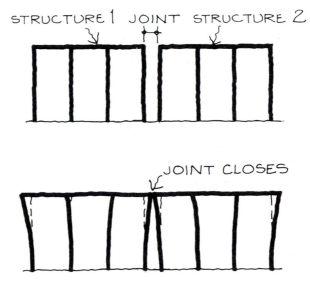

Fig.5.37

Structural materials also behave differently when exposed to fire. Steel, masonry and concrete are all **incombustible** when exposed to 'ordinary' fires but timber **burns**. But oddly, timber structures can be more fireproof than steel structures. When large timber sections burn the fire chars the outer surface and the charring rate is known. The timber behind the charred surface maintains its structural strength so, during a fire, timber members lose strength for geometric reasons.

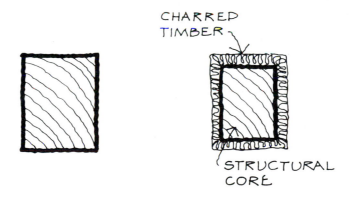

Fig.5.38

Whilst steel does not burn its structural behaviour changes at temperatures of about 550°C, quite a usual temperature in ordinary fires. At these temperatures steel loses most of its strength and stiffness and ceases to act structurally, hence the 'mass of tangled steelwork' after a fire.

If structures are required to be fireproof, as they often are, then steel and timber structures need special attention. Timber structures have to be checked for strength using the structural member sizes after they have been charred, and steel structures need some form of protection to keep the steel below the critical temperature.

Nothing lasts forever but structures have to be **durable**. How durable varies with the use of the structure and it is not easy to make accurate predictions for durability. Again when exposed to climatic changes the common structural materials behave differently.

In the presence of moisture and oxygen steel will **corrode** (or rust). Unlike other metals, such as copper or aluminium, the corrosion does not form a protective layer but is progressive until the steel literally rusts away. The products of corrosion, iron oxides, are less dense than steel so the corroded steel expands, this can crack or spall any material, such as masonry or concrete, in which it is embedded. To prevent this corrosion steel can be coated with materials which inhibit the corrosion process. These materials can be other metals, such as zinc or aluminium, or special corrosion inhibiting paints. Ordinary paints do not have any corrosion inhibiting properties.

Whilst masonry and concrete may last for hundreds of years they may also deteriorate in a short time if attacked by frost and chemicals. If moisture is present in small cracks and it freezes then it expands. This can cause further cracking and possibly spalling of the face of the concrete or masonry. Also many chemicals can attack masonry and concrete causing various forms of deterioration. These chemicals may be present in the atmosphere, ground, be part of an industrial process or even be present in the constituents (for instance polluted mixing water or contaminated aggregates).

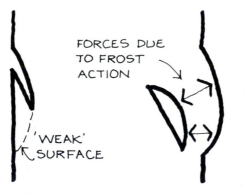

Fig.5.39

Although concrete may be attacked by chemicals and frost it is more frequently attacked by the corrosion of the steel with which it is commonly reinforced. It is perhaps illogical to strengthen concrete with steel reinforcement only to find the rusting reinforcement destroying the concrete! This only happens if moisture and oxygen can penetrate the concrete sufficiently to allow this corrosion to occur. The growing interest in the repair of concrete structures indicates that this is neither a small nor rare problem. This problem could be solved by using stainless steel reinforcement but unfortunately, except for special circumstances, this material is not cheap enough.

Rather like masonry and concrete, timber can last for hundreds of years. But timber can also deteriorate, usually due to attacks from animals or plants. Various animals, such as insect larvae or termites, eat the timber. Various plants, mainly fungi, can grow in the timber. The action of these plants and animals alters the structure of the timber. This alteration usually means that the timber can no longer serve its constructional purpose. Some species of timber are more readily attacked than others and susceptible timbers can be preserved with various forms of chemical treatment. But the best way of ensuring timber is durable in building is to avoid using it in positions where attack is possible.

Not only do the material properties affect the choice for a particular structure, the choice is also affected by the process of building with the material. The four main structural materials are available in quite different forms.

The shape and size of steel structures is almost unlimited (think of super-tankers). Steel is generally available in various standard forms, these are plates of standard thicknesses and rolled members of particular cross-sectional shapes and sizes. Whilst these can be assembled into structures of any size they are usually fabricated in workshops rather than the final site. The size of the largest part is usually limited by the maximum size that can be transported.

Like steel, concrete structures are unlimited by size or shape. Concrete can either be formed on site, in-situ concrete, of made off site in special pre-casting yards — pre-cast concrete. Again like steel, the maximum size of pre-cast parts is limited by transport restrictions.

As timber sizes are determined by the natural size of trees. Larger timber structures can made by laminating timber. This technique involves gluing natural sized timber together to form large structures. Laminated timber can also be made into curved or bent structures.

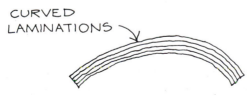

CURVED
LAMINATIONS

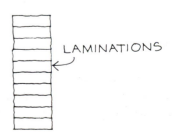

LAMINATIONS

Fig.5.40

Theoretically, the size of masonry bricks and blocks is not limited, but masonry is constructed manually. These mean the size of individual units is limited by human dimensions of the bricklayers, both their size and strength. Strangely this has resulted in bricks sized to be held in one hand whilst blocks come in a range of sizes, including some dense concrete blocks that are so heavy that it takes two people to lift them!

This section shows that the choice of a particular structure, made from a particular structural material, cannot be made without consideration of the non-structural behaviour. For example, the non-structural behaviour may restrict choice in highly corrosive or highly flammable environments. Again restrictions of size may require joints or complete separation of structural elements, thus altering the structural behaviour. When proposing a structural system for a particular application, the structural designer must be aware that the chosen system satisfies the requirements of the non-structural behaviour.

CHAPTER 6   *Safe structures and failure*

A major aim of structural design is to provide structures that are strong enough, that is they can carry the loads imposed on them by their use without failure. This may seem obvious but there are many difficulties associated with this simple requirement, and unless they are resolved the possibility of failure remains.

6.1   Basic concepts of safety

In industrial societies building structures are expected to be very safe and the occurance of failures, especially causing loss of life, must be almost unknown. To achieve this the possibility, or more correctly the probability, of failure must be quantified. This is attempted by using a **statistical approach**.

The first question to be answered is how big is the load on a particular structure. If this question cannot be answered then all attempts at structural design will be meaningless. But accurate answers can only be obtained if the use of the building is somehow controlled. For example the density of water does not vary so, for a water tank, the load from the liquid can be known accurately, unless someone decides to store mercury in the tank! This illustrates the difficulty of knowing how a structure will be loaded during its life which may be 100 years or more.

Other important loads such as those from snow or wind are beyond the control of humans so can never be 'known'. To overcome this serious problem attempts are made to estimate possible loads from natural phenomenon by making a statistical analysis of past records. In many areas of the world no useful records exist so the prediction of these loads becomes hazardous.

To understand how real structural design is done the basic principles of the statistical approach must be understood. These principles attempt to use past data to predict **probable future data**. Because the prediction is one of **probability** it is, by definition, uncertain. To illustrate the principles a non-structural engineering example is used. Anyone who has visited ancient buildings may have noticed that the height of doorways are often lower than those of modern buildings. This is often explained by the 'fact' that people were smaller when these buildings were constructed. So how high should a doorway be? Should every doorway be high enough for the tallest person who ever lived, Robert Wadlow who was 272cm — 8ft 11in tall, to walk through upright?

Fig.6.1

As this person was so tall 'most' people would agree that all doorways do not need to be this high. But what percentage of doorway users should be able to walk through the doorway upright? For convenience most users should be able to walk through the doorway upright. To arrive at an actual height some data are needed. Suppose 100 randomly chosen adults have their heights measured. There will be an average height, but how much shorter or taller than the average height will any person be? The first step is to draw a **histogram** of the data. This is a diagram that shows how many of the 100 people there are of each height. If the heights are taken for 4cm intervals and the number of people in each height interval are recorded the histogram can be drawn.

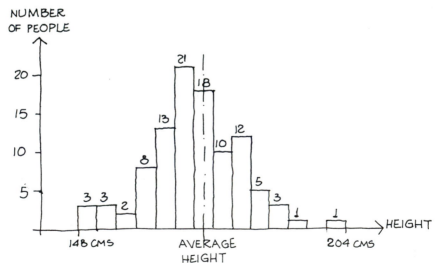

Fig.6.2

All the histogram does is to record the **distribution** of the heights of the **population**, as the sample is called. In this population there is one person over 2m tall, so if all doorways used by the group were made 204cm high everyone could walk through all doors upright but if they were made 192cm high 98 people could walk through upright and 2 could not.

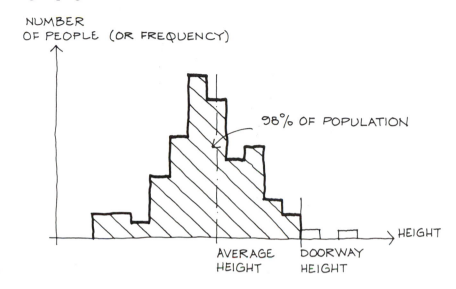

Fig.6.3

It may seem reasonable that 98% of the population can walk through all the doorways upright and the chosen door height is 14cm higher than the average height. This choice has not used probability because the heights of **all** the users are known but can the data be used to predict anything ? Is a random sample of 100 people enough? In Fig.6.3 the histogram is 'heaped' around the average height but would this always be true and would the average height be 174cm? Suppose the top of the histogram is made into a smooth curve by joining the middle of each step to the next.

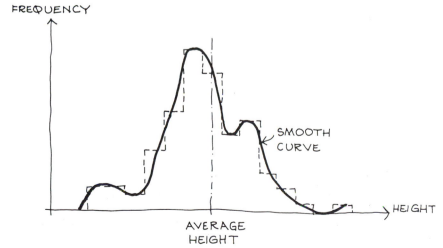

Fig.6.4

If a mathematical expression could be found for this rather odd shaped curve it would be called a **probability density function**. From the mathematical expression for the curve the **mean** can be calculated and so can something called the **standard deviation**. In this case the standard deviation would be a length in centimetres. By adding or subtracting a number of standard deviations to the mean a relationship can be established between the mean, a number of standard deviations and a percentage of the population.

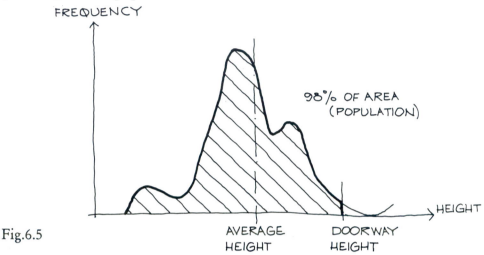

Fig.6.5

As the population is increased in size the size of the interval can be reduced and the smooth curve may become simpler. Anticipating this a particular probability density function in the shape of a bell is often used. This is called the **normal** curve and it is the probability density function of the **normal** (or Gaussian) **distribution**. This is used as it is straightforward to calculate the standard deviation, and two standard deviations from the mean give 98% of the population.

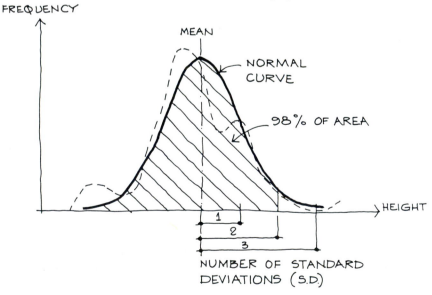

Fig.6.6

Using the standard calculations for the normal distribution (often available on pocket calculators) any data can be processed to produce the **mean** and the **standard deviation**. So the data used to draw the histogram could be processed as a normal distribution to give the mean and the standard deviation.

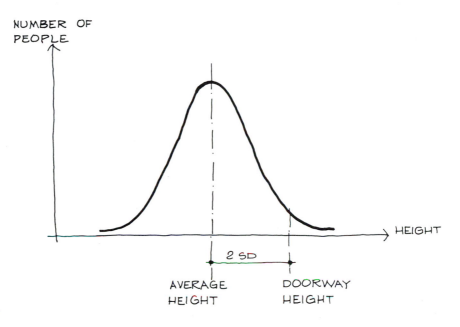

Fig.6.7

This approach is used to decide what loads a structure should carry and how strong the structure should be. Instead of measuring the heights of people a population of 'identical' structures could be tested. Suppose the structure is a solid rectangular cube of a particular size. If 100 of these cubes were made and then tested by loading them in some way, opposite faces for instance, the results could be analysed statistically.

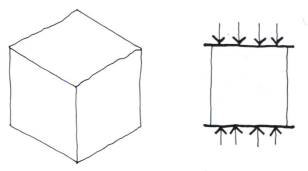

Fig.6.8

If the failure strength of each cube is recorded it may seem reasonable to expect the histogram of the failure loads to approximate a normal distribution.

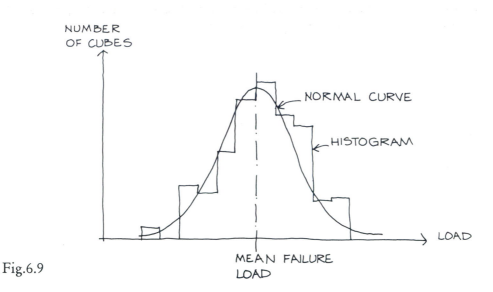

Fig.6.9

Now, unlike the door, it is the **lowest** strength that is required. Using the same 98% criterion used for the doors this would be two standard deviations from the mean.

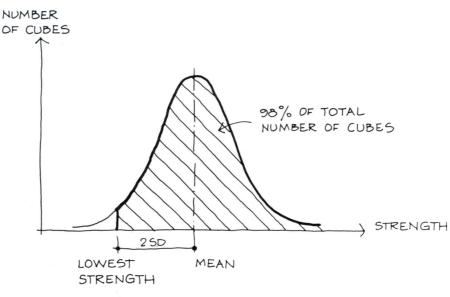

Fig.6.10

The **lowest strength** is the one which 98% will attain. So it is reasonable to assume for these concrete cubes, that if they are always made in the same way, there will be a 98% probability that they will be at least as strong as the lowest strength. As this can be calculated, it provides some information on the likely strength of these cubical structures.

164   **Safe structures and failure**

As structural materials are regarded as **linear elastic/perfectly plastic** (see Fig.5.6) the test on the concrete cube finds point B of Fig.5.6.

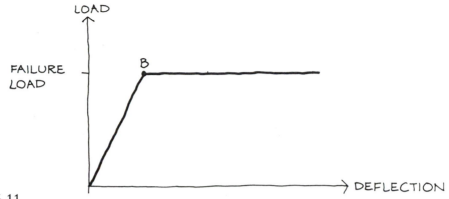

Fig.6.11

This statistical approach could be used to find the 'lowest strength' of any structure provided a large enough number of identical structures could be tested. Practically this means that only very simple structures, like the cube, can be tested. These simple tests are used to give information about structural materials rather than whole structures.

As well as knowing the lowest strength that a structure may have the **highest load** that a structure has to carry must also be decided. The loads that a structure has to carry are the weight of the construction, the loads from the use of the building and the loads from natural phenomena. How much the weight of the construction varies can be found in the same way as the strength of the cubes.

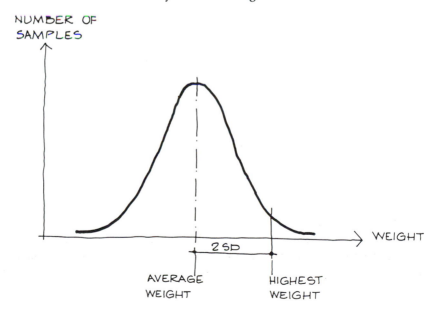

Fig.6.12

To establish the loads applied to buildings from their use surveys have to be carried out over a period of time. This period is called the **return period**.

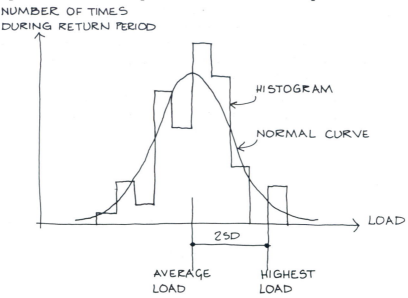

Fig.6.13

Naturally to carry out these surveys thoroughly is a vast undertaking. The results of these are now codified in many countries and these loads are available as standard data.

A similar approach is used for natural phenomena such as wind or snow loading if sufficient data is available over a long return period. Twenty years is the minimum return period. For wind, the maximum daily wind speed is recorded and the data histogram is approximated by a normal distribution.

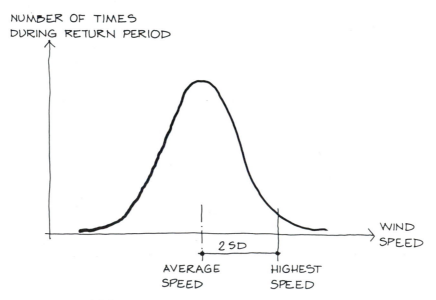

Fig.6.14

The same approach can be taken with other natural phenomena, like the depth of snow or height of sea waves. This again assumes that the data is collected over a sufficiently long return period and the data exhibits the characteristic of the normal distribution. There are other natural phenomena, such as earthquakes, that are hard to predict statistically. Although areas of seismic activity can be mapped, earthquakes are a geological phenomenon so the statistical analysis has to be carried out over geological time! This problem also occurs with 'freak' weather conditions such as hurricanes which occur regularly but too infrequently to provide enough data for accurate prediction. So, whilst it is valid to attempt to predict loading by statistical methods it is not surprising that for some occurrences these may be inaccurate.

By using the normal distribution to describe what is meant by a highest load (Fig.6.13) and a lowest strength (Fig.6.10) the concept of a **safe structure** is available. This concept combines two bell-shaped curves, one for the **structure strength** and one for the **structure load**.

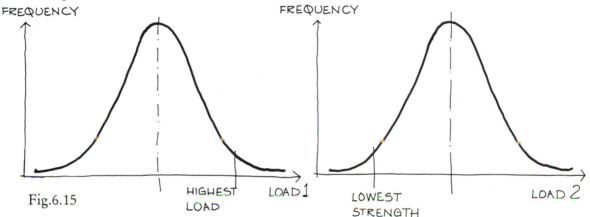

Fig.6.15

LOAD1 is the load the structure **has to carry** and LOAD2 is the load the structure **can carry**. Provided LOAD1 (the highest load) is greater than LOAD2 (the lowest strength) the structure will not fail, so the two diagrams can be drawn overlapping.

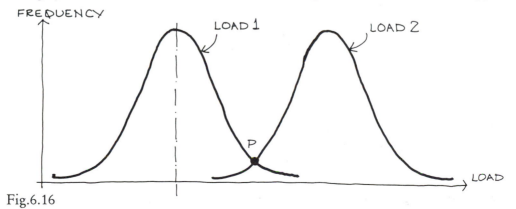

Fig.6.16

Basic concepts of safety 167

At point P the highest load coincides with the lowest strength so the structure will fail. This is a statistical possibility and depends on the accuracy of the data used for the curves and on how many standard deviations are used to relate the highest/lowest values to the mean. As the failure condition, point P, has been found the concept of **factor of safety (F.o.S)** can be used. The factor of safety is actually a number. As the load at P is a real possibility and the strength at P is also a REAL possibility there is a **real possibility of failure**. For building structures this is unacceptable as society has decided they should be very safe, hence sayings such as 'safe as houses'. The factor of safety moves the curves of Fig.6.16 apart by the numerical factor. This means LOAD1 (the highest load) and LOAD2 (the lowest strength) are now **numerically different**.

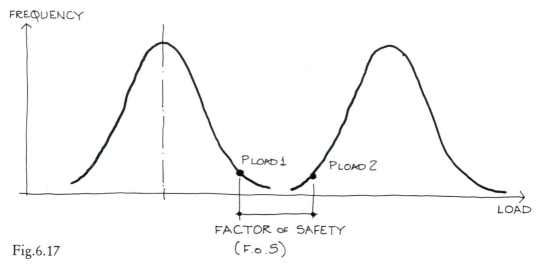

Fig.6.17

The idea of **designing**[*] the structure can now be used, in other words somehow matching the loads which are expected to be applied to the structure with the strength of the structure and the factor of safety. This can be done in three ways, which are:

- Elastic (or Permissible Stress) Design
- Collapse (or Plastic) Design
- Limit State Design

Basically this means moving the two curves of Fig.6.15 together in three different ways to find a position for P that is a **design criterion**.

For the **elastic** method the actual load (LOAD1) is used but the failure strength, (LOAD2) is divided by the factor of safety to give an **elastic strength**.

---

[*] Here the word **designing** means only matching loads, strength and the factor of safety.

This is the same as moving the point B of Fig.6.11 down the elastic part of the graph of the load/deflection behaviour to a point that is the failure strength divided by the factor of safety.

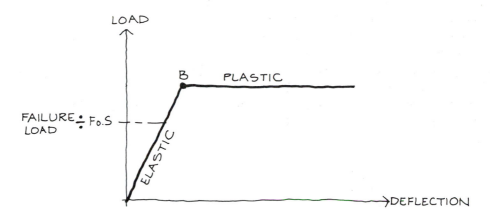

Fig.6.18

This also has the effect of moving the 'P_{LOAD2}' curve of Fig.6.17 to the left, so P_{LOAD1} and $P_{LOAD2} \div$ F.o.S coincide.

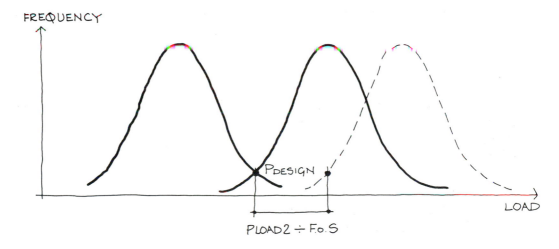

Fig.6.19

Now the structure is designed to make sure that $P_{LOAD2} \div$ F.o.S is greater then P_{LOAD1}. This gives the **design criterion** represented by P_{DESIGN} on Fig.6.19. Because for design, the structure is on the elastic part of the load/deflection graph (see Fig.6.18) this design procedure is called **elastic design**.

The **collapse** method is the opposite procedure, that is P_{LOAD1} is multiplied by the F.o.S to give the **collapse load**. That is the real load is multiplied by the factor of safety to give the load at which the structure is expected to collapse. This has the effect of moving the 'LOAD1' curve of Fig.6.16 to the right so that P_{LOAD2} and $P_{LOAD1} \times$ F.o.S coincide.

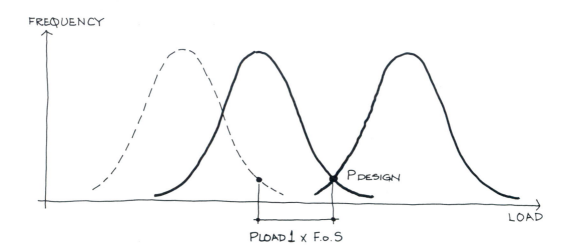

Fig.6.20

Now the structure is designed to make sure that P_{LOAD2} is greater than $P_{LOAD1} \times$ F.o.S which gives the **design criterion** represented by P_{DESIGN} on Fig.6.20. As, for design, the structure is now at the collapse point (point B of Fig.6.18) of the load/deflection graph this design procedure is called **collapse design**.

The third method, called **limit state design**, moves both the LOAD1 and the LOAD2 curves of Fig.6.17, one to the right and one to the left. Now the overall factor of safety is composed of two **partial safety factors** and these are:

- **Partial load factor called gamma f (γ_f)**

- **Partial material (strength) factor called gamma m (γ_m)**

With this combined method the position of P_{DESIGN} is found by multiplying P_{LOAD1} by γ_f and dividing P_{LOAD2} by γ_m. This effectively moves both curves of Fig.6.17, one to the right and one to the left.

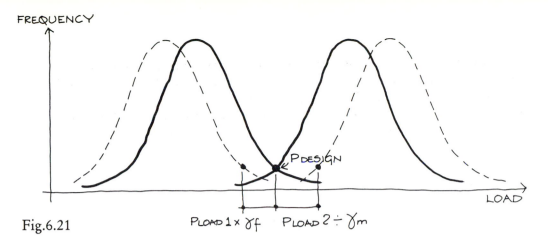

Fig.6.21

$P_{LOAD}1 \times \gamma_f$ $P_{LOAD}2 \div \gamma_m$

In Limit State design the partial safety factors can be varied to take account a number of factors that affect the variability of both the loading and the strength. The point called P_{DESIGN} is a **limit state** and the limit state method allows a number of different limit states to be considered. This is done by varying γ_f and γ_m.

The existence of three methods of designing structures suggests there is a choice of method giving three different designs and there is some truth in this. The choice of method depends on the designer's preference although the choice may be dictated by legislation in some places. All three methods ensure a safe structure is designed but there may be some slight variation in the actual designs.

The complexity of the numerical design of structures can often lead to a desire to achieve a high degree of numerical accuracy. This can obscure the fact that all the ideas of designing safe structures are based on the statistical interpretation of what may be quite inadequate basic data. Furthermore the histograms of the data may not be accurately modelled by the shape of a normal distribution probability density function. This point is made by JG Gordon (on page 328 of his book *Structures*) who, on statistically analysing the strength of airframes tested during World War II found the probability density function was not the normal curve but approximately square!

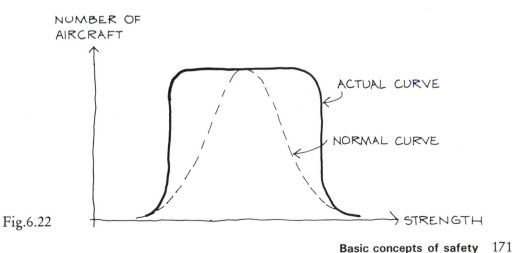

Fig.6.22

6.2 Types of structural collapse

For structures to collapse under load they have to become a mechanism. That is the structure will undergo a gross movement before coming to rest in its collapsed state. For example if a portal frame (see Fig.2.27) has four hinges and is loaded by a horizontal load it will collapse sideways as they rotate. When the frame has collapsed it is no longer a mechanism as it can no longer move.

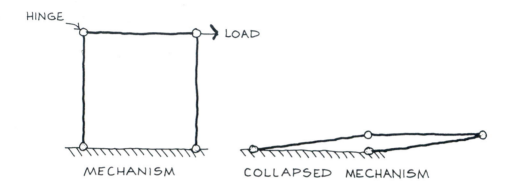

Fig.6.23

In this example the four-hinged portal is not a structure but a mechanism. For structures to collapse they have to **become mechanisms**. This can happen suddenly or gradually. These two types of collapse can be compared to two types of material behaviour described in Chapter 5. The sudden collapse can be compared to the sudden failure of **brittle** materials and gradual collapse to the **plastic** phase of elastic/plastic materials.

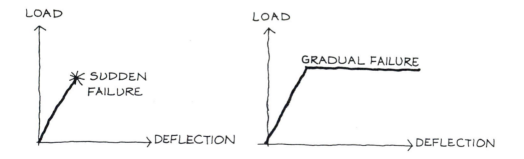

Fig.6.24

Sudden collapse can occur for two reasons:

• **The structural material is brittle**

• **The structure loses overall stability**

Structural designers try and avoid using brittle materials but this is not always possible. Although masonry and concrete exhibit some plastic behaviour the plastic phase is quite short (compared to ductile materials such as steel) so collapses can be sudden. Because of this the factor of safety for these materials are high. Ductile metals such as steel can also become brittle, this can happen due to a very high number of repeated loading or high loading rates at low temperatures. With steel these problems are avoided by limiting the types of steel used in building structures.

The loss of overall stability can occur when the disturbing force, the loading, exceeds the restoring force due to gravity. Suppose a cantilever structure is anchored by a counterweight.

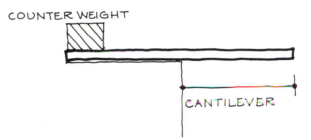

Fig.6.25

Gravity acting on the counterweight causes a force which can balance loads on the cantilever.

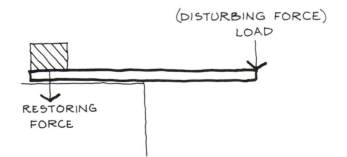

Fig.6.26

If the load is increased until the disturbing force exceeds the restoring force the cantilever structure will tip, becoming a mechanism and collapse.

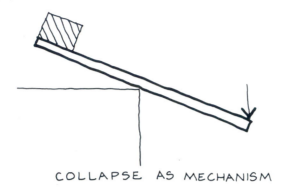

COLLAPSE AS MECHANISM

Fig.6.27

This can also happen horizontally, for example a retaining wall can slide.

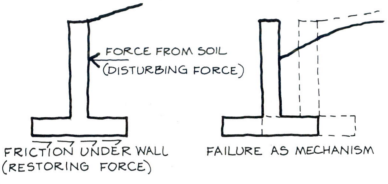

FORCE FROM SOIL
(DISTURBING FORCE)

FRICTION UNDER WALL
(RESTORING FORCE)

FAILURE AS MECHANISM

Fig.6.28

The wall moves until the load on the back of the wall is reduced to the restoring force. Strangely structures can also collapse due to a loss of overall stability due to their own weight. This is what happens when a 'tall' stack of bricks suddenly collapses.

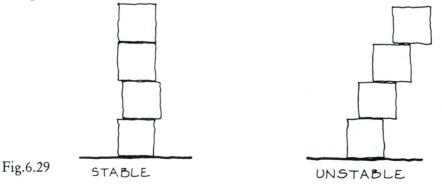

Fig.6.29   STABLE   UNSTABLE

This happens due to the **Pe effect** shown in Fig.3.75. As the stack grows higher the centre of gravity of each brick starts to deviate from the centre of gravity of the brick below.

Fig.6.30

The lowest brick of the toppling stack provides the restoring force and the bricks above the disturbing force.

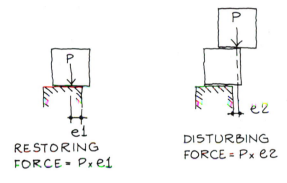

Fig.6.31

And, as before, when the disturbing force exceeds the restoring force the structure collapses.

COLLAPSE AS MECHANISM

Fig.6.32

Really Fig.6.32 is just another version of Fig.6.27. What is important to notice in these overall stability collapses is that the structural elements do not fail but the load path loses stability. So the cantilever, the wall and the individual bricks have not failed by losing strength as structural elements but they have become part of an unstable load path. For overall stability the factor of safety can be expressed as:

•   **F.o.s = Restoring force ÷ disturbing force**

6.3   Plastic behaviour

For structures to collapse 'gradually' they have to be behaving plastically on some part of the load path and this plastic behaviour must cause the structure to become a mechanism. To see how this happens look again at the beam shown in Fig.2.26.

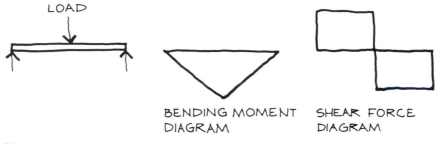

BENDING MOMENT DIAGRAM   SHEAR FORCE DIAGRAM

Fig.6.33

In Chapter 3, the linear elastic stress distribution (Fig.3.39) was given. It was noted that there was a point of maximum stress at the top and bottom faces at the point of maximum bending moment (Fig.3.50). As the load on the beam is increased the stress at these points will eventually reach point B of Fig.5.6. That is the maximum elastic stress, this is often called the **elastic limit**.

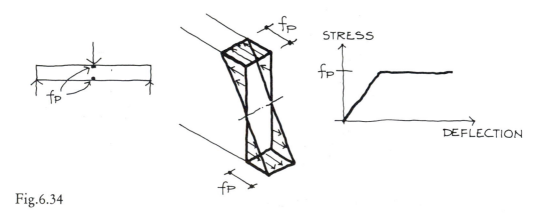

Fig.6.34

176   **Safe structures and failure**

The stress F_p (force per unit area) is the stress at which the structural material starts to act plastically. As the load is further increased the point becomes a **zone of plastic stress**. This zone occurs as parts of the beam adjacent to the original point of maximum stress reach the elastic limit and become plastic.

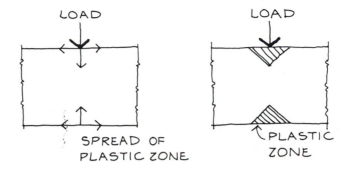

Fig.6.35

Because the stress cannot exceed the elastic limit the stress distribution in the plastic zone changes from that shown in Fig.3.49.

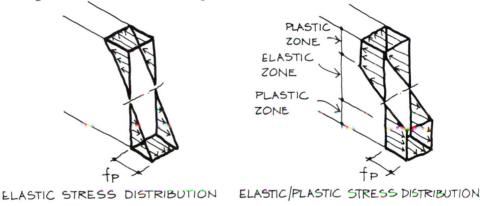

ELASTIC STRESS DISTRIBUTION   ELASTIC/PLASTIC STRESS DISTRIBUTION

Fig.6.36

As the load is further increased the depth of the plastic zone increases until the beam achieves **full plasticization**.

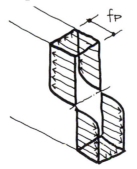

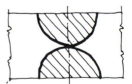

PLASTIC ZONE

Fig.6.37   PLASTIC STRESS DISTRIBUTION

When full plasticization is reached the beam cannot be stressed further and a **plastic hinge** has formed. The beam now collapses 'gradually' as it becomes a mechanism rotating about the plastic hinge.

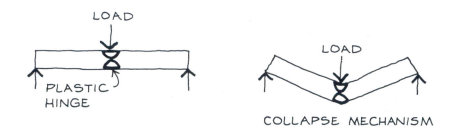

Fig.6.38

The bending moment at the formation of the plastic hinge is called the **plastic moment**. The ratio between the elastic moment, M_e, the moment at the elastic limit, and the plastic moment, M_p, varies with the cross-sectional shape. For a rectangular cross-section the ratio is 1.5. The behaviour of the beam through the loading range can be illustrated by drawing a graph of the bending moment plotted against the central deflection.

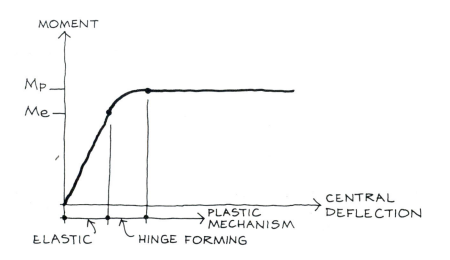

Fig.6.39

What happens to the structure is that a local failure of an element in the load path causes the structure to become a plastic mechanism. The prediction of the plastic mechanism forms the basis of the **collapse design method**. For the simple beam the elastic behaviour directly predicts the plastic mechanism.

178   **Safe structures and failure**

ELASTIC BENDING
MOMENT

PLASTIC HINGE
AT Mᴘ

Fig.6.40

But for slightly more complicated structures, such as a two-span beam, the formation of one plastic hinge will not cause the structure to be a plastic mechanism.

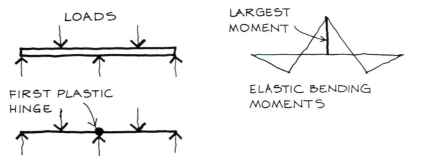

LOADS

LARGEST
MOMENT

FIRST PLASTIC
HINGE

ELASTIC BENDING
MOMENTS

Fig.6.41

Here the first plastic hinge forms at the central support but the structure is not yet a mechanism.

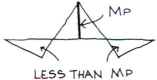

Mᴘ

LESS THAN Mᴘ

Fig.6.42

The load on the structure can be increased until one of the span moments reaches the plastic moment. A second plastic hinge now forms and the structure becomes a mechanism and collapses.

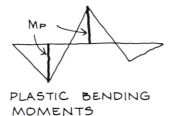

Mᴘ

PLASTIC BENDING
MOMENTS

SECOND PLASTIC
HINGE
COLLAPSE MECHANISM

Fig.6.43

For a pitched portal frame loaded both horizontally and vertically there are three different possible collapse mechanisms. Which one will form depends on the rates of loading for each load.

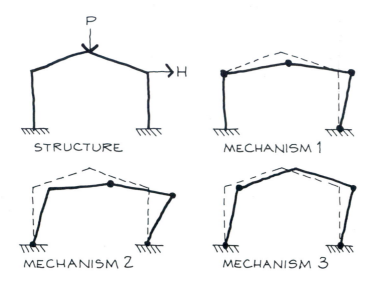

Fig.6.44

This idea of plastic hinges can be used for laterally loaded two dimensional structures to predict collapse mechanisms. The plastic moment, instead of being at a point forming a plastic hinge, is along a line. This 'line of plastic moment' is usually called a **yield line**. For a rectangular slab spanning between opposite supports the yield line position is similar to that of the hinge in the beam shown in Fig.6.38.

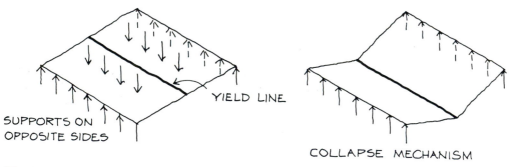

Fig.6.45

For this simple case the position of maximum bending moment is in a straight line across the slab which gives the position of the yield line. A plan of the slab showing the yield line (or lines) is called the **yield line pattern**. For the slab shown in Fig.6.45 the yield line pattern has just one line.

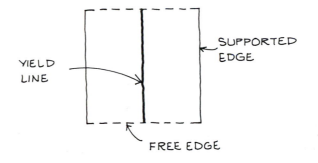

Fig.6.46

A 'free edge' of a laterally loaded slab is one which is unsupported. If the rectangular slab is supported on all sides then, as explained on pages 57 and 58, the slab will span two ways (Fig.2.44). This will cause bending moments in two directions (Fig.2.47).

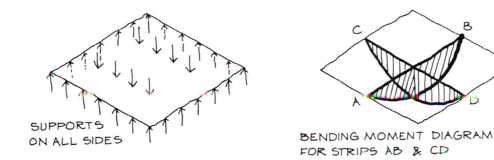

Fig.6.47

But what is the yield line pattern? Whilst the slab is acting elastically the maximum bending moment will be at the centre, but as the load is increased the slab will become plastic at this point, the moment cannot be increased (see Fig.6.39) and a yield line begins to form.

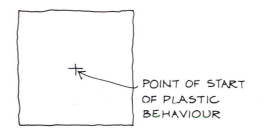

Fig.6.48

But how will the yield lines 'grow' into a yield line pattern that allows the slab to collapse? For the one dimensional structure shown in Figs.6.43 and 6.44 the hinges allowed the structure to 'fold' into a collapse mechanism. Similarly the slab must be able to fold to be able to collapse. As the supported sides must remain level the fold lines (yield lines) must go to the corners.

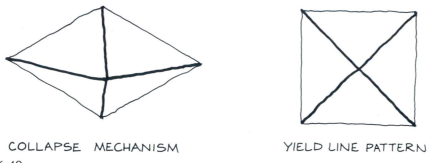

COLLAPSE MECHANISM   YIELD LINE PATTERN

Fig.6.49

The fact that the yield lines go diagonally across the slab is because, not only is this necessary for the fold pattern but these are lines of **principal moments**. The idea of principle moments is not described here but it similar to the idea of principal stresses (page 99 et seq). Moments are applied to the 'sides of a small element' and this is rotated in plan to find the maximum and minimum moments on each side.

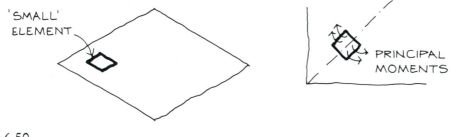

'SMALL' ELEMENT

PRINCIPAL MOMENTS

Fig.6.50

For a square slab with a uniform load the yield line pattern may be 'obvious' but a rectangular slab can be folded in several different ways.

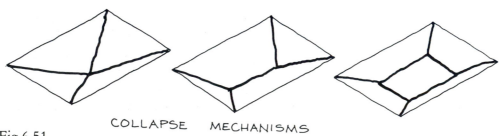

COLLAPSE MECHANISMS

Fig.6.51

These three different foldings of the slab give three different yield line patterns and three different collapse loads.

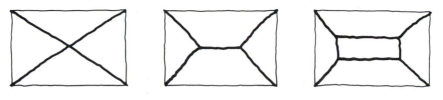

YIELD LINE PATTERNS

Fig.6.52

Because the mathematical prediction of the elastic behaviour of slabs (usually called plates in the technical literature) is difficult or often impossible, the elastic analysis of slab structures is not usually carried out as part of structural design. In contrast, **yield line analysis**, developed for reinforced concrete by the Danish engineer FW Johanssen, is relatively simple to carry out. Of course the correct yield line pattern must be chosen to make sure that the lowest collapse load is calculated.

The collapse mechanisms for these one and two dimensional structures rely on the formation of plastic hinges (yield lines) at positions of maximum bending moments. The formation of these hinges allows geometrically simple foldings of the structure into a collapse configuration. This means that these simple types of structural collapse are only possible if internal axial forces are absent or negligible and the geometry of the structure allows a simple folding.

For instance the ideas of plastic hinges and folding does not give any guidance on how a simple column collapses. Again the ideas of yield lines give no guidance on how the curved shell shown in Fig.4.22 collapses. To see how these structures collapse the effect of **axial forces** must be examined.

6.4   Axial instability

When a straight one dimensional structural element is loaded by axial end loads it either stretches or squashes (see pages 41 to 43). If the structural material is linear elastic/perfectly plastic (Fig.5.6) the element deforms elastically as the load is increased until the elastic limit is reached. The element then becomes plastic and deforms without limit under the collapse load. Because the axial stress distribution is assumed to be uniform (Fig.3.29) the whole of the cross section becomes plastic at the collapse load.

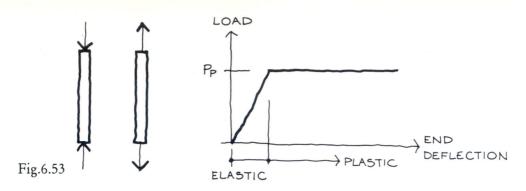

Fig.6.53

At collapse load P_p the element fails by 'endless' stretching or squashing. This is always true for elements in tension but for elements in compression it is only true for certain types of element. This is because compressed elements can be affected by the 'Pe effect' which caused the stack of bricks, shown in Fig.6.29, to topple. If there are two columns of the same cross-section and made of the same material and one is 'short' (stocky) and the other is 'long' (slender) then the difference in length will not alter the collapse load, P_p of Fig.6.53. Both will resist the axial forces by uniformly distributed axial stresses. As the cross-sections and the material are the same both columns will become 'plastic' at the same load.

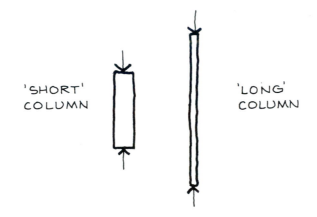

Fig.6.54

But a simple experiment with a slender rod will show as the end load is increased a slender rod begins to bow, that is it starts to bend.

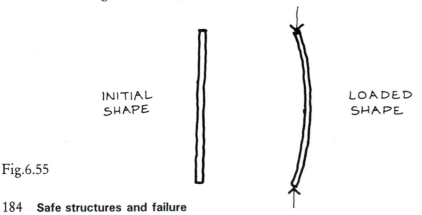

Fig.6.55

184 **Safe structures and failure**

The rod (column) is still carrying load but because the rod is bent the internal forces are axial and bending moments. The size of the bending moment depends on how much the axial load bends the column. So far the behaviour of structures has been described using the **unloaded shape** of the structure and the deflection has not altered the behaviour. This assumption is part of the Engineer's Theory mentioned on page 75, and this theory makes no distinction between stocky and slender columns. For this distinction to be made a more sophisticated theory is required. The general name for this bending behaviour under axial load is **buckling** (from 'to buckle' — 'to bend out of shape'). Because of the technical difficulties of buckling it has fascinated and frustrated mathematicians and engineers for over 200 years. The first mathematical analysis was carried out by the great Swiss mathematician Leonhard Euler (1707—1783) who used it as an illustration of the calculus of variations which he was developing. His work remained unknown to engineers for over 100 years but such was its importance Euler's name, pronounced 'oiler', is still associated with the buckling behaviour of structures.

But why has the initially straight rod (column) buckled? According to Euler's analysis the **perfectly straight** rod will remain straight under increasing load until the **Euler buckling load** is reached. The rod can then either buckle or stay straight! The Euler buckling load is often called the **elastic critical load** and the point on the load/deflection graph where the rod can buckle is call the **bifurcation point**. The deflection is now the lateral deflection and not the axial deflection of Fig.6.53.

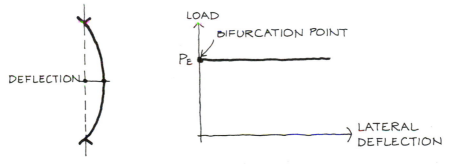

Fig.6.56

Euler's analysis was based entirely on mathematical theory and the fact that the rod has a choice at the bifurcation point is a 'quirk' of the mathematics, no real rod behaves like this. Euler's analysis also required that the rod is perfectly straight but real rods are not, they are **imperfect**. The reason that a stack of bricks topples (Figs.6.30, 6.31 and 6.32) is that it cannot be perfectly made, stacked or loaded. These imperfections cause the e of Fig.6.30 and the toppling of the stack. Similarly columns cannot be made perfectly or loaded perfectly. This means columns are never perfectly straight, as Euler's theory requires but are always bent (imperfect).

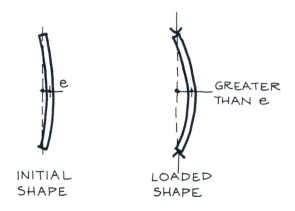

Fig.6.57

This imperfection e has the same effect on the column as that shown in Fig.3.75.

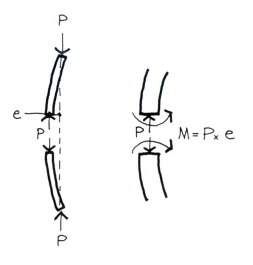

$$M = P \times e$$

Fig.6.58

In the case of the eccentric loading shown in Fig.3.75 the eccentricity e remains constant no matter how big the axial load P becomes, and the Engineer's theory applies. For the imperfect column, as the axial load increases the dimension e increases and so the bending moment, $M = P \times e$, also increases. If the Engineer's theory is used for an imperfect column the bending moment in the column is Pe where e is the initial imperfection. As the axial load increases the increase in e is ignored and the moment increases in direct proportion with the load.

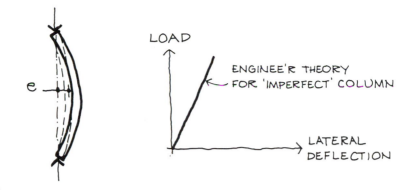

Fig.6.59

If the effect of the increase in e due to increasing load is taken into account the load/deflection behaviour is not represented by the straight line of Fig.6.59 but by a curve. As the axial load reaches the Euler buckling load (P_E, the Elastic critical load) the curve meets the horizontal line of Fig.6.56.

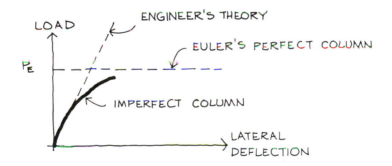

Fig.6.60

The **slenderness** of a column depends on the length, the structural material and the cross-sectional shape. As the buckling effect causes a bending moment in the column the better the column is at resisting bending the less slender it will be. Unlike a beam which is loaded in a particular direction a column can buckle in any direction, so columns that are good at resisting bending in any direction will be the least slender. For the same reasons for preferring I sections to + sections for beams (see pages 86 and 87) columns with circular tubular sections are the least slender and with + sections the most slender. This was not realised by 19th century engineers who frequently used + section columns. And as the column becomes more slender the elastic critical load P_E reduces.

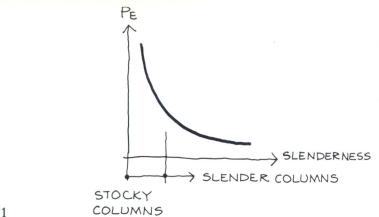

Fig.6.61

This figure indicates a point on the slenderness axis where a column alters from a stocky column to a slender column. For a stocky column the buckling effect can be ignored and the Engineer's theory can be used to predict the column behaviour. As is explained later the reason that this distinction can be made is because stocky columns fail at loads well below their elastic critical loads.

Columns that are cantilevers or horizontally restrained within their height will have buckled shapes that are different to each other and to the column shown in Fig.6.57.

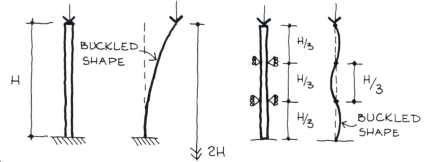

Fig.6.62

For the cantilever the slenderness would be based on a length of 2H whereas for the column restrained at third points the length would be H/3, a sixfold difference. So, depending on how a column is joined to the rest of the world, a column could be stocky or slender. To make sure that the appropriate theory is used the following questions must be answered for **all parts of structures in compression**.

•   **what is the buckled shape?**

•   **is the structure slender?**

And as with many structural engineering questions they are easier to ask than to answer!

188   **Safe structures and failure**

For columns the whole structure buckles into a shape that depends on how the column is joined to other parts of the total structure. But how does a beam buckle? As is explained on pages 80 to 83 when a beam is loaded part of the beam is in compression and part is in tension (Fig.3.36).

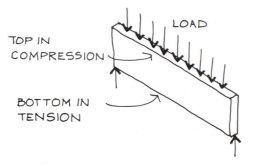

Fig.6.63

For this simple beam the whole of the top of the beam is in compression, so it will be the top part of this beam that will buckle. As the bottom is in tension it can only be displaced by an external force so the top can only buckle sideways.

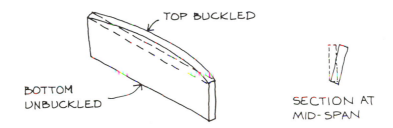

Fig.6.64

If, like the column in Fig.6.62, the top of the beam is restrained at third points the top of the beam will buckle into a different shape.

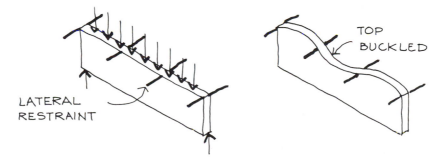

Fig.6.65

Having found the buckled shape it has to be decided whether the compressed part of the structure is slender or stocky. As with the column this depends on the (buckled) length, the structural material and the cross-sectional shape. The compressed part of the beam buckles by a combination of sideways bending and twisting (Fig.6.64). Beams that have cross-sections that are good at resisting this combined action are the least slender. For solid rectangular beams deep narrow sections are more slender than square ones, for non-rectangular sections tubes or sections with wide flanges are less slender and + sections are more slender.

Where stress effective sections (see page 86) are used flanges or webs that are in compression may have buckled shapes in part of the element, this is often called **local buckling**. If an I beam is used for a simple beam compressive stresses will be high in the top flange at the centre of the beam and in the web at the supports.

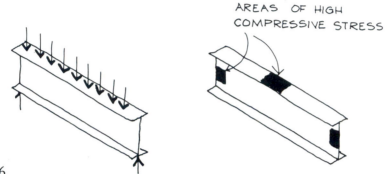

Fig.6.66

So the top flange or the web could buckle locally in these areas of high compressive stress.

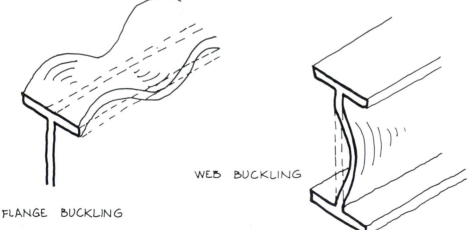

Fig.6.67   FLANGE BUCKLING

This local behaviour can happen anywhere in a structure if there are high compressive stresses and the structure is **locally slender**. This could happen in the wall of a box column or the crown of a cylindrical shell.

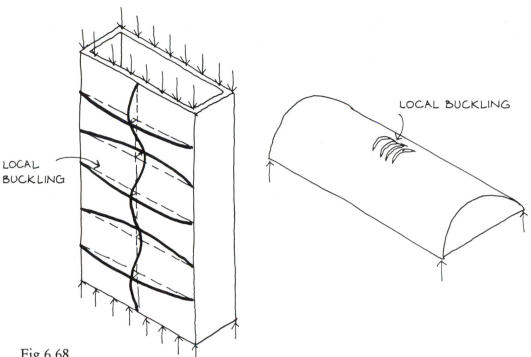

LOCAL BUCKLING

LOCAL BUCKLING

Fig.6.68

These various forms of buckling can be combined by considering slenderness in the compressed part of the structure. Whether it is local is then a matter of definition rather than concept. For the box column the whole of the wall has buckled locally.

As with other structural engineering concepts slenderness has to be quantified before it can be a factor for making structural decisions. The importance of identifying slenderness is shown by redrawing Fig.6.60.

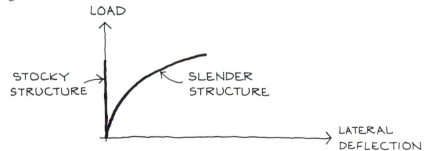

LOAD

STOCKY
STRUCTURE

SLENDER
STRUCTURE

LATERAL
DEFLECTION

Fig.6.69

Although a stocky structure will not be perfect the imperfections can be ignored for structural design and axial forces only cause axial shortening and uniform axial stress. For a slender structure imperfections cannot be ignored for structural design and axial forces cause axial shortening and lateral displacement hence non-uniform axial stresses.

Most importantly the bending of slender structures under axial forces means the type of collapse will be different from a similar stocky structure and **at a lower load**.

Whether elastic, collapse or limit state design methods are used (see pages 165 to 171) to be successful they all depend, in one way or another, on collapse strength of the structure. Structures collapse by becoming mechanisms (see pages 172 to 183) and if they are slender, the bending due to axial forces must be considered in the formation of these mechanisms. This bending may cause a slender structure to collapse in quite a different way to a similar but stocky structure. For example the two columns shown in Fig.6.54 will collapse differently. The stocky structure, the short column, will collapse by squashing as the axial stress reaches the elastic limit and becomes plastic. The slender structure, the long column, will collapse when a plastic hinge (see page 178) forms in the column bent by the effect of the axial load.

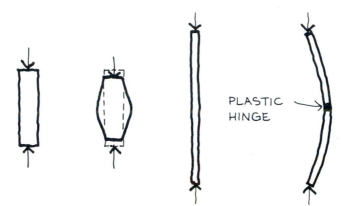

Fig.6.70

A structure will always collapse due to plastic behaviour before the elastic critical load is reached. The more slender the structure the nearer the collapse load will be to the elastic critical load. Recent research into the behaviour of steel columns has been collated to produce a graph showing the relationship between the collapse load and the elastic critical load.

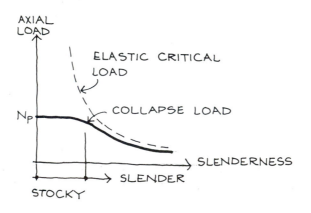

Fig.6.71

Here N_p is the squash load of a stocky column, the maximum collapse load of the column. As the column becomes more slender the collapse load reduces and is nearer the elastic critical load which is also reducing with increased slenderness. For beams the situation is similar, that is a stocky beam will collapse with a plastic hinge when the bending moment reaches M_p (see Fig.6.40). As the beam becomes more slender the effect of buckling on the part of the beam in compression (see Fig.6.65) reduces the collapse moment. A diagram similar to Fig.6.71 can be drawn for beams.

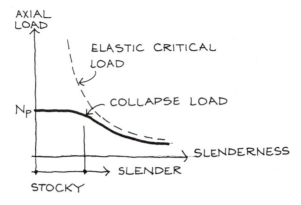

Fig.6.72

These diagrams show that if the failure strength of a column or a beam (P_{LOAD2} of Fig.6.17) is calculated without considering slenderness, then the factors of safety used in the design process may be dangerously wrong. In fact safe structures have collapsed for this reason. One of the best known collapses of this type was the failure, in 1907, of the St. Lawrence bridge in Canada. This bridge collapsed twice during construction with the loss of 88 lives. As the bridge structure was being cantilevered out one of the compression elements failed as a mechanism caused by the buckling effect.

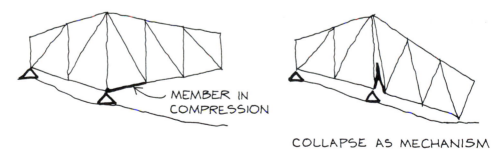

Fig.6.73

There is often pressure on structural designers from other members of the design team to produce slender structures for visual reasons. Even without this pressure slenderness in structures presents the designer with a number of practical difficulties:

- The theoretical analysis is mathematically difficult and at present incomplete.

- The matching of theoretical predictions to laboratory experiments is also incomplete and has only been attempted for elementary structures such as beams and columns.

- The design process does not automatically identify parts the structure that are slender.

The first two difficulties mean that the structural designer does not have reliable technical data for use in quantitative analysis. The third difficulty means that the structural designer must be able to **identify** structures, or parts of structures, that are slender.

The various aspects of the effect of buckling on structures has generated a vast technical literature. Unfortunately in most introductory texts the buckling effect on structures is either ignored or treated as an isolated topic. Although the basic behaviour of structures can be understood without considering the buckling effect it leads to a naive understanding of structural design. This is because both overall conceptual design and detail design are concerned with the control of slenderness by either the choice of element or the specific introduction of slenderness controlling elements or systems.

A simple example explains how this happens. At the end of a simple beam the shear force is at it maximum (see Fig.2.26). If the chosen beam has an I section then this shear force is mainly carried by the web (see Fig.4.35) and the web may buckle locally (see Fig.6.67)

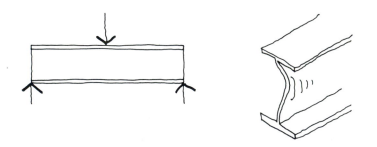

Fig.6.74

This buckling behaviour may have to be controlled by making the web thicker, choice of element, or by adding slenderness controlling elements. As the web wants to bend sideways these extra elements need to stiffen the web against this bending.

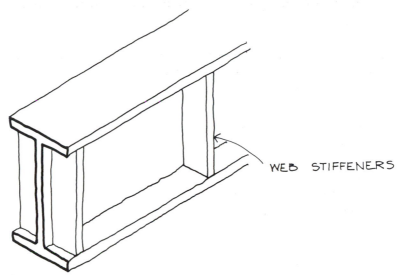

Fig.6.75

In effect the stiffener now acts as a beam spanning between the top and bottom flanges and because it is stiff in the direction that the web wants to buckle it prevents the web buckling. These web stiffeners can often be seen on steel railway bridges or other large steel beams.

Although the most widely used structural materials are still steel, concrete, timber and masonry (see page 141) there is an increasing availability of these materials with higher strengths. This results in more slender structures but to use the higher strengths more slenderness controlling strategies are needed.

6.5   Relationship of structural theories

No matter what theories of structural behaviour are proposed a real loaded structure will behave in a way that suits the structure and not the theory! To design structures by using a theory there are two conditions. The predictions of the theory must have a **reasonable correlation** with the behaviour of real structures and the theory must be **simple enough** to be usable as a part of the design process. But how close is a reasonable correlation and how simple is simple enough? There is no definitive answer to these questions but by comparing how the various theories apply to a simple structure an opinion can be informed.

The simple structure used for this comparison is the portal frame shown in Fig.2.27. The loads are applied both vertically and horizontally.

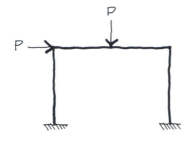

Fig.6.76

The structural material is idealised as linear elastic/perfectly plastic (see Fig.5.6). The behaviour shown in Fig.5.10 indicates the reasonable correlation obtained by this idealisation. Under the loading shown in Fig.6.76 the portal frame will deflect sideways at the beam level.

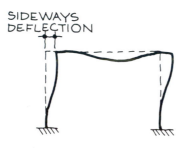

Fig.6.77

As the size of the loads P are varied the size of the horizontal deflection will also vary. The response of this deflection to the variation of the load will indicate how the frame is behaving. The most widely used theory for the prediction of structural behaviour is the **linear elastic theory**, this uses the assumptions of the Engineer's theory. This analysis predicts that the size of the deflection will vary in **direct proportion** to a variation in the size of the load. There is no limitation to the size of load, that is there is no prediction of collapse. This theory predicts a **linear** response.

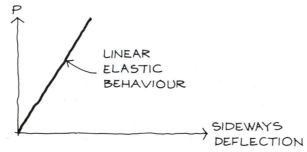

Fig.6.78

For simple framed structures the **rigid/perfectly plastic theory** can be used. This assumes a collapse mechanism from which a collapse load is predicted. For the portal frame with the loading shown in Fig.6.76 the collapse mechanism would have four hinges.

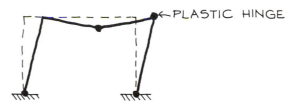

Fig.6.79

This theory predicts a collapse load and at this load the frame would deflect without limit. This theory would not predict the frame's behaviour before collapse.

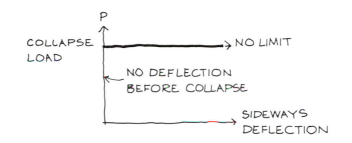

Fig.6.80

The predictions of these two theories can be combined to give a **linear elastic perfectly plastic** response.

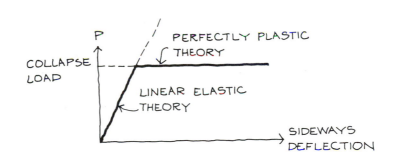

Fig.6.81

These theories can also be combined to predict **linear elasto-plastic** behaviour. Really this is just alternating applications of the two theories. The linear elastic theory is used until the largest elastic moment equals the plastic moment (see Figs.6.41 and 6.42). The structure used for analysis is now modified by the formation of the first plastic hinge but acts elastically until the second plastic hinge forms. Again the structure for elastic analysis is modified and another hinge forms, this process is repeated until the frame becomes a mechanism. Each phase of elastic analysis will only predict the position of the next plastic hinge and will not automatically identify the collapse mechanism. The response alters with the formation of each hinge.

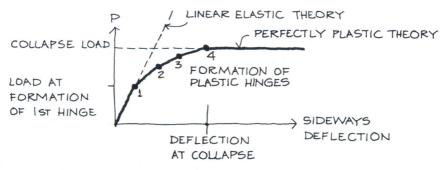

Fig.6.82

This elasto-plastic analysis gives additional information such as the loads at which each hinge forms. The formation of the first hinge, which is a form of local failure, may occur at a load that is much lower than the collapse load. Because now there is a deflection history the rotations at each hinge are predicted.

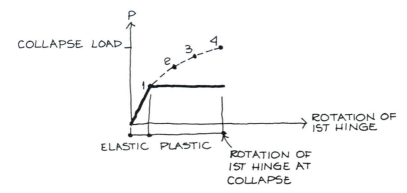

Fig.6.83

In a real structure there may be a limitation on the rotation of a plastic hinge due to a lack of ductility. This may cause the first hinge to fail due to excessive rotation before the final hinge forms to cause the collapse mechanism. In this case the failure would not be the frame collapse but a local collapse and the collapse load would be lower.

Alternatively an elastic analysis can be carried out for simple frames that takes the buckling effect into account, this is a **non-linear elastic** analysis. The analysis will take into account the bending moments and deflections caused by the Pe effect (see Figs.6.57 and 6.58). The response will be non-linear and will follow a similar curve to that shown for the imperfect column in Fig.6.60. An elastic critical load can also be predicted for the frame under the specific loading and this limits the size of the load the frame can carry.

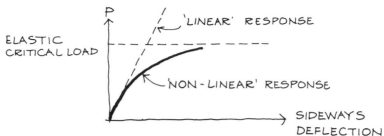

Fig.6.84

The elastic critical load will always be greater than the collapse load as Figs.6.71 and 6.72 show for columns and beams. However the elasto-plastic analytical process can use the non-linear elastic analysis between the formation of plastic hinges. The response will be similar to that shown in Fig.6.82 except the behaviour between hinge formation will now be non-linear.

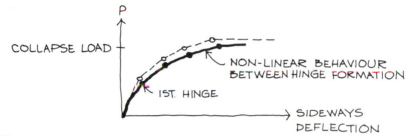

Fig.6.85

This theory may predict a collapse load that is lower than the one predicted by the linear theory as the buckling effect may increase the bending moments at critical sections. This will cause the hinges to form at lower loads. The responses predicted by the five types of analysis can be compared by combining Figs.6.81, 6.82 and 6.85 into one diagram.

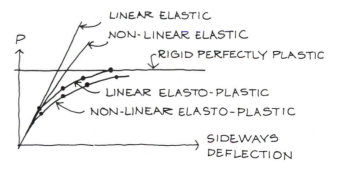

Fig.6.86

The analytical dilemma facing the structural designer is now clear. A reasonable correlation between theory and real behaviour is best obtained by the use of the non-linear elasto-plastic analytical process which predicts the response shown in Fig.6.85. The only general theory that is simple enough for general use is the linear elastic theory which predicts the response shown in Fig.6.78.

The reasonable correlation of the non-linear elasto-plastic theory is approximate as it idealises the true material behaviour, ignores local buckling effects, ignores the effect of residual stresses and ignores the effect of axial and shear stresses on the formation of plastic hinges. Theories that take account of these effects are in the realm of research rather structural design. The linear elastic theory is only simple enough for quite simple structures unless computing facilities are available. In spite of these shortcomings the linear elastic theory can be used because the difference in the predicted behaviour and the actual behaviour is small in the phase before the formation of the first plastic hinge.

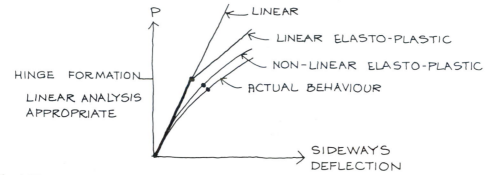

Fig.6.87

As the majority of building structures are expected to behave elastically during ordinary use their behaviour is adequately predicted by the linear elastic theory. However safe structures can only be designed by using factors of safety against collapse (see page 169). The factors of safety are applied to linear elastic analysis by the use of a range of numerical coefficients. These coefficients are based on current analytical and experimental research and take account of the non-linear effects of material and structural behaviour. These coefficients are published in technical documents specifically prepared for structural design and are called **Codes of Practice**. In countries that have sufficient technical resources these are prepared as National codes and their recommendations are often legal requirements as they are part of national building laws. In Europe the national codes are being superseded by trans-national European codes.

CHAPTER 7 *Structural geometry and behaviour*

A structure may be considered to be an assembly of elements and these elements can be one, two or three dimensional. Depending on whether the loading is lateral or axial, each element had a particular type of structural behaviour (see Chapter 3). This behaviour may also be affected by the slenderness of parts of the structures that are axially loaded, as this can lead to instability (see pages 183—195).

The structural behaviour of any structure is dependent on a number of factors and these are:

- **The shape of the structure.**
- **The type of loading on the structure.**
- **The slenderness of the structure.**

To conceive structures the structural designer must be able to understand the consequences of structural geometry and structural assembly. This can be achieved by knowing how structures can be varied geometrically and understanding the overall behaviour of different assemblies of elements.

7.1 Geometry of structures

For structures to exist in the real world they must have a shape or **form**. Not only must the overall structure have a **geometry**, but also each part of the structure must have a shape or form.

Fig.7.1

For a simple goal post structure there is a choice for the cross-sectional shape for the posts and the cross-bar. They could be rectangular, circular or any other shape. Furthermore the posts and cross-bar could have the same (constant) cross-section throughout their length, or a variable (that is tapered etc.) cross-section.

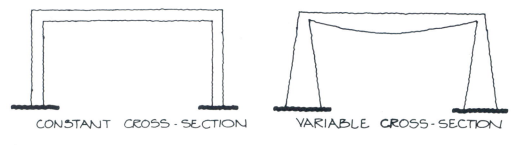

CONSTANT CROSS-SECTION   VARIABLE CROSS-SECTION

Fig.7.2

Or again the basic goal post geometry could be altered by sloping the posts or curving the cross-bar.

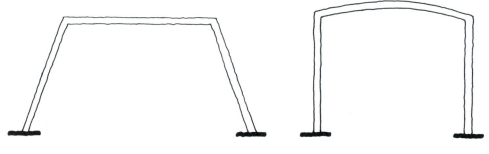

Fig.7.3

It is worth making a distinction between **defined** and **organic geometry**. What is meant by a defined geometry is one whose shape can be expressed mathematically. Examples are rectangles, circles, ellipses and so on. Thus with a defined geometry the exact shape can be determined by mathematical calculation. This contrasts with organic geometry which has no mathematical basis. All natural objects such as trees, fish, humans, rocks and beetles have this geometry. This geometry can be created by drawing or modelling the structure without mathematical constraints. The exact numerical geometry can, if necessary, be obtained by measuring the drawing or model. This is often done for such natural objects as car body shapes!

Traditional building tends to use organic geometry, for example tepees, igloos and thatched cottages, and this is part of their charm and 'naturalness'. This is not to say traditional building has random geometry, often traditional geometry complies to a strict geometry but it is not mathematically based.

This contrasts with civilised building which has a strict defined geometry. Often the

202   **Structural geometry and behaviour**

geometry is something of a fetish. Research has highlighted the amazing accuracy of the geometry of the ancient Egyptian Pyramids and Classical Greek temples. Indeed the main secrets of the masons who built the great Gothic cathedrals were geometric.

Many attempts have been made to build modern civilised organic buildings, such as the original scheme for Sydney Opera House. However these attempts appear contrived rather than natural.

Fig.7.4 Sydney Opera House

There are obvious advantages for a civilised society to use defined geometry. This is because civilisation uses extended lines of communications and a defined geometry is easier to communicate than an organic one. The majority of civilised building structures are based on rectilinear forms and there are practical and economic reasons for this. Due to the lack of skill of the designers the vast array of non-rectilinear but still mathematically based geometries are rarely used. Again because the engineering analysis of non-rectilinear structures is difficult, therefore time-consuming and costly, engineering designers prefer rectilinear geometries.

7.2   The behaviour of structural systems

To understand the overall behaviour of any structural system it must be clear how the basic concepts apply. These concepts are:

1	**The function of a structure is to transfer loads** (see page 3)
2	**The load path is the structure for each load** (see page 38)
3	**The structure transfers loads by forces in the structure** (see page 41)
4	**Forces in the structure can be considered as a combination of direct forces, shear forces and bending moments** (see pages 41—49)
5	**The structure must have overall stability** (see pages 173—175)
6	**Collapse initiated by slender structures must be avoided** (see pages 183—195)

The choice of structural materials, concepts of structural safety and the stress distribution all affect the actual design but not the overall behaviour of the structural concept.

The first step towards understanding the overall behaviour is to extend the concepts of direct forces, shear forces and bending moments to more complex structures than the beam element. The behaviour of a simple spanning beam can be characterised by drawing the bending moment and shear forces diagrams (see pages 48 and 49). The shape of these diagrams will depend of the pattern of loading and the magnitude on the size of the span and the loads. Looking yet again at the simple beam with a central point load the bending moment and shear force diagrams are those shown in Fig.7.5

BENDING MOMENT
DIAGRAM

SHEAR FORCE
DIAGRAM

Fig.7.5

These diagrams plot the size of the internal forces which balance slices of the beam (Figs.2.9 and 2.18).

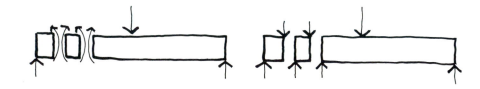

Fig.7.6

It is important to understand the equivalence of bending moments with push/pull forces acting a lever arm apart (Figs.3.40 and 3.43).

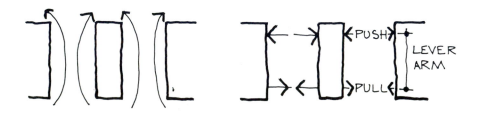

Fig.7.7

These concepts have been explained by their effect on a simple beam but a more general statement is:

- **When any structure carries loads over a span, bending moments and shear forces or their equivalent will be present.**

The key is to find 'their equivalent'. Suppose that instead of using a beam to transfer the load P to the support points a 'loose' cable is used. As anyone who has hung out washing knows the line changes shape as each item is hung up. For a central point load the shape is particularly simple.

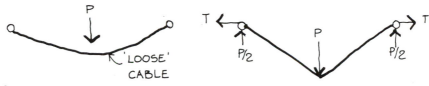

Fig.7.8

The cable will be in tension (a direct force) and the supports must be capable of resisting vertical and horizontal loads. This seems to be a completely different structure from a beam, so where is the equivalent of the bending moment and shear force? Where is the push force and where is the pull force? Using the slicing technique of a section what happens to a slice of cable?

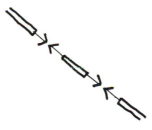

Fig.7.9

Everything is nicely balanced but suppose the sloping forces are thought of as a combination of horizontal and vertical forces.

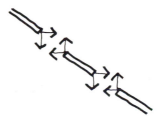

Fig.7.10

The behaviour of structural systems 205

Now the vertical forces on the slice look rather like shear forces.

Fig.7.11

But where is the bending moment? All there is are some pull forces and these are not in the same line!

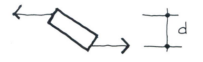

Fig.7.12

The push force is in mid-air in line with the supports.

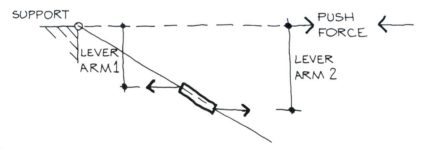

Fig.7.13

This seems completely unreasonable, after all how can there be a push force in mid-air? Clearly it isn't there as such, only conceptually, and this allows the comparison with a bending moment and bending moment diagram.

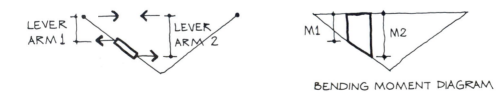

Fig.7.14

Because the force in the cable cannot vary the variation in the size of the bending moment is achieved by the variation in lever arm. This rather fantastic concept makes more sense if a strut is introduced 'to hold the supports apart'.

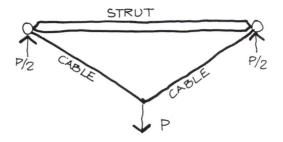

Fig.7.15

Now the supports only resist vertical forces and the tension force T of Fig.7.9 becomes a compression force in the strut.

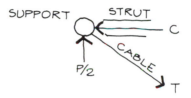

Fig.7.16

Now the strut/cable assembly can be sliced.

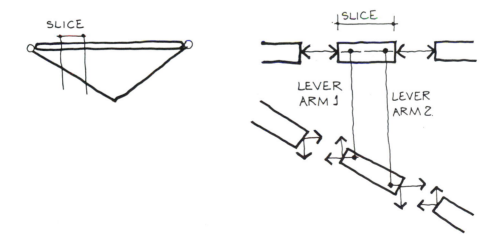

Fig.7.17

The whole structure could be turned upside down, with sloping struts and a horizontal tie.

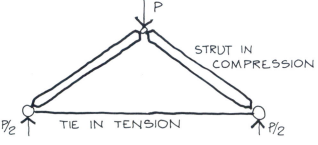

Fig.7.18

Here a slice would show that the shear is now carried by the vertical force in the sloping strut and the tensile force in the tie. This is the pull force of the bending moment. If the supports can resist horizontal forces then the tie could be removed.

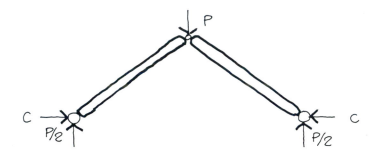

Fig.7.19

A slice of this structure would now require a pull force in mid-air to allow comparison with a bending moment. These five different structures, all carrying the same load over the same span provide a basic palette of structural types. These five structures are:

1   **A beam**

2   **A hanging cable**

3   **A hanging cable with a compression strut**

4   **Sloping struts with a straight cable**

5   **Sloping struts**

Structures 3 and 4 are **trusses** and are simple forms of the structure shown in Fig.3.9. Structure 5 is an **arch**, these are usually curved shapes.

These five structures can now be compared for the structural actions of bending moments and shear forces.

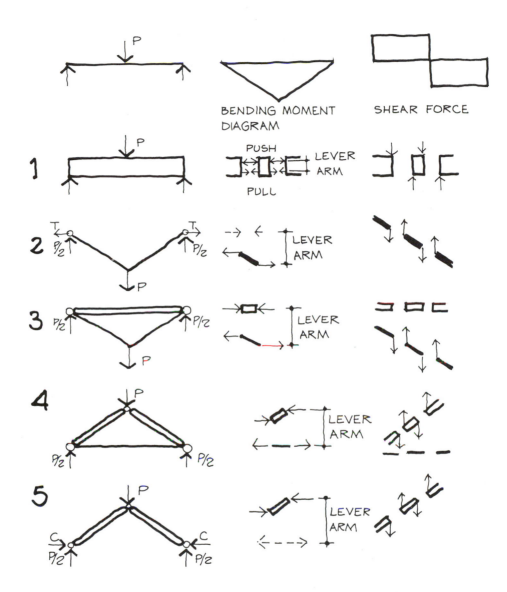

Fig.7.20

It is worth noting that in structures 3 and 4 the shear forces are carried by the sloping members, the horizontal member making no contribution. The stress distributions for the bending can also be compared.

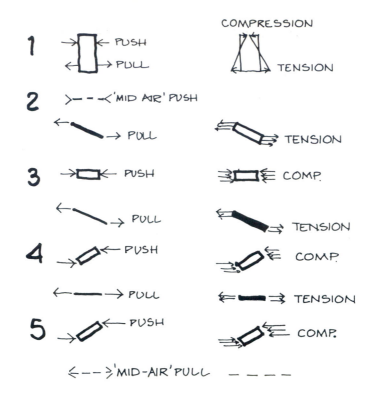

Fig.7.21

Similarly the stress distribution for shear for structures 2, 3, 4 and 5 is the 'vertical' stress in the sloping member.

Fig.7.22

For a beam the paths of principle stress give arch-like curves for tension and compression (see Fig.4.19).

PRINCIPAL COMPRESSION   PRINCIPAL TENSION

Fig.7.23

Because of the simplicity of the stress paths of the structures only crudely approximate the beam patterns. For comparison they are drawn on beam shapes.

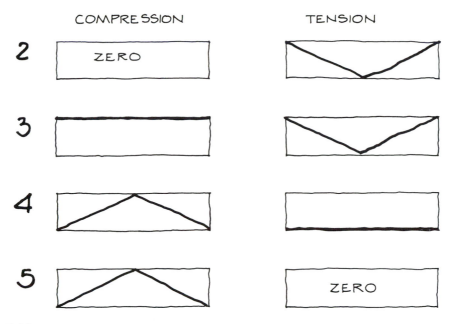

Fig.7.24

All these structures are in two dimensions but they can be extended to form similar three dimensional structures.

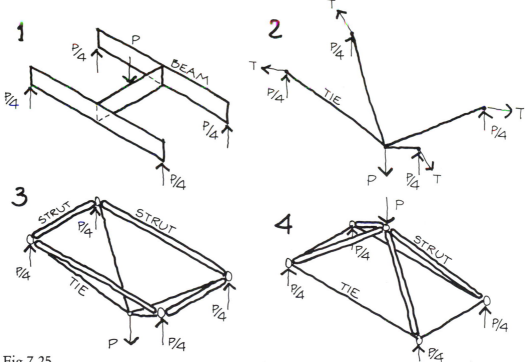

Fig.7.25

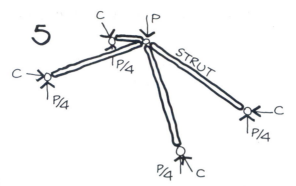

Fig.7.25 continued

Structure 1 now has bending moments and shear forces in two directions.

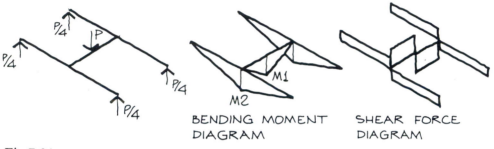

BENDING MOMENT
DIAGRAM

SHEAR FORCE
DIAGRAM

Fig.7.26

For the tetrahedron shaped structures it is difficult to draw the slices and the push and pull forces but M1 and M2 must exist. These structures can be thought of as having four simple triangles.

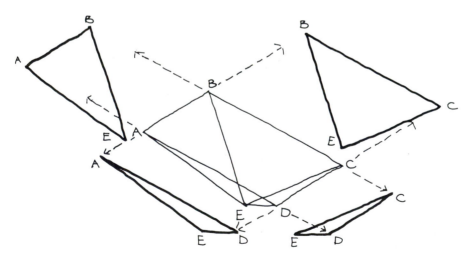

Fig.7.27

212 **Structural geometry and behaviour**

The inclined triangles share the inclined members AE, BE, CE and DE. The inclined trusses ABE and DCE resist the bending moment M1 and ADE and BCE resist the bending moment M2. This is achieved by the horizontal part of the tension force in the inclined ties AE, BE, CE and DE. The push forces are supplied by the compression forces in the struts AB, BC, CD and DA.

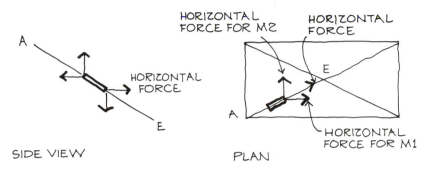

Fig.7.28

Because the structure is now three dimensional the five basic two dimensional structures can be combine to form many different structural systems. Here are three (The bold numbers indicate the type of structure used — see Fig.7.20):

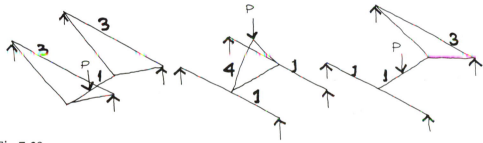

Fig.7.29

These simple structures can also be used to illustrate concepts 5 and 6 (see page 203). Structures 2 and 5 depend for their action on the existence of the support reactions T and C shown in Fig.7.20. These reactions could be resisted by massive blocks.

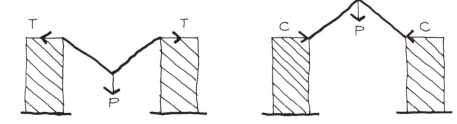

Fig.7.30

The massive blocks must be stable under the disturbing forces that tend to turn the blocks over.

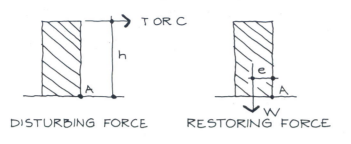

DISTURBING FORCE   RESTORING FORCE

Fig.7.31

From page 176 the Factor of Safety would be:

- **F.o.s = Restoring force ÷ disturbing force**

The structure could fail by the blocks overturning or sliding.

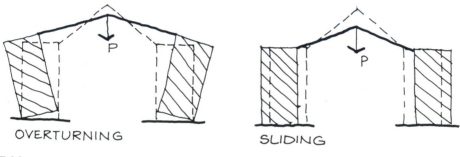

OVERTURNING   SLIDING

Fig.7.32

Again structures 4 and 5 could fail by falling over sideways if there was eccentricity in the construction.

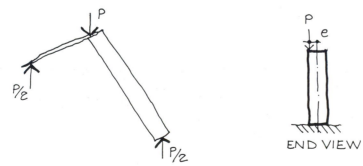

END VIEW

Fig.7.33

If the dimension e was significant then the truss would lose overall stability.

In structure 1, if the beam was slender then a collapse could be initiated by lateral buckling of the top of the beam (see page 189). In structures 3, 4 and 5 if the compression struts are slender then a collapse could be initiated by overall buckling of the strut (see page 184). This is what happened in the collapse of the Quebec bridge (see Fig.6.73).

7.3   Trusses and frames

It is now possible to see how the concepts of bending moments and shear forces enable the structural action of a variety of physically dissimilar structures to be understood. In Fig.7.20 the structures 3 and 4 are trusses and trusses can be made in a range of **triangulated** arrangements of straight members.

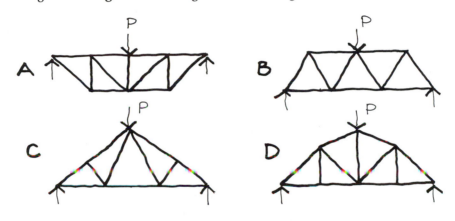

Fig.7.34

These trussed structures are used widely and can be seen in all types of buildings, particularly as roof structures. As with the simple trusses, the sloping members carry the shear forces and also part of the push/pull forces of the bending moment whilst the horizontal members only carry the push/pull forces. This can be shown by examining the forces in truss type A.

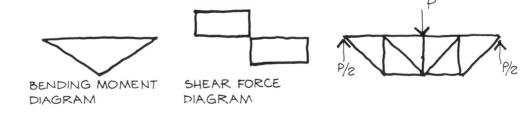

BENDING MOMENT DIAGRAM   SHEAR FORCE DIAGRAM

Fig.7.35

If the truss is sliced then the slice of the truss must be in equilibrium with the bending moment and the shear force.

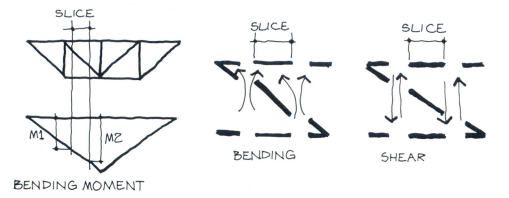

BENDING MOMENT

Fig.7.36

Of the three truss members cut by the slice, only the sloping member has a vertical force and can carry shear.

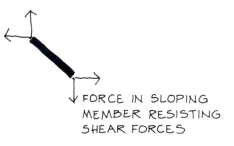

Fig.7.37

The forces in the top and bottom members only contribute to the push/pull forces, but there is also a contribution from the sloping member. So there are three push/pull forces!

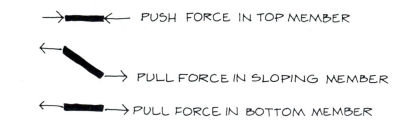

Fig.7.38

As the forces do not vary along each member the variation from M1 to M2 comes from the variation in the lever arm caused by the different positions of the pull force in the sloping member.

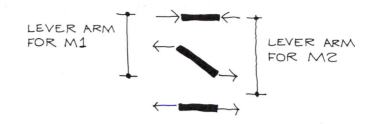

LEVER ARM FOR M1

LEVER ARM FOR M2

Fig.7.39

This shows the top member in compression and the bottom and sloping members in tension. The complete distribution of compression and tension forces for such a simple truss is relatively easy to discover.

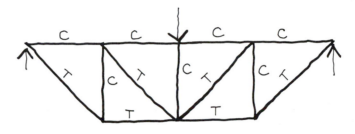

Fig.7.40

Again the forces in the members can be considered to be paths of principal stress (see Figs.7.22 and 7.23). Because the truss is now more beam-like the paths are more beam-like.

PRINCIPAL COMPRESSION   PRINCIPAL TENSION

Fig.7.41

For this truss there is overall stability but there are several possibilities that slender parts could initiate collapse. The whole of the top part of the truss could buckle laterally, similarly to the top of a beam.

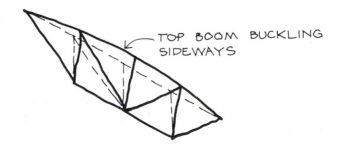

TOP BOOM BUCKLING SIDEWAYS

Fig.7.42

Or any of the seven members that are in compression could buckle individually.

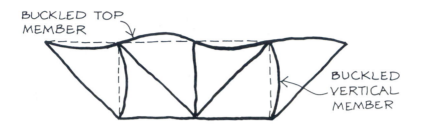

Fig.7.43

Sometimes it is more convenient, for practical reasons, to support this type of truss at the level of the bottom member.

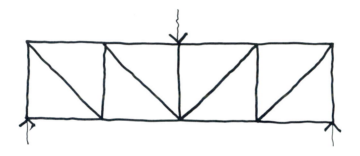

Fig.7.44

The pattern is not altered, but the extra vertical members are in compression, basically just transferring the reaction force. The extra horizontal members are unloaded.

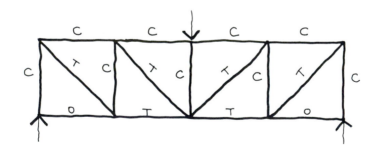

Fig.7.45

This would be altered if the diagonals were reversed.

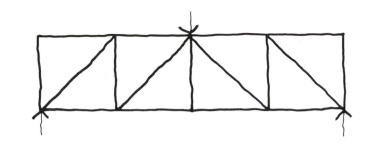

Fig.7.46

The force pattern is similar for the top and bottom members but the forces in the diagonals now change from tension to compression and vice versa for the verticals.

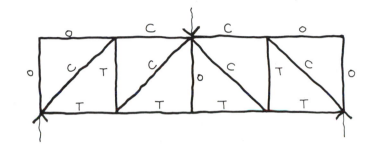

Fig.7.47

This shows how a structural designer can alter, to some extent, the force pattern by choice of structural arrangement. But the truss still has to provide vertical forces for shear and push/pull forces for bending moments. This means the top and bottom members will always have tension and compression forces.

The trusses have axial forces in the individual members of the truss but a beam has bending moments and shear forces. As has been explained there are similarities between the structural action of a spanning trusses and beams but physically they are quite different. It is possible however to physically change them into one another. Suppose a beam has small holes drilled through it and a truss has thicker members with large joints.

Fig.7.48

These two structures do not appear to be similar and it would quite reasonable to expect the beam to act like a beam and the truss like a truss. In the region of the small holes the beam stresses would be slightly altered and in the region of the joints the direction of the direct forces may be altered. But the overall behaviour would be beam-like and truss-like. However if the holes in the beam were made larger and the members of the truss made thicker the behaviour would change.

Fig.7.49

Both these structures have to carry bending moments and shear forces but the stress distributions are no longer like beams or trusses. The large holes in the beam will invalidate the assumptions made for a beam (pages 81—82). The thick members and the large joints mean that the truss members will no longer only carry axial forces because the joints are no longer pinned. By making the beam holes square or removing the truss diagonals the structures become the same — a **frame**.

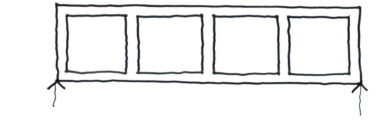

Fig.7.50

But how does this unbeam-like/untruss-like structure carry the overall bending moments and shear forces? Again slice the structure.

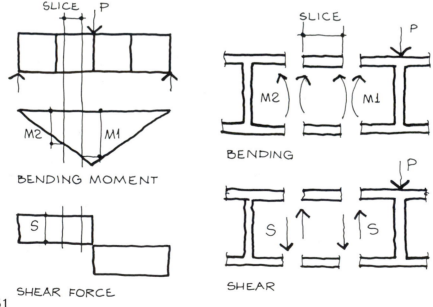

Fig.7.51

220 **Structural geometry and behaviour**

Now the top and bottom parts of this structure have to carry the effects of M1 and M2 by axial push/pull forces and also the shear forces.

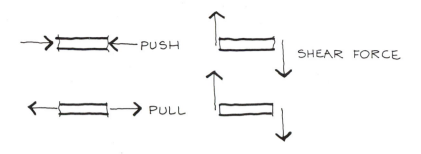

Fig.7.52

It may appear that these are the only forces that act on the structure, but by carrying the shear forces the top and bottom members are also subjected to bending moments — this is far from obvious. In the truss with diagonals the individual members may be joined to each other in such a way that they are hinged to one another. This is called **pin-jointed**. However if the frame was pin-jointed it would be a mechanism and collapse.

Fig.7.53

But if the frame members have stiff joints the structure will not collapse. What is preventing the collapse is the stiffness of the joint stopping each panel lozenging, but to do this the stiff-jointed members must bend.

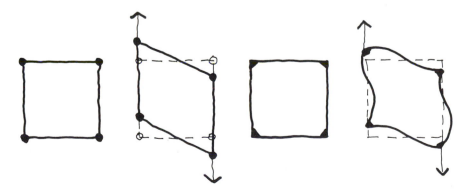

Fig.7.54

Trusses and frames 221

Each member bends into an S shape, with the maximum bending moments at each end and a zero bending moment in the middle. Drawing the bending moment on the tension side of each member gives a rather confused bending moment diagram for the whole panel.

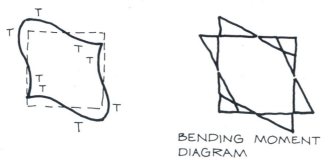

BENDING MOMENT
DIAGRAM

Fig.7.55

Not only are there bending moments in all members of the structure but there are also (horizontal) shear forces in the vertical members.

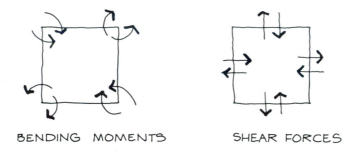

BENDING MOMENTS   SHEAR FORCES

Fig.7.56

This should not be too surprising as this is similar to the horizontal shear forces that were required for the beam (see page 112).

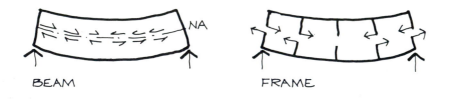

BEAM   FRAME

Fig.7.57

For the whole frame the bending moments are a sequence of those shown in Fig.7.55 for one panel. For clarity the bending moment diagram is split into one for the top and bottom members and one for the vertical members.

222   **Structural geometry and behaviour**

 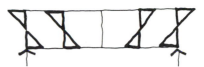

BENDING MOMENTS IN
TOP & BOTTOM MEMBERS

BENDING MOMENTS IN
VERTICALS

Fig.7.58

In the truss the variation in the overall bending moment either side of the slice was catered for by the variation in the lever arm (see Fig.7.38). The lever arm varied because of the varying position of the force in the sloping member. In the frame this is achieved by the bending moments in the top and bottom members. The axial forces are constant in each panel and cater for the overall moment at the point of zero moment in the top and bottom members.

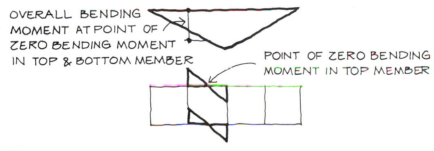

OVERALL BENDING
MOMENT AT POINT OF
ZERO BENDING MOMENT
IN TOP & BOTTOM MEMBER

POINT OF ZERO BENDING
MOMENT IN TOP MEMBER

Fig.7.59

For each panel the overall bending moment is the sum of the moment due to the axial forces **plus** or **minus** the bending moments in the top and bottom members.

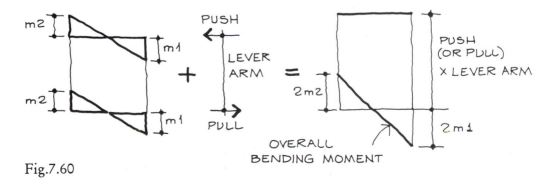

Fig.7.60

This frame action with bending moments at the stiff joints which connect the individual members of the frame is used widely in structural engineering. The portal frame (see Fig.2.27) is a common example of a framed structure. It is the loss of joint stiffness by the formation of plastic hinges (see Fig.6.44) that causes frame structures to collapse.

Three types of structure have been identified, beams, trusses and frames. Each type carries the overall bending moment and shear forces of Fig.7.5. Beams by internal forces of bending moments and shear forces, trusses by internal forces of axial tension and compression and frames by internal forces of bending moments, shear forces and axial forces. This means that if any part of a load path has to carry an overall bending moment and shear forces then any of these types of structure can be used. For example the vertical legs of the sign board shown in Fig.1.66 could be beam-like, truss-like or frame-like.

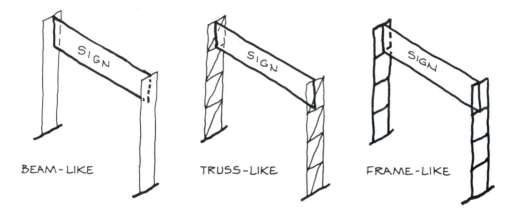

Fig.7.61

Or again the portal frame (see Fig.2.30), whilst itself a frame could also be beam-like, truss-like or frame-like.

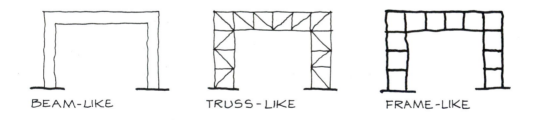

Fig.7.62

The types can be mixed to make a portal frame with beam-like legs and a truss-like beam, or any other mixture.

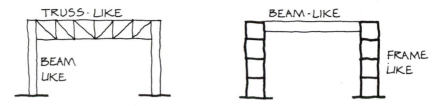

Fig.7.63

All these portal frames are the same! That is they all have to carry the applied load and do so by overall bending moments and shear forces. Where part of the structure is beam-like they are carried by internal bending moments and shear forces, where it is truss-like they are carried by internal axial forces and where it is frame-like they are carried by frame action. Even one structural element could be a mixture of structure types.

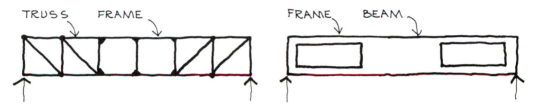

Fig.7.64

By using these mixtures a great variety of structural systems is available to the structural designer.

7.4   Cables and arches

There is another type of structural behaviour which it not beam-like, truss-like or frame-like but **funicular**. Funicular comes from the Latin for rope — funis. The behaviour has already been described for the washing line/cable structure (see Fig.7.8). For a cable (or rope) the shape of the structure changes with a change in the load pattern.

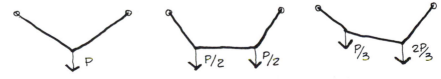

Fig.7.65

This is because the cable is flexible and can only have internal forces of axial tension. It would be rather surprising if the cable took up different shapes from those shown in Fig.7.65.

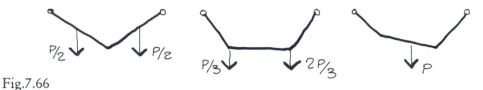

Fig.7.66

The shapes shown in Fig.7.66 would require that the structure was stiff rather than flexible, then the structure would be a frame — but a cable is not a frame but a funicular structure. Like any spanning structure it has to carry the overall bending moment and shear forces. For a cable this has already been described on pages 208 and 209. If a cable is loaded by a uniformly distributed load the cable will take up a parabolic shape. This is the **funicular shape** for this load pattern.

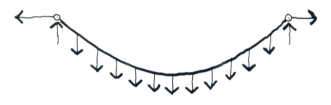

Fig.7.67

If the load is non-uniform then other curved shapes would be the funicular shapes.

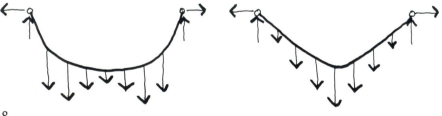

Fig.7.68

Because all these cables are in direct tension if they were turned upside down they would be in direct compression!

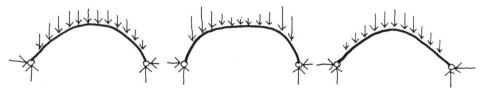

Fig.7.69

Of course this would not be possible for a cable but if the structure could carry compression then the funicular shape obtained from the hanging cable gives the correct shape for an arch that is in direct compression everywhere. Although the arch was the main spanning structure for construction from the Roman period to the nineteenth century the idea of inverting cables to find arch shapes was only stated in 1675 by the English genius and eccentric Robert Hooke. There is little evidence that this concept was used directly for actual design although some historical domes and arches were built in funicular shapes. The first application of this principle was by G. Poleni in 1748 as part of his investigation into the structural behaviour of the dome of St. Peter's in Rome. He used a correctly loaded chain to determine the funicular shape of the dome.

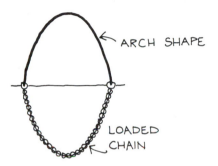

Fig.7.70

If an arch is built to the shape of the funicular line for a particular loading the whole of the arch will be in direct compression. If, however, the loading changes, or the arch is built to the wrong shape and the funicular line moves outside the arch then the arch will have to maintain its shape by frame action or collapse!

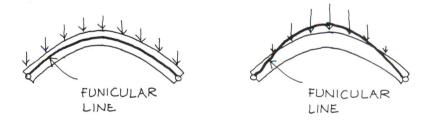

Fig.7.71

Because funicular arches are in direct compression they are suited to materials that are good in compression but have little tensile strength, that is brick, stone or mass concrete. To ensure that tensile stresses, or cracks do not occur with arches made of these materials it is important to keep the funicular line within the middle third of the cross-section (see Fig.3.78).

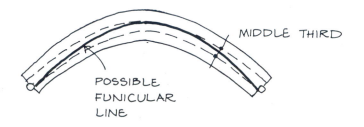

MIDDLE THIRD

POSSIBLE
FUNICULAR
LINE

Fig.7.72

As the funicular line changes shape with a change in loading, for compression only arches the load variation can only be small. For heavyweight structures the permanent load is usually large compared to the applied load. If this is not the case the arch structure must be capable of resisting the bending moments and shear forces that result from the frame action required to maintain the arch shape. It must be remembered that funicular structures need supports that can provide a horizontal reaction. In fact funicular structures must be seen as a combination of the funicular part and the horizontal restraint. Casual viewing of a curved structure does not always reveal whether the structure is funicular or just a curved beam.

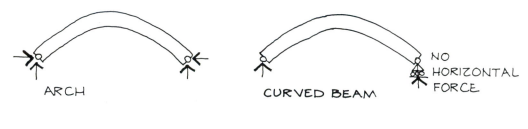

ARCH

CURVED BEAM

NO
HORIZONTAL
FORCE

Fig.7.73

7.5   Three dimensional structures

Beam-like, truss-like, frame and funicular structures can be two dimensional or three dimensional. For three dimensional structures the basic principles of the different types of behaviour still apply. The structure now has overall bending moments and shear forces in two directions. Schematically this can be illustrated for a structure, rectangular in plan and supported at the corners.

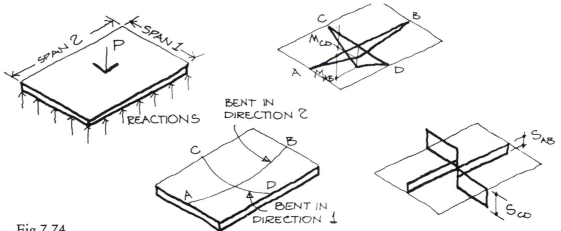

Fig.7.74

This has already been described for slabs (see pages 59—60). The basic pattern of behaviour will be the same. The different types of structure can be used to span a rectangle and be supported at the corners.

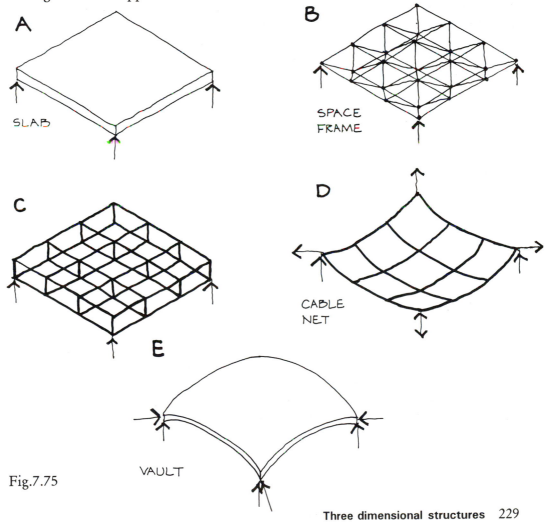

Fig.7.75

The three dimensional truss is often called a **space frame**, the cable system a **cable net** and the curved surface a **shell** or **vault**. Structures D and E are funicular surfaces which will be a different shape for each different loading pattern if bending moments and shear forces are to be avoided.

The action of each type of structure follows from the two dimensional types. The slab resists the loads by internal forces of bending moments and shear forces like a beam. The space frame resists load by axial forces in the individual members, the top and bottom members resisting the bending push and pull forces and the diagonal members resisting the shear and the bending. The three dimensional frame has axial forces with bending moments and shear forces at the stiff joints. The cable net only has axial tension forces and the shape varies with loading pattern. The shell is the cable net 'turned upside down'. Provided the shell is a funicular shape the loads will be resisted by compression forces only. Like the two dimensional funicular structures the supports of the cable net and the shell must be able to resist horizontal as well as vertical forces.

The variety of structures that can be derived from these basic types is almost limitless. Not only is there a choice for the overall structural system but every part of the structure can be one of the different types. This is just an extension of the ideas shown in Figs.7.61 to 7.64. However these structures must not be conceived visually but the conception must be based on an understanding of the structural behaviour. This is illustrated by Fig.7.73, as it is no good expecting a curved structure to be a funicular structure unless the supports can resist horizontal forces, again a truss without diagonals has to behave as a frame therefore must have stiff joints (Fig.7.54).

7.6 Prevention of axial instability

Even if the conception of a structural system is based on an understanding of structural behaviour the structure may be slender and prone to buckling initiated collapse. Part of conceptual design is to provide stiffness against these slenderness induced failures. The designer must ensure that parts of the structural system that are in compression have **stiffening structures** to keep the slenderness within sensible limits. The example of a beam with a U-shaped cross-section illustrates this point.

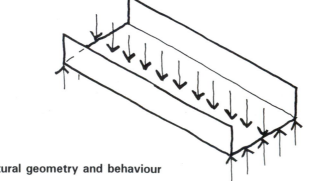

Fig.7.76

The structure has to resist the overall bending moment due to the load. As it is a beam-like structure this bending moment will cause longitudinal tension and compression stresses and the compression stress will be in the top part of the structure.

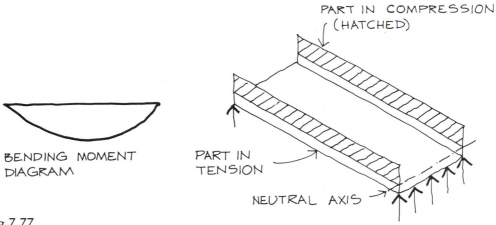

BENDING MOMENT DIAGRAM

PART IN COMPRESSION (HATCHED)

PART IN TENSION

NEUTRAL AXIS

Fig.7.77

If the top part is slender it could buckle sideways initiating collapse. To prevent this the top of the structure must have some lateral stiffness. This stiffness could be continuous or discrete. Continuous stiffness can be provided by giving the top lateral stiffness or by making the joints between the vertical and horizontal parts of the 'U' stiff.

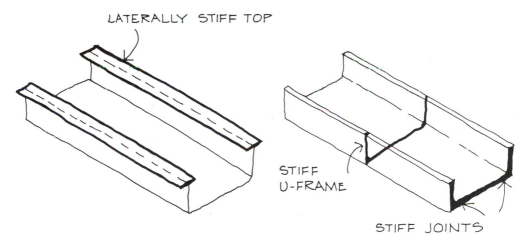

LATERALLY STIFF TOP

STIFF U-FRAME

STIFF JOINTS

Fig.7.78

For the stiff top structure to buckle sideways the top must deflect sideways and this is resisted by the top acting as a horizontal beam. For the stiff jointed 'U' to buckle the U must open or close and this is resisted by bending moments at the stiff joints.

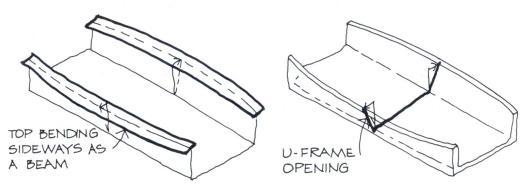

TOP BENDING SIDEWAYS AS A BEAM

U-FRAME OPENING

Fig.7.79

Alternatively the structure can have discrete stiffening structures which have the effect of providing lateral restraint at each point.

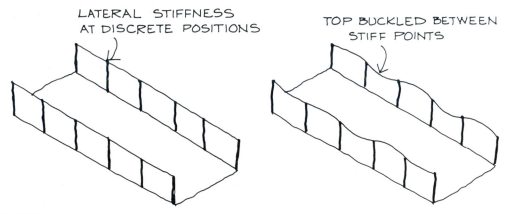

LATERAL STIFFNESS AT DISCRETE POSITIONS

TOP BUCKLED BETWEEN STIFF POINTS

Fig.7.80

Again these stiffening structures can be beam-like or truss-like.

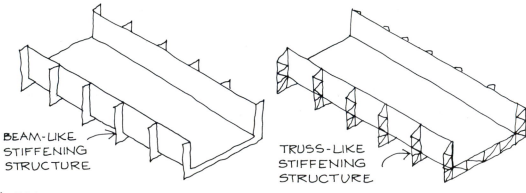

BEAM-LIKE STIFFENING STRUCTURE

TRUSS-LIKE STIFFENING STRUCTURE

Fig.7.81

The stiffening U-frames provide stiffness in the same way that the continuously stiff-jointed structure does, but at discrete points. This shows that if the structural concept was the U-shaped structure it would be incomplete **as a concept** without the provision of stiffness against buckling. How any structure is stiffened against buckling initiated collapse is a matter of choice for the designer but it must be part of the concept rather than something that is added at a later stage to 'make the structure work'. If the structural designer is unable to conceive where this stiffening is required then the original concept is likely to be flawed. Radical re-design may be required at the detail design stage often with unfortunate results for the initial concept.

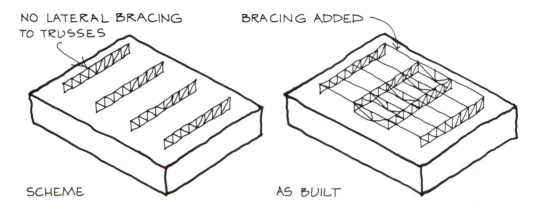

NO LATERAL BRACING TO TRUSSES

BRACING ADDED

SCHEME

AS BUILT

Fig.7.82 WD & HO Wills Factory : Bristol

Using all the concepts that have been described it is possible to understand how building structures behave when they are loaded. This understanding does not give any quantitative information about the structures. It does not answer questions about the sizes of the individual structural elements, this information can only be obtained by numerical calculations.

Because structures are built into buildings it is not usually possible to see how the structure acts without additional information such as drawings or written descriptions. If this information is available, usually from technical journals, then the concepts can be used to understand how any particular building structure works. Investigating the behaviour of existing structures gives the inexperienced designer important insights into how building structures are designed and built. Because there is such an enormous variety of possible structures this knowledge does not mean that all designs need be slavish copies — but perhaps a 'good' copy is better than an ill-conceived 'innovation'!

CHAPTER 8 *Behaviour of a simple building*

Buildings are constructed to alter the environment locally by enclosing space and building structures give strength and stiffness to the enclosing elements. The simplest building is a single enclosed space or a single space building. If the function and behaviour of the structure of a single space building is understood then understanding building structures of more complex buildings is relatively straightforward. Although many buildings have many spaces, factories, sports halls, theatres and churches are all examples of buildings which are often essentially single spaced.

The shapes of single spaces could be cubic, spherical or any defined or organic geometry (see page 203). However the majority of new buildings are rectilinear for a number of practical reasons so the **basic structure** is the structure for a cubic single space. The explanation for the behaviour of the structure for this single space uses the six basic concepts which are:

1   The function of a structure is to transfer loads.

2   The load path is the structure for each load.

3   The structure transfers loads by forces in the structure.

4   Forces in the structure can be considered to be a combination of direct and shear forces and bending moments.

5   The structure must have overall stability.

6   Collapse initiated by slender structures must be avoided.

An understanding of how these six essential concepts apply to the structure of a single space can be used to understand the structures of more complex buildings such as houses, hotels, offices or arts centres. Not only does the application of these basic concepts give an understanding of structural behaviour but it also provides a basis for the more difficult process of structural design. The design process is more difficult than understanding the behaviour of existing structures as the concepts have to be used simultaneously to produce the design.

8.1 Basic structure and loading

As these concepts apply to the whole of the structure they must be applied to every part of the structure; from each weld or bolt to the whole structure. So that the concepts can be applied to a specific example the basic shape of the building is assumed to be rectangular with a simple pitched roof.

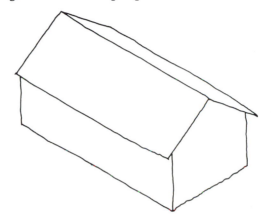

Fig.8.1

The building has a roof covered with corrugated metal sheeting with walls of brickwork. The main structure is steelwork, the floor is of pre-cast concrete, and the foundations are of in situ concrete. This type of building is used widely throughout the world for factories and warehouses.

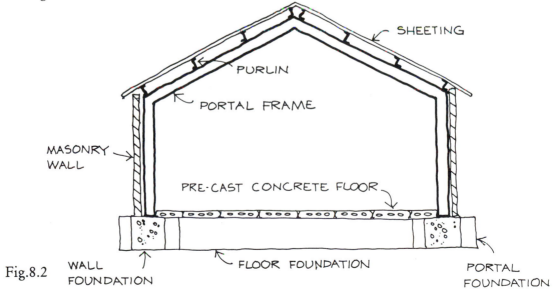

Fig.8.2

To avoid the endless use of the word concept in the rest of this section concepts are put into square brackets. **So [2] in the text will mean concept 2** — the load path is the structure — applies.

To start at the beginning [1], what are the loads? The sources of loads will be gravity, the wind and the use of the space. Gravity and use will apply vertical loads (see Figs.1.27 to 1.32).

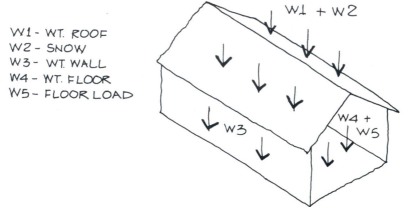

W1 - WT. ROOF
W2 - SNOW
W3 - WT. WALL
W4 - WT. FLOOR
W5 - FLOOR LOAD

Fig.8.3

Wind will apply loads at right-angles to the roof and walls.

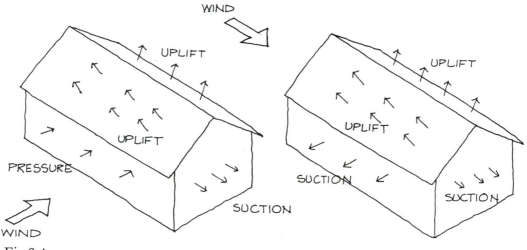

Fig.8.4

Whether the wind causes an uplift force on the roof depends on the slope angle of the roof.

Although all these loads are applied to the building at various times not all the loads will be applied simultaneously, so the structure must be safe under all **load combinations** (see pages 17 to 21). Even for such a simple building there can be numerous different combinations. Here three combinations will be considered.

Loadcase 1   Maximum vertical load on the roof and floor.

Loadcase 2   Minimum vertical load on the roof and floor plus wind load on the side elevation.

Loadcase 3   Minimum vertical load on the roof and floor plus wind load on the end elevation.

Because of [2] the structure for each loadcase may be different so [2] has to be applied to each loadcase. As the space is three dimensional the structure has to be three dimensional, however each element is either one or two dimensional (see pages 65 to 69) and will act as one dimensional or two dimensional structures. For this structure the elements can be identified as one or two dimensional and so can their actions.

ELEMENT	TYPE	ACTION
Roof sheet	2D	1D
Wall	2D	2D
Steel frame	1D	1D
Pre-cast floor	2D	1D
Foundations	1D	1D (?)

It may seem odd that two dimensional elements like the roof sheeting or the floor units act as one dimensional structures but this is because of the way they are connected to the rest of the structure.

Before each load path [2] is identified the structural behaviour, [3] and [4], of each element can be clarified. Firstly the roof sheeting, this is two dimensional but spans unidirectionally.

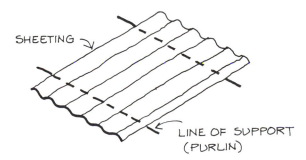

Fig.8.5

The wall is connected vertically for vertical loads and is connected laterally for horizontal loads.

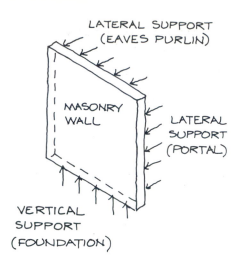

Fig.8.6

The steel frame consists of several different parts. The purlins, the portal frames, the roof wind bracing, the wall wind bracing and the gable posts.

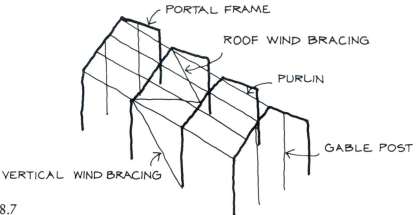

Fig.8.7

The pre-cast concrete floor units are two dimensional elements but span unidirectionaly.

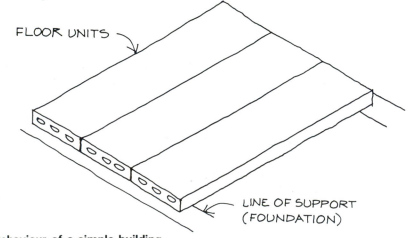

Fig.8.8

The foundations are one dimensional elements but their structural action, rather surprisingly, is one or two dimensional!

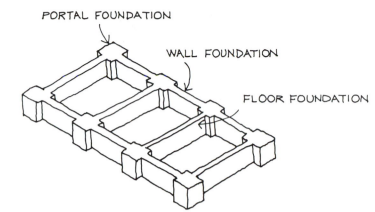

PORTAL FOUNDATION

WALL FOUNDATION

FLOOR FOUNDATION

Fig.8.9

The identification of the structural elements often provides important clues to the behaviour of the structure, but for built structures this identification usually requires more information than can be provided by visual inspection. Having identified all the structural elements it is possible to see how they become parts of load paths [2], how the structure transfers loads [3] and what type of internal forces there are in each element [4].

For Loadcase 1, maximum vertical load, every element will be involved because all the elements have self-weight due to gravity. Is usual to 'chase' loads down a building so the roof load path has to be identified.

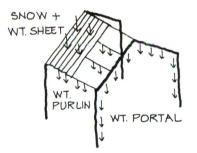

SNOW +
WT. SHEET

WT.
PURLIN

WT. PORTAL

Fig.8.10

The vertical load on the roof, snow load and the self-weight of the sheeting, is supported by the roof sheeting which spans from purlin to purlin.

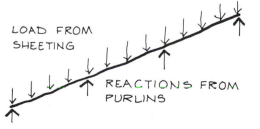

LOAD FROM
SHEETING

REACTIONS FROM
PURLINS

Fig.8.11

The reactions to the sheeting becomes loads on the purlins, the self-weight of the purlins must be added to the sheeting reactions. The purlins span between the portal frames.

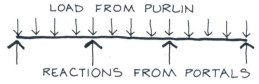

Fig.8.12

Now the reactions to the purlins become loads on the portal frames, again the self-weight of the frames must be added to these loads. These loads are carried by the frame action of the portal frames to the foundations.

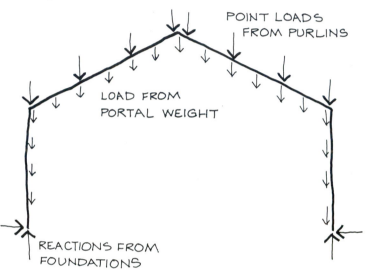

Fig.8.13

The foundations are loaded by the reactions to the portal frames plus the reactions to the self-weight of the walls and the reactions to the floor units.

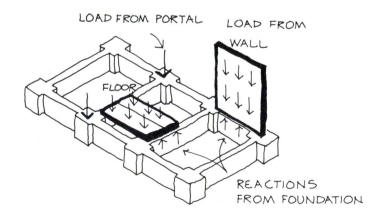

Fig.8.14

240 **Behaviour of a simple building**

The loadcases for the wind load include the minimum vertical loads, that is the self-weight of the building construction. As the load paths for these loads are the load paths for loadcase 1 only the load paths due to the wind loads are described. When the wind blows on the side elevation the walls are loaded horizontally and the roof sheeting is loaded at right-angles to the roof slope — these loads are shown in Fig.8.4. Again the roof sheeting spans between the purlins but the walls span both vertically, from the ground to the eaves, and horizontally between the portal frames or gable posts.

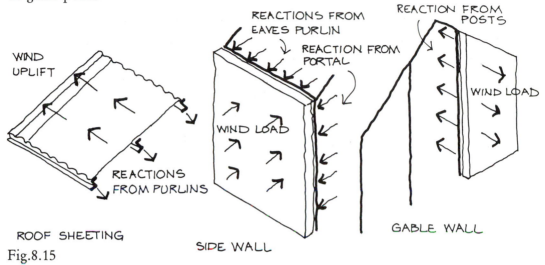

Fig.8.15

The loads on the intermediate portals are due to the reactions to the purlins and the side walls. The self-weight of the sheeting, purlins and the portal frames must be added to the wind loads.

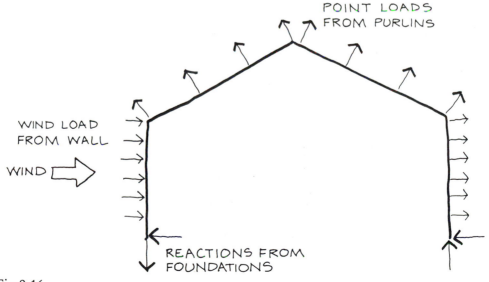

Fig.8.16

For the end portals the reactions from the wind load on the gable walls must be added to the loads from the wind on the side walls shown in Fig.8.16.

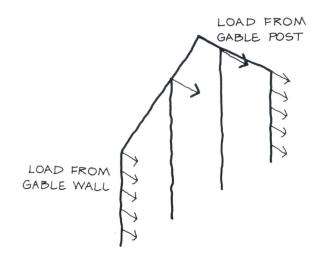

LOAD FROM
GABLE POST

LOAD FROM
GABLE WALL

Fig.8.17

Because the outward loads on the end walls are approximately equal there is no overall effect along the building. The loads across the building do have the overall effect of a horizontal load.

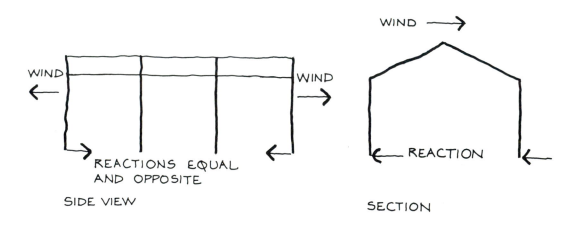

WIND

WIND

WIND

REACTIONS EQUAL
AND OPPOSITE

SIDE VIEW

REACTION

SECTION

Fig.8.18

When the wind blows on the end wall there is uplift on the roof and equal and opposite outward wind loads on the side walls. The loads on the intermediate portals is similar, but not the same as that shown in Fig.8.16.

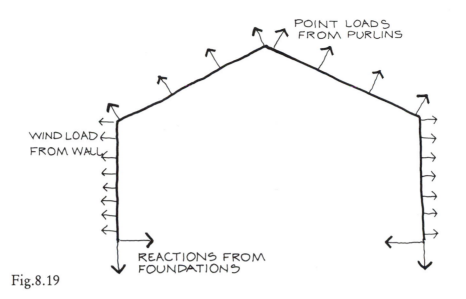

Fig.8.19

The loads on the end portals are similar to those on the intermediate portals plus loads from the gable wall. The gable wall loads are similar to those shown in Fig.8.17. However the overall load situation is the opposite to that shown in Fig.8.18, there is now an overall force along the building but no overall force across the building.

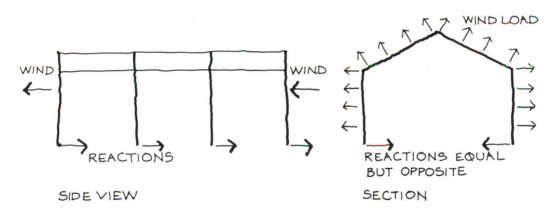

SIDE VIEW   SECTION

Fig.8.20

For the wind loads the foundation loads are the reactions required by the portal frames, the gable posts and the wall panels. Again it must be remembered that the self-weight loads must be added to these wind loads.

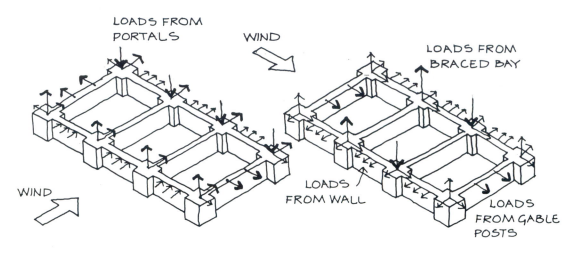

LOADS FROM PORTALS

WIND

LOADS FROM BRACED BAY

WIND

LOADS FROM WALL

LOADS FROM GABLE POSTS

Fig.8.21

8.2   Structural action and stability

It is now possible to see how each part of the structure carries the loads [4] and how and stability [5] and [6] effects are dealt with. There are two approaches to this, either the whole of the load path for each loadcase can be investigated or each part of the structure can be investigated for all the loadcases. Because it is usual to design structures element by element the second approach will be used here. As structures are usually designed **roof down** the order of elements would be:

1   Roof sheeting
2   Walls
3   Purlins
4   Portal frames
5   Windbracing
6   Pre-cast concrete floor
7   Foundations

For the roof sheeting only two of the three loadcases will apply because there will be a maximum downward loadcase and a maximum upward loadcase.

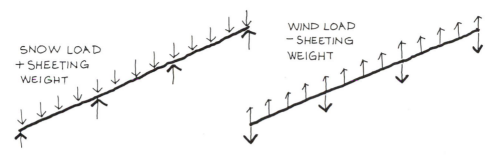

Fig.8.22

The sheeting spans as a three span beam between the four rows of purlins, and this spanning action will cause shear forces and bending moments in the sheeting. Shear force and bending moment diagrams can be drawn for these internal forces [3]. For brevity only the downward loadcase is shown.

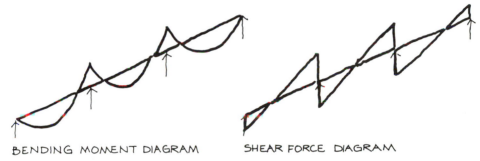

BENDING MOMENT DIAGRAM   SHEAR FORCE DIAGRAM

Fig.8.23

As the sheeting is beam-like there will be bending stresses and shear stresses in the sheeting. The sheeting is corrugated so that it can carry these stresses in an efficient way, the bending stresses will be at a maximum at the top and bottom of the corrugations and the shear stresses will be a maximum at the mid-depth of the section [4].

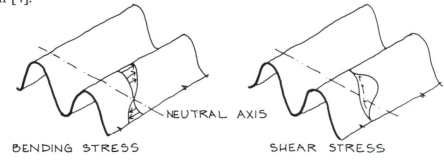

BENDING STRESS   SHEAR STRESS

Fig.8.24

The overall stability [5] of the sheeting is provided by the fixings to the purlins. These must be strong enough to prevent whole sheets being sucked off by the upward wind loads. Due to the shape of the sheets lateral buckling (see page 191), will not occur but local buckling [6] could initiate collapse. This could occur at the point of maximum compressive stress or at the point of maximum shear stress.

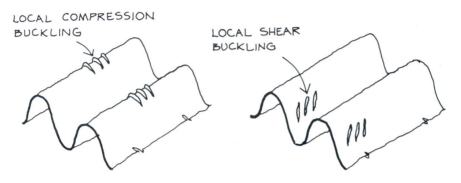

Fig.8.25

Possible problems due to local buckling are prevented by providing a suitable thickness for the roof sheeting.

The walls are not loadbearing in the sense that they are part of the main structure however they do have to transfer [1] wind loads to the portal frames. They also have to carry their own weight.

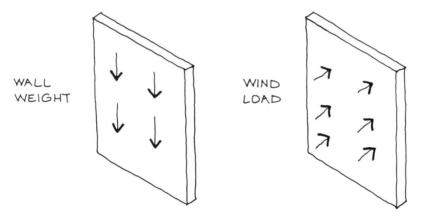

Fig.8.26

The self weight load is applied vertically and causes direct forces [3] and compressive stresses [4] in the wall. The wind load is applied horizontally and causes shear forces and bending moments [3] in the wall. As the wall is connected horizontally on all sides (Fig.8.6), the wall spans in two directions. This means that these internal forces [3] will also be in two directions (see page 57).

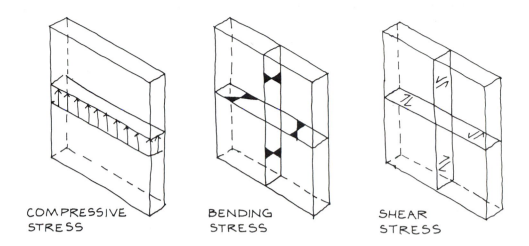

COMPRESSIVE
STRESS

BENDING
STRESS

SHEAR
STRESS

Fig.8.27

Because brickwork has very limited tensile strength (see page 143) the size of the bending moments in the wall are limited by the tensile bending stress. The bending stress depends on the span of the wall and the thickness of the wall. As walls can only be built in specific thicknesses it is usual to choose a thickness and then limit the span. If the spacing between the main portal frames means the span of the wall is too big then additional supports can be used to reduce the wall span.

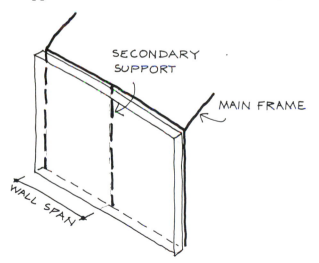

SECONDARY
SUPPORT

MAIN FRAME

WALL SPAN

Fig.8.28

The windload can cause bending in the wall panels in either direction so the walls must be fixed positively to the support framework, otherwise a panel could just be blown (actually sucked) over [5]. The wall could also collapse by buckling [6] under its own weight if it is too thin. This form of buckling would be similar to the buckling of the wall of a box-column (Fig.6.68).

The function of the purlins is to transfer the sheeting loads to the portal frames [1]. How much load depends on the spacing of the purlins along the sheet.

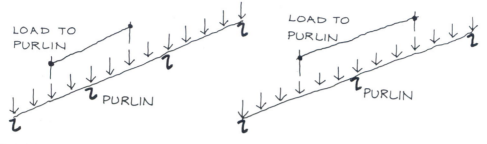

Fig.8.29

The purlins are beams spanning between the portal frames so they have shear forces and bending moments like any other beam [3] and [4].

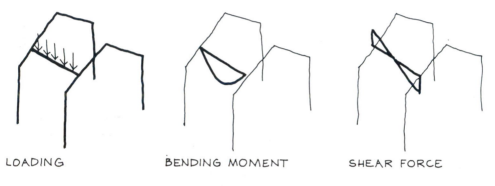

LOADING   BENDING MOMENT   SHEAR FORCE

Fig.8.30

There is a range of cross-sectional shapes that can be used for purlins.

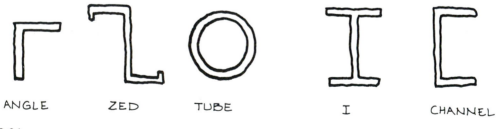

ANGLE   ZED   TUBE   I   CHANNEL

Fig.8.31

If the chosen purlin is slender then the possibility of the compression flange buckling sideways [6] must be examined. Under downwards load the roof sheeting acts as a stiffening structure (page 233) to prevent lateral buckling of the compression flange. Under upward wind loading the bottom flange is in compression and could buckle between the supports.

248   **Behaviour of a simple building**

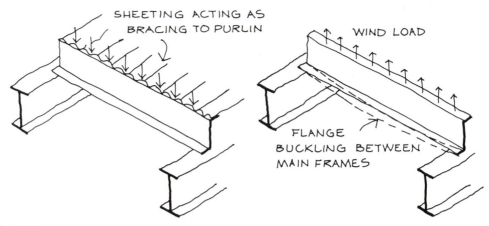

Fig.8.32

If the span is long then a discrete stiffening structure can be used to provide lateral restraint to the bottom flange. This is often done by bracing the bottom flange of each purlin to the top flanges of the adjacent purlins.

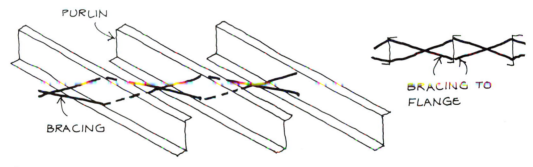

Fig.8.33

This bracing reduces the slenderness of the bottom flange of the purlin which now has to buckle between support points.

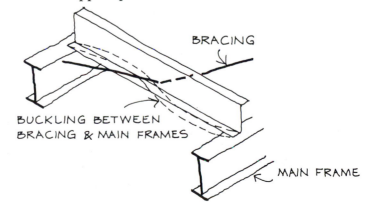

Fig.8.34

The portal frames carry the loads from the purlins (Fig.8.30) and the lateral loads from the walls [1]. This is done by frame action of the portal, this frame action only acts across the building. This means that the portal can only carry loads that are applied across the building, not loads that are applied along it.

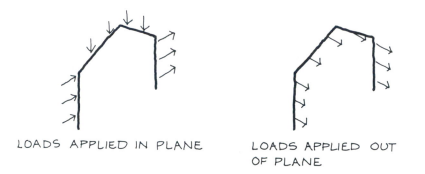

LOADS APPLIED IN PLANE   LOADS APPLIED OUT
                                OF PLANE

Fig.8.35

The three loadcases cause different load patterns on the portal frame [1].

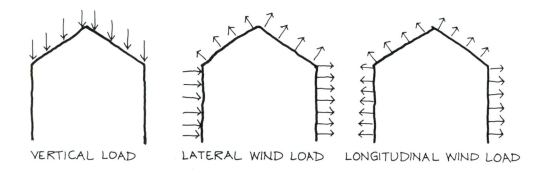

VERTICAL LOAD   LATERAL WIND LOAD   LONGITUDINAL WIND LOAD

Fig.8.36

These load patterns will cause axial forces, shear forces and bending moments in the beam-like members that make up the portal [4]. The size of these internal forces will vary along the members of the frame and can be represented by axial force, shear force and bending moment diagrams similar to those shown in Fig.2.42. There will also be vertical and horizontal reactions at the base of the portal frame.

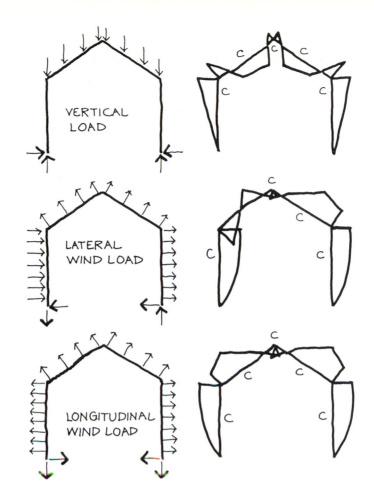

VERTICAL
LOAD

LATERAL
WIND LOAD

LONGITUDINAL
WIND LOAD

Fig.8.37

This figure only shows the bending moment diagrams, but there will be a direct force and shear force diagram associated with each of these bending moment diagrams. The positions of the tensile and compressive stresses are also shown on the diagrams. It should be noted that these vary quite dramatically from loading to loading as do the directions of the reactions at the support of the frame. Under wind loading one vertical reaction is up and the other is down! This indicates that the whole frame could overturn under wind loading [5].

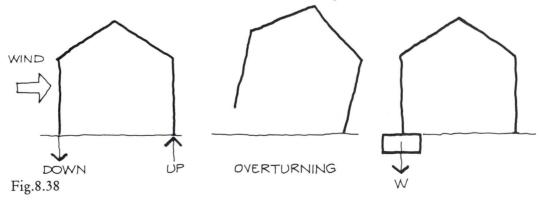

WIND

DOWN   UP   OVERTURNING   W

Fig.8.38

If the frame and the cladding is 'light' the frame may need to be held down by the weight of the foundations. Where there are compressive stresses in the frame the possibility of buckling initiated collapse [6] must be investigated. Because different loadcases cause compressive stresses in different parts of the structure each case must be considered separately. For compressive stresses in the top of the roof part of the frame the purlins act as discrete stiffening structures and, depending on the connection, the walls may prevent the outside of the legs buckling.

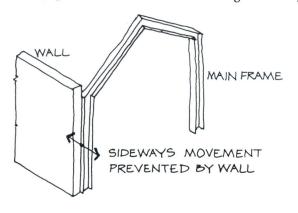

Fig.8.39

Under vertical load the inside of the legs, the eaves and the ridge have compressive stresses and are not restrained in an obvious way.

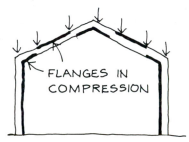

Fig.8.40

Under sideways wind load different parts of the frame have compressive stresses and again some of these are unrestrained.

Fig.8.41

Any of these areas of compression could buckle laterally if they are too slender.

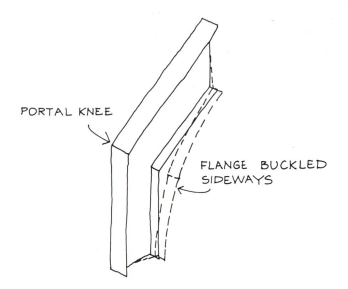

PORTAL KNEE

FLANGE BUCKLED
SIDEWAYS

Fig.8.42

The steel portals resist the force due to the wind acting on the side of the building but they cannot resist horizontal loads caused by wind loads on the gable walls (Fig.8.35). The forces along the building are resisted by truss-like structures called **wind bracing**. These truss-like structures are a combination of the members of the portal frame and bracing members specifically introduced to resist the longitudinal wind forces — hence wind bracing.

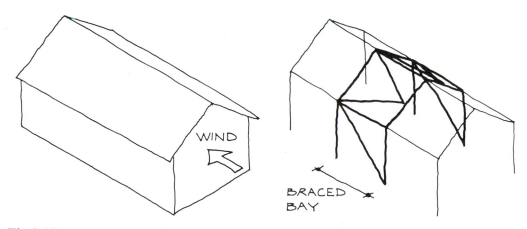

WIND

BRACED
BAY

Fig.8.43

The wind force on the end walls has to be strutted or tied to the braced bay.

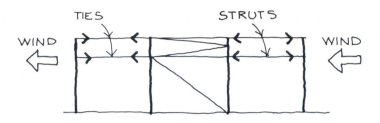

Fig.8.44

These struts and ties may be the purlins [2], in which case they have to be designed to act as part of this load path, or they may be extra members added to the roof structure solely for this purpose. The bracing in the roof is a truss-like structure often called a wind girder. The vertical bracing is also a truss-like structure which acts as a cantilever from the ground.

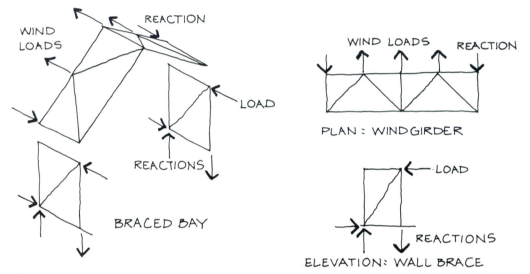

Fig.8.45

The portal frames become part of the truss-like structures [2], the roof parts of the frames become the top and bottom members of the wind girder and legs of the portal frames become the vertical members of the cantilever trusses.

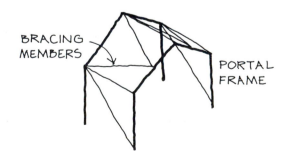

Fig.8.46

The cantilever side bracing requires upward and downward reactions. These are the push/pull forces of the cantilever bending moment.

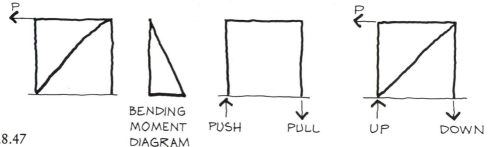

BENDING
MOMENT   PUSH   PULL   UP   DOWN
DIAGRAM

Fig.8.47

As with the portal frame the whole frame could overturn [5]. If the self-weight is low then the downwards reaction is provided by the weight of the foundations.

UP   DOWN   OVERTURNING   W

Fig.8.48

These truss-like bracing structures resist the shear forces and bending moments [4] caused by their spanning action by tensile and compressive forces in the individual elements of the trusses. As the wind direction is usually reversible all the members of the bracing system will be in compression or tension for one of the wind directions. This means all parts of the bracing system have to be checked for the possibility of buckling initiated collapse [6] (pages 185—187).

Like the purlins, the floor units span as simple beams between the lines of foundations [1] and [2]. The units are beam-like so the shear forces and bending moments are carried by shear stresses and bending stresses in the units [3] and [4].

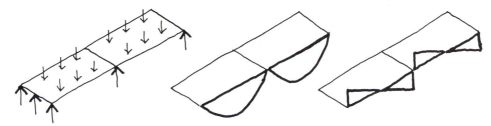

LOADING   BENDING MOMENT DIAGRAM SHEAR FORCE DIAGRAM

Fig.8.49

As concrete is a heavyweight material and floors usually only have downwards loads there is no problem of overall stability [5], and as no part of the structure is slender there will be no slenderness initiated collapse [6].

The main role of the foundations is to alter the stress level (pages 74—75). As the ground below the structure is usually weaker than the structural materials the stress level has to be reduced, rather like the use of snow shoes (Fig.3.23).

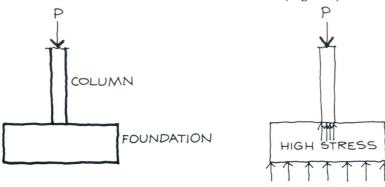

Fig.8.50

In the case of this building the foundations also have to provide weight against uplift and resistance to horizontal forces.

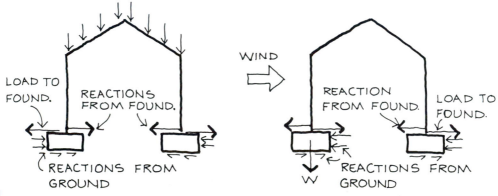

Fig.8.51

The horizontal forces due side wind are resisted by friction on the underside of the foundation and earth pressure on the sides of the foundations.

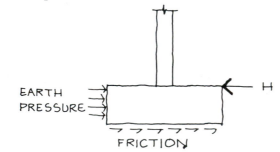

Fig.8.52

256   **Behaviour of a simple building**

Where the horizontal forces are acting in opposite directions the friction and earth pressure can resist them, but if the force is high then a specific tie member may be required to resist spreading of the portal supports.

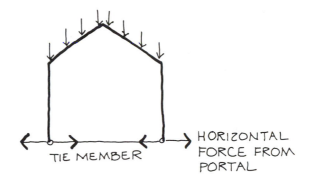

Fig.8.53

If the supports of a portal frame move the distribution of bending moments will alter radically. This is similar to the difference between an arch and a curved beam (Fig.7.73).

Depending on the proportions of the foundations they may act as one or two dimensional structures.

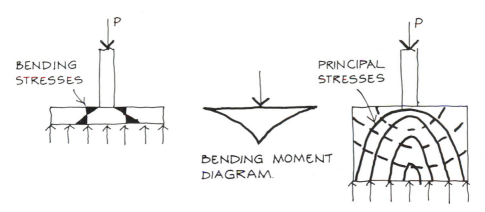

Fig.8.54

Usually the behaviour of the ground away from the structure is not considered. This is because the stress level in the ground diminishes rapidly with distance from the foundations.

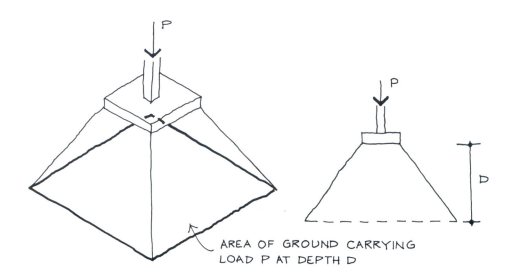

AREA OF GROUND CARRYING
LOAD P AT DEPTH D

Fig.8.55

Whilst the ground is part of the structure it is usual to consider that the structure ends at the underside of the foundations.

This example of a structure for a single space building illustrates how different load paths are needed for different loadings and how concepts of axial forces, shear forces and bending moments are used to understand the behaviour of each load path. The type of stress in each part of the structure depends on whether it is part of a beam-like or truss-like structure.

How any building structure behaves can be found by using the conceptual analysis used for this simple example. **It also shows how a structural designer has to choose the structure for every part of the structural system**. For instance the chosen purlins were steel and beam-like, but truss-like steel or timber purlins could have been chosen. It is these choices and their consequential effect on the structural behaviour of the whole structural system that is the essence of structural design.

CHAPTER 9 *Real structures*

The way any structure behaves under loading can be understood by using the six basic concepts (see page 234). The behaviour of the **basic structure** for a single space building was analysed in detail by repeatedly applying these concepts to each part of the building. This process can be used to analyse any structure provided sufficient technical information is available.

Because the process of structural design currently used for building structures is relatively recent the structures of older buildings are often different in concept from more recent ones. Any building structure will act in the way that suits the structure rather than the designer's concept if the concept is wrong. Recent designs answer questions raised by considering the six basic concepts but for structures built before about 1850 the process was different. In older structures the design was based on traditional practice (rule of thumb; experience) and by the use of geometric concepts rather than structural ones. The geometry was used to size structural elements by using relationships based on proportions rather than structural behaviour. This means that the behaviour of structures conceived in this way is often difficult to clarify, their exact behaviour can be a matter of debate amongst interested academics.

The six structures chosen for conceptual analysis are mainly from the period of engineering design because structural behaviour tends to be easier to clarify. The chosen structures are:

- **Durham Cathedral**, England, completed 1133
- **The Palm House**, Kew Gardens, England, completed 1848
- **Zarzuela Hippodrome**, Madrid, Spain, completed 1935
- **CNIT Exposition Palace**, Paris, France, completed 1960
- **Federal Reserve Bank**, Minneapolis, USA, completed 1973
- **Bank of China**, Hong Kong, completed 1990

These projects have been chosen because they all have very clear but different structural forms. Each structure is conceptually analysed in outline using the six basic concept process. These analyses demonstrate how these universal concepts apply to structures that are quite different geometrically and materially.

9.1   Durham Cathedral

The period of the early middle ages, that is from the 11th to 15th centuries, saw an enormous programme of church building in Western Europe. The buildings ranged from small parish churches to the famous, and not so famous, cathedrals. Their style is now know as Gothic and Gothic architecture has been, and still is a subject of considerable academic and popular interest. This interest covers the historical, symbolic and aesthetic aspects of these churches and cathedrals.

There is also an interest is how the cathedrals were built and what technical knowledge the builders had. But the study of these aspects is hampered by the lack of documentary evidence of the building process. Although written material survives from this period none of it relates to technology so either it was considered unimportant or never existed. As there was no concept of scale technical drawings the masons and carpenters must have worked from models and full-size templates.

The modern concepts of structural engineering had not been formulated so the builders could not have know about stress or bending moments but they must have known about gravity and force. What technical knowledge that did exist came from the Greeks but this had been lost in Western Europe during the so-called Dark Ages so the builders of the cathedrals were really pioneers.

The plan of Durham Cathedral follows the usual Latin cross plan of the Gothic style.

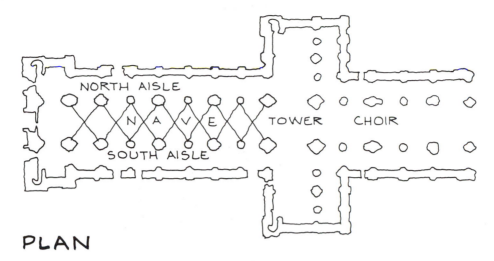

PLAN

Fig.9.1

The cross-section also follows the usual pattern for Gothic cathedrals.

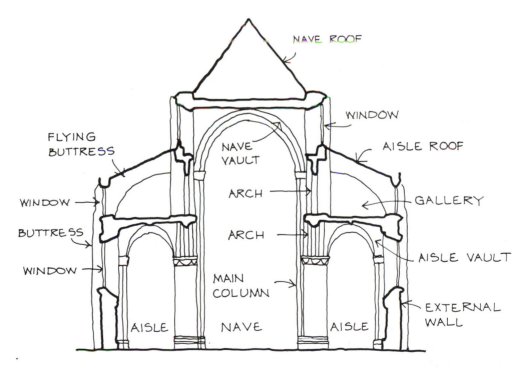

Fig.9.2

The main parts of the cross-section are the roof, the main vault (ceiling), the internal and external 'walls', the side aisle roofs and vault.

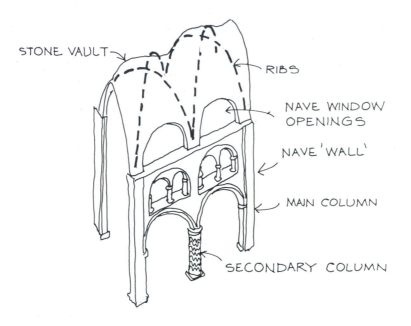

Fig.9.3

One of the main ambitions of the builders was to flood the cathedrals with natural light so the internal and external walls have numerous perforations which means the walls often became colonnades.

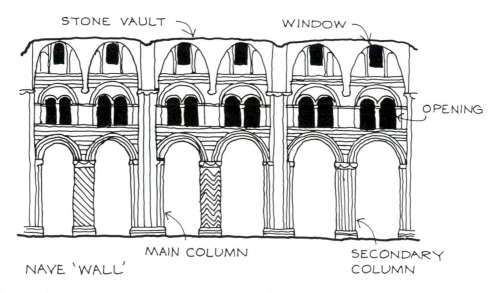

Fig.9.4

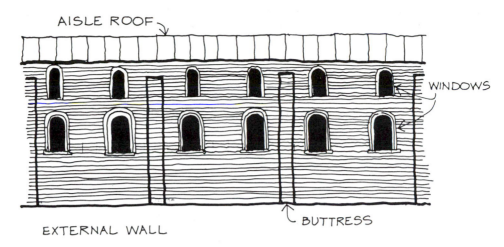
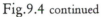

AISLE ROOF

WINDOWS

EXTERNAL WALL

BUTTRESS

Fig.9.4 continued

The structures of the roofs of the nave and the side aisles are of timber. These structures spanned between the internal and external walls.

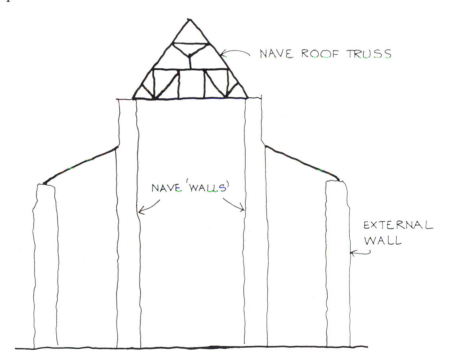

NAVE ROOF TRUSS

NAVE 'WALLS'

EXTERNAL WALL

Fig.9.5

Below these roofs are stone vaulted ceilings and it this vaulting that is one of the main interests in cathedral architecture. To allow light into the cathedral and to permit circulation at ground level each bay of the nave vaulting is only supported at the corners.

Durham Cathedral 263

Fig.9.6

Most of the cathedral structure is built of masonry and because masonry can only carry compressive forces most of the structure must be in compression. The exception is the timber roof structures. The cathedral is essentially a single space with the main loading being from self-weight, snow and wind. As masonry is a heavyweight material and the structure is massive, self-weight is the major load. Compared to this load, snow and wind loads are negligible.

The main roof structure and the stone ceiling vaulting are independent structures spanning across the nave. The timber roof structure is a rather complicated truss which spans unidirectionally across the nave whereas the stone ceiling vault spans in two directions (Fig.7.75 E). As both are spanning there will be associated bending moment and shear force diagrams.

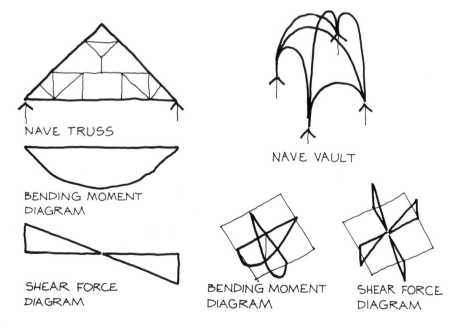

NAVE TRUSS

BENDING MOMENT
DIAGRAM

SHEAR FORCE
DIAGRAM

NAVE VAULT

BENDING MOMENT
DIAGRAM

SHEAR FORCE
DIAGRAM

Fig.9.7

The roof structure is truss like so the push/pull forces are taken by the sloping and bottom members and the shear resisted by the sloping member (Fig.7.18).

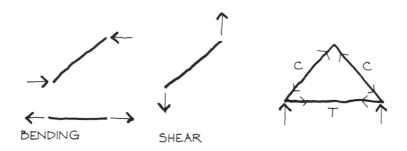

BENDING   SHEAR

Fig.9.8

The vault however is funicular (see page 225 et seq) and the push/pull forces are carried by compression in the vault and by tension in mid-air (Fig.7.21 - 5). The shear is carried by the vertical component of the sloping compression force.

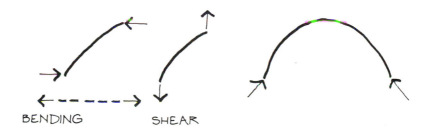

BENDING   SHEAR

Fig.9.9

Because the vault acts in two dimensions these forces will also be in two dimensions. The span of these vaults are not great, only 9.75m across the nave at Durham, smaller than many ancient Islamic mosques. However the height of the nave is quite considerable, 21.4m at Durham. It is this height that causes the major structural difficulty as the 'tension in mid-air' is supplied by a sloping thrust at the level of the vault supports.

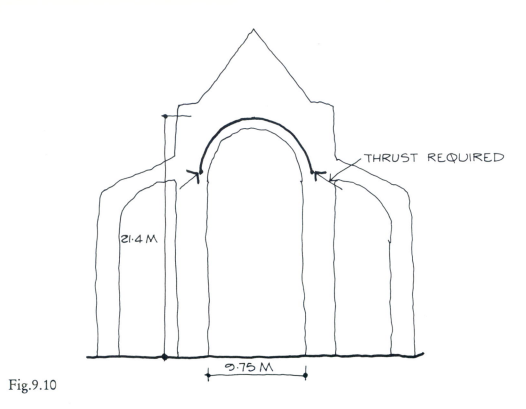

Fig.9.10

And this thrust becomes a load on the nave/external wall structure.

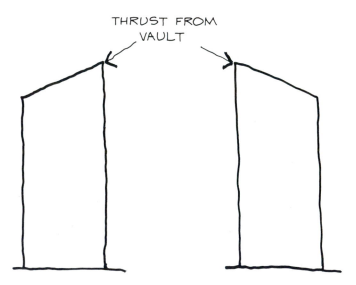

Fig.9.11

These walls are cantilevers from the ground and the sloping thrust can be regarded as a combination of a vertical and a horizontal forces applied to the top of the wall. This causes axial forces plus a bending moment and a shear force.

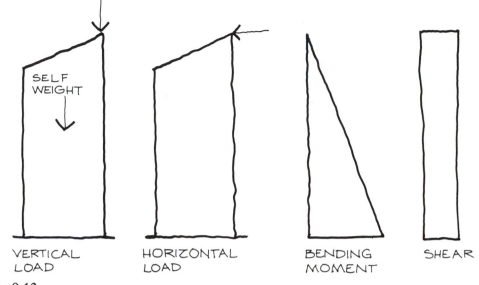

SELF WEIGHT

VERTICAL LOAD   HORIZONTAL LOAD   BENDING MOMENT   SHEAR

Fig.9.12

This action is just another example of an axial load acting at an eccentricity to cause a moment (Figs.3.75 — 3.78). Because the wall is of masonry the thrusts must be kept within the wall section.

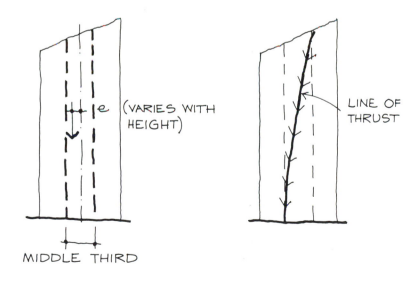

e (VARIES WITH HEIGHT)

LINE OF THRUST

MIDDLE THIRD

Fig.9.13

The line of thrust cannot be as shown in Fig.9.13 as the nave/external wall is not solid across the building, so the thrust is carried by a **flying buttress** which joins the tops of the nave and external walls.

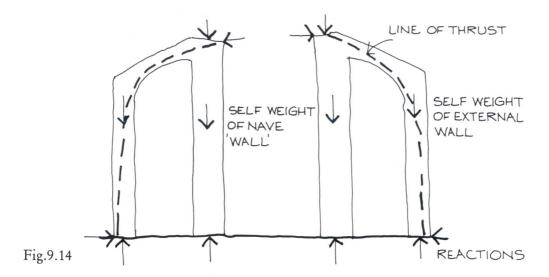

Fig.9.14

In this way the wall can be perforated. This system of flying buttresses became more and more complex as the Gothic period progressed and culminated with the cathedral at Beauvais. Here the height of the nave was 48m and the vault thrust was taken by three tiers of buttresses.

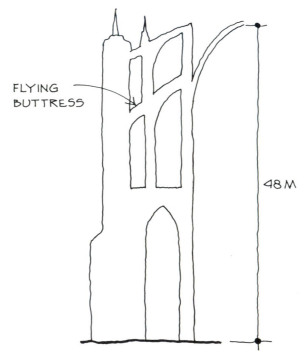

Fig.9.15

Beauvais is often considered the final achievement of the Gothic builders though this view must be tempered by the fact that various parts of the cathedral collapsed and it was never completed.

Whilst the forces across the structure are taken by the nave and external walls and the flying buttress, because the vault is two dimensional there are also forces along the nave.

'UNBALANCED' THRUST

Fig.9.16

As the main force is due to self-weight the forces along the nave balance one another that is until the end! At the ends are more solid constructions, the main tower and the West tower and the weight of these resist the end thrusts.

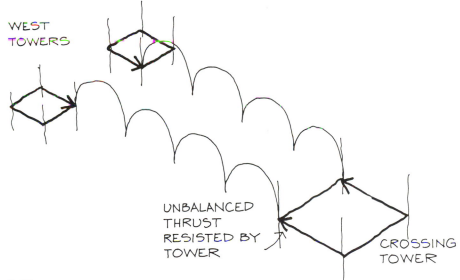

WEST TOWERS

UNBALANCED THRUST RESISTED BY TOWER

CROSSING TOWER

Fig.9.17

The marvel of these cathedrals' structures is how the builders, without concepts of stress and moments were able to balance the various thrusts and keep them within the funicular lines. They occasionally failed to manage this with consequent collapses!

9.2   The Palm House

Glasshouses were a building type that came into existence in the nineteenth century being an extension of the eighteenth century orangeries and conservatories. As with all new building types their emergence depended on a number of factors, technical, economic and social. The first substantial structure built of iron was the Ironbridge at Coalbrookdale in 1779 (see page 141), by the 1840s iron, both cast and wrought, were routinely used for structures. During this period there were also advances in the production of glass. It was the availability of iron and glass at reasonable prices that were the technical and economic factors that made glasshouses possible. During the nineteenth century there was also a rise in interest in science and this gave the impetus to the expansion of numerous scientific establishments. It was under these circumstances that plans for a palm house at the Botanic Gardens at Kew were drawn up. These initial plans were abandoned and Decimus Burton, the designer of the Winter Gardens in Regent's Park, was asked to drawn up plans for a new design.

Decimus Burton had already worked with the Irish iron founder Richard Turner, an astute and ambitious businessman, who ensured that the Commissioner of Works for the new palm house asked him for a proposal for the new building. His proposal was quite different to Burton's design and was to the close final design. For many years the design was attributed to Decimus Burton but it is now recognised that the main influence on the design was that of Richard Turner.

The design was influenced by the work of G.S.MacKenzie and John Louden who had both promoted for horticultural reasons the advantages of curved glasshouses and the Palm House is curved in all directions !

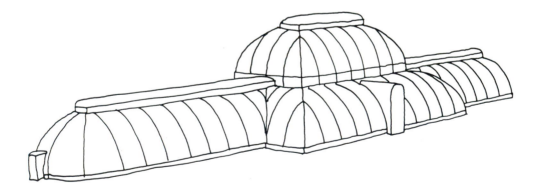

Fig.9.18

Turner's design also used the recently patented wrought iron **deck beam**. The production of these beams were, in turn, made possible by the invention of the steam hammer by Naismith in 1839. The deck beam was the forerunner of the ubiquitous I beam (see pages 86-88).

Fig.9.19

The deck beam was so-called as it was used to support decks in the new iron ships. The Palm House was the first building to use this new structural element.

Like the builders of Durham cathedral, the builders of the Palm House were principally concerned with natural light. But Turner and Burton had a new structural material, wrought iron, which was much stronger than stone and could also resist substantial tensile stresses. In the 1840s structural design was in its infancy and no evidence for the existence of technical calculations for the Palm House has ever been found. It seems likely that Turner acted very like his medieval counterparts in designing a structure using intuition and a knowledge of his material.

Whether a designer understands the structural behaviour of his structure or not does not affect the behaviour of the actual structure. Because of this the **conceptual approach** can always be used to understand the actual behaviour of the structure rather than the structural behaviour considered by the designer. The first step is to simplify the complex three dimensional shapes into three parts; the end 'caps', the barrel vaults and the central transept.

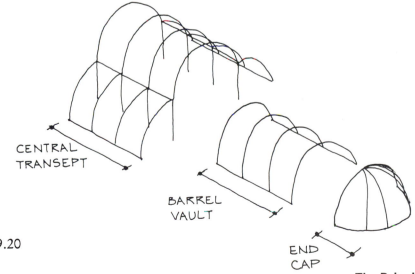

CENTRAL
TRANSEPT

BARREL
VAULT

END
CAP

Fig.9.20

Although these parts are connected together they do act fairly independently. The major loads on the Palm House are self-weight, snow and wind loads. Due to the curved shapes the intensity of these loads vary continuously. The loading is conceptually similar to that on the **basic structure** (Figs.8.3 and 8.4), but with no differentiation between wall and roof.

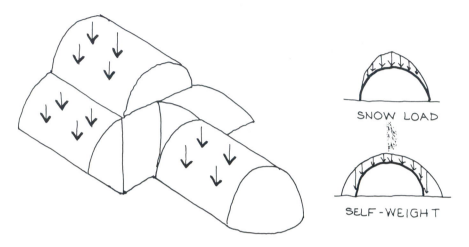

SNOW LOAD

SELF-WEIGHT

Fig.9.21

The overall distribution of wind pressure is complex and can only be obtained from wind tunnel tests, a technique not available to the original designer! Across the barrel vault sections the pressure distribution is similar to Fig.8.4

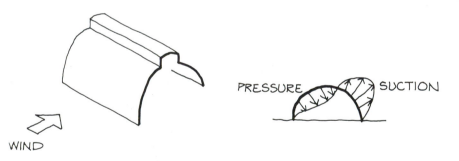

WIND

PRESSURE   SUCTION

Fig.9.22

Around the end caps and the central transept the wind pressure distribution is more complicated but there will be areas of positive pressure and areas of suction. Again, the structural behaviour of the end caps and the transept is more complicated than the barrel vaults. By regarding the barrel vaults as separate structures a conceptual analysis can be carried out on this area. This closely follows the analysis of the roof and portal frame of the Basic Structure (see pages 245—251).

Initially the loads are carried by the glazing (glass cladding). These loads are self-weight, snow and wind loads and the glass carries these loads by spanning between the curved glazing bars.

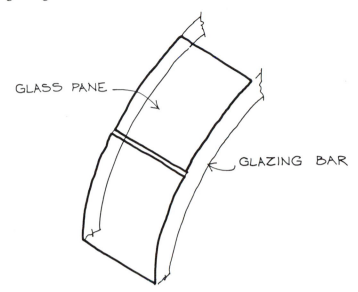

GLASS PANE

GLAZING BAR

Fig.9.23

The load and the structural behaviour of the glass varies from area to area. The self-weight and the snow load are always vertical whereas the wind load is normal (at right angles) to the surface.

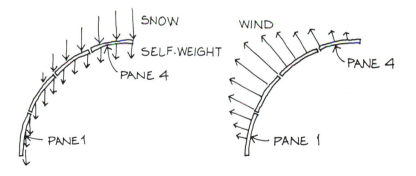

SNOW

SELF-WEIGHT

PANE 4

PANE 1

WIND

PANE 4

PANE 1

Fig.9.24

For example pane 2 may have the highest wind load whilst pane 4 had the highest snow load. All the panes have the same self-weight but near the crown this loads the pane across its width (a beam) but at the ground it loads the pane along its length (a wall).

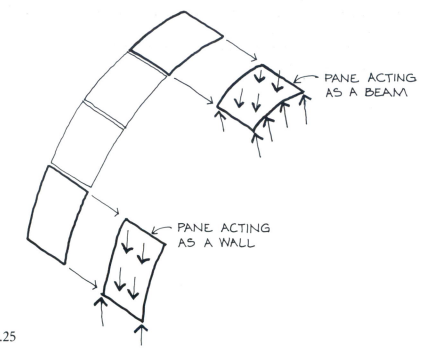

PANE ACTING
AS A BEAM

PANE ACTING
AS A WALL

Fig.9.25

To cater for the changing loading patterns and structural behaviour the glass panes, as structures could be altered throughout the glass house. For a building this is too complicated so the **worst** case will control the glass design. Depending on the numerical values this could be at the crown under self-weight and snow load or at an intermediate point under self-weight and wind load. In each of these cases the pane will act as a beam-like structure spanning between the glazing bars. This means the glass pane will have a bending moment and a shear force with the associated stresses.

LOADING

BENDING MOMENT
DIAGRAM

BENDING
STRESSES
IN GLASS

Fig.9.26

Like the spacing of the purlins of the Basic Structures (Fig.8.5) the spacing of the glazing bars is chosen by the designer. Greater spacing means less glazing bars but thicker glass to keep the stresses in the glass within set limits; closer spacing means thinner glass but more glazing bars. There is no correct spacing!

The glazing bars are curved and run from the ground to clerestory windows. The glazing bars are supported by the intermediate tubular purlins for 'inward' loads but not for 'outward' loads. An outward load is a wind suction force. The reason for this one-way support is because the glazing bars just rest on rods which in turn just rest on the tubular purlins.

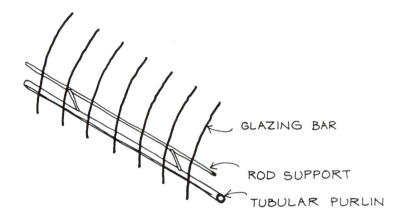

GLAZING BAR

ROD SUPPORT

TUBULAR PURLIN

Fig.9.27

This odd arrangement of glazing bar support shows that the designers were unaware of the suction effects of wind load. It also means that under inward load the glazing bar spans, as a beam, from purlin to purlin but for net outward load they have to span from ground to clerestory level. This is done by the glazing bar acting as a funicular structure in tension — a hanging cable (Fig.7.8).

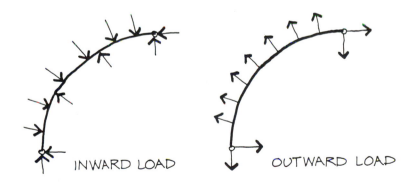

INWARD LOAD

OUTWARD LOAD

Fig.9.28

When the purlins are loaded they span between the arch frames, but they also have a rather strange feature as they are prestressed (see page 130 et seq). Prestressing is common for concrete but rare for steelwork. At the Palm House the purlins are stressed by the stretching of an internal iron rod.

Fig.9.29

Under inward load the purlin system is the rod and the prestressed tubular purlin.

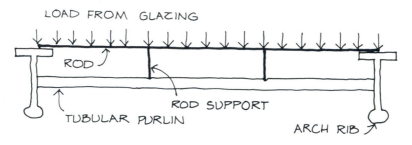

Fig.9.30

The rod spans as a three span beam loaded by the reactions from the glazing bars. The rod support reactions become point loads on the prestressed tubular purlins.

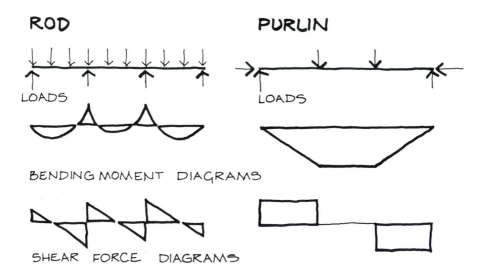

Fig.9.31

The stresses in the rod are as for a beam but those in the purlin are altered by the prestress compression (Fig.3.49 and 3.72).

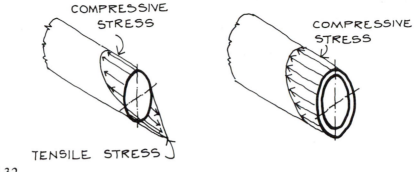

COMPRESSIVE STRESS

COMPRESSIVE STRESS

TENSILE STRESS

Fig.9.32

The different inward/outward load behaviour of the purlin system means the loads on the arch frame are very different for the snow load and wind load cases.

SELF-WEIGHT + SNOW

SELF-WEIGHT + WIND

Fig.9.33

These frames act like curved portal frames and not like funicular arches so their behaviour is similar to the portals of the Basic Structure. This behaviour can be represented by axial force, shear force and bending moment diagrams. Only the bending moment diagrams are shown (Fig.8.37)

SELF-WEIGHT + SNOW
BENDING MOMENT DIAGRAMS

SELF-WEIGHT + WIND

Fig.9.34

The behaviour of the central transept is quite different and has to be viewed three dimensionally.

Fig.9.35

The cross-section has an arch frame, two half-arch frames and two columns.

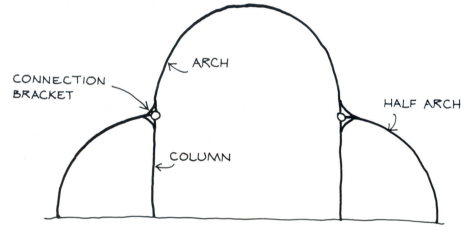

CONNECTION BRACKET

ARCH

HALF ARCH

COLUMN

Fig.9.36

There are six of these frames and each is loaded by loads that are similar to those applied to the barrel vaults.

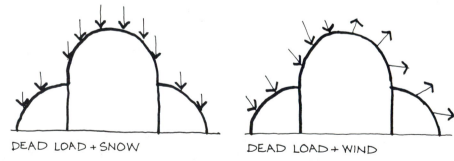

DEAD LOAD + SNOW

DEAD LOAD + WIND

Fig.9.37

These frames could act independently, rather like more complicated versions of the barrel vault arch frames. However the structure of the central transept acts as a three dimensional structure and this means that not only are the cross frames supported at the ground in the vertical and horizontal directions but they are also supported horizontally at the gallery level.

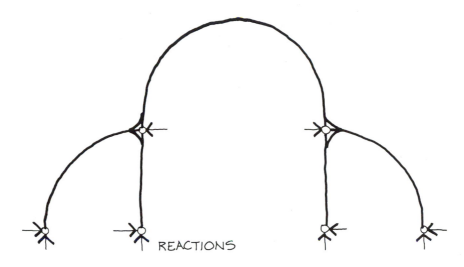

REACTIONS

Fig.9.38

This additional horizontal support allows the top arch frame to act in the same way as the barrel vault arch (Fig.9.34) and the side arch frames to act in a similar way. Again this behaviour can be represented by axial force, shear force and bending moment diagrams and again only the bending moment diagrams are drawn.

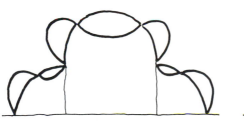

BENDING MOMENT DIAGRAM
SELF-WEIGHT + SNOW

BENDING MOMENT DIAGRAM
SELF-WEIGHT + WIND

Fig.9.39

The horizontal reactions from the frames at gallery level become loads on the gallery which acts as a horizontal beam spanning between the main arch frames at each end of the transept.

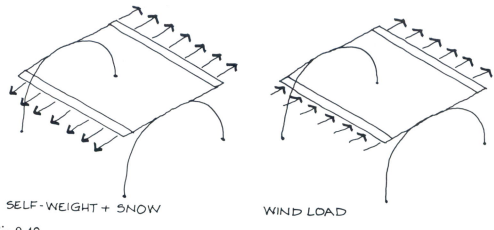

SELF-WEIGHT + SNOW   WIND LOAD

Fig.9.40

The gallery acts as a simple beam spanning the length of the central transept. Like any other beam it has bending moments and shear forces.

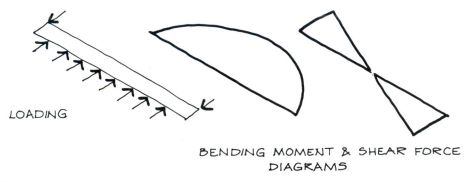

LOADING

BENDING MOMENT & SHEAR FORCE
DIAGRAMS

Fig.9.41

The reactions from the beam become loads on the main arch frames. In the case of the vertical load the reactions from the gallery beams do not produce any load on the arch frame but the reactions from the wind load case do cause a horizontal load applied to the arch crown.

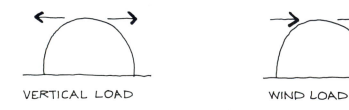

VERTICAL LOAD   WIND LOAD

Fig.9.42

The main arch frames resist these loads by acting as curved frames. The structure for the wind load on the central transept acts like the bracing system used for the wind load on the end wall of the Basic Structure (Fig.8.45).

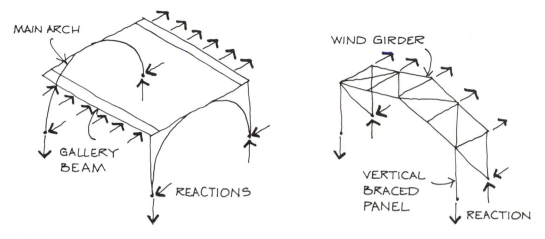

Fig.9.43

The gallery beam spans horizontally as does the wind girder of the Basic Structure, and each cause horizontal loads on the vertical structural elements — the main arch frames and the vertical braced panels. This is another example of similar structural behaviour but quite different structural geometries. It is the ability to recognise these systems of structural action rather than geometry that is a key to understanding how whole structures act.

The wind load acting on the Palm House when the wind blows along it is resisted by the end caps and the transition structures at the central transept.

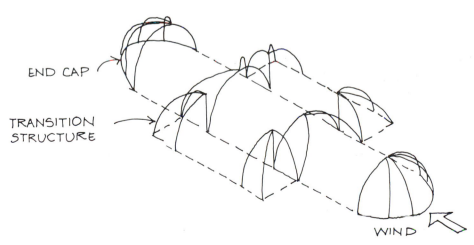

Fig.9.44

These wind forces cause internal forces in the various half-arch frames which again could be represented by axial force, shear force and bending moment diagrams.

As the structure is of iron it is quite slender so all parts that are in compression under any loading must be examined for the possibility of buckling initiated local or overall collapse (see page 183 et seq). The structure must be examined element by element as was the Basic Structure.

The Palm House looks like a modern structure and is renowned for its beauty and elegance however its designer has not used the current rational approach. After all none of the arches are near to the correct funicular shape for the loadings so a portal frame would have been much more structurally appropriate. This approach can be seen at Kew with the more recent Australian and Princess Diana glass houses.

At the time of the design, the 1840s, there was considerable technical knowledge about the theoretical behaviour of structures. This knowledge was not widespread and consequently not routinely used for structural design. It is probably for this reason that no calculations were done by the original designers but in the 1980s the Palm House was completely dissembled, refurbished and re-assembled. As part of this process the structure was checked using modern analytical and wind tunnel techniques. This work showed that the original design is adequate and that no structural strengthening was required. The term re-assembled is used rather than rebuilt because the Palm House is a kit of over 7000 iron parts and the refurbishment allowed the technical and organisational genius of Richard Turner to be seen in its totality for the first time.

9.3   Zarzuela Hippodrome

The engineered structures of the nineteenth century were predominately of cast and wrought iron, and towards the end of the century, of steel. The first use of reinforcing concrete with metal is usually attributed to Lambot with his boat in 1849 and Monier with his garden boxes in 1865 but the idea was proposed by Coignet in 1828. But it was only at the end of the nineteenth century that concrete, reinforced with steel, began to be used widely. This was due to the pioneering work of the French engineers Hennebique and Perret. By the 1930s the use of reinforced concrete structures was commonplace in Europe.

Because concrete structures can be formed **in situ** by pouring wet concrete into moulds virtually any shape can be made. Again, the reinforcing bars can be placed anywhere in the concrete and the density of the bars can continuously varied. This means that these in situ reinforced concrete structures are quite different in concept from iron or steel ones. They are no longer an assembly of elements as the one-, two- or three-dimensional parts can be joined by smooth geometric transitions. If the structure if formed into complex shapes the conceptual analysis can be very difficult, so where possible the structure may be approximated to an assembly of elements.

The structure of the Zarzuela Hippodrome was designed by the celebrated Spanish engineer Eduardo Torraja and was built in 1935, just in time to be damaged but not destroyed in the Spanish civil war. The building is essentially a grandstand with a betting hall underneath the seating.

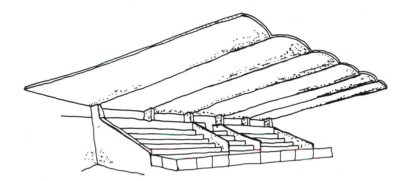

Fig.9.45

A cross-section through the building shows the functions of the various parts more clearly.

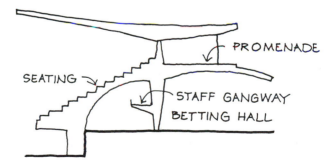

Fig.9.46

This section can also be used to show where the loads are applied to the structure. As the structure is of reinforced concrete, a heavyweight material, the self-weight of the structure is a major load. Even though the roof structure is thin its self-weight is still greater than any upward wind load.

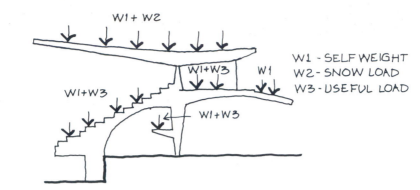

W1 - SELF WEIGHT
W2 - SNOW LOAD
W3 - USEFUL LOAD

Fig.9.47

The main supporting structures are frames which are spaced regularly along the building.

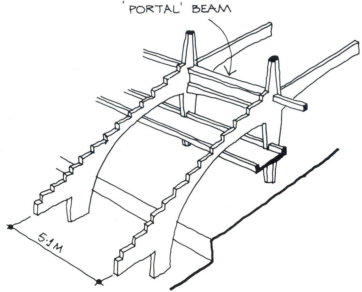

Fig.9.48

Although much more complex in shape these frames can be compared to the portal frames of the Basic Structure (Fig.8.7).

The roof of the grandstand is a shell (Fig.3.4). Concrete shells were pioneered by the German engineers Dischinger and Finsterwalder in the 1920s and are examples of funicular structures (E of Fig.7.75). Because the shell is thin it cannot resist significant bending moments so shells are only successful if they are good funicular shapes. If the shape of a shell deviates from a funicular shape it may have to be thickened to resist the internal stresses caused by the bending moments which makes a shell an inappropriate structural form. Sydney Opera House and the TWA terminal at Idlewild airport are well-known examples of inappropriate shapes for shell roofs. As the roof is spanning overall bending moments and shear forces exist.

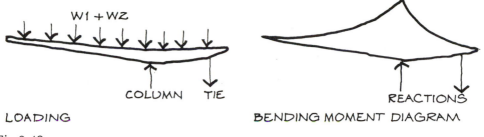

LOADING   BENDING MOMENT DIAGRAM

Fig.9.49

A shell is a two-dimensional structure so this shell roof spans along the building as well as across it.

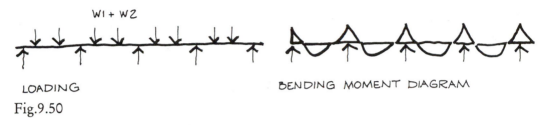

LOADING   BENDING MOMENT DIAGRAM

Fig.9.50

For the roof to act as a funicular structure rather than a beam like structure these bending moments and shear forces must be carried by internal axial forces [4]. The pattern of these axial forces is complex and was too difficult to be found by the mathematical techniques available at the time of the design. This meant that the designers had to resort carrying out a load test on a large scale model. Testing was extensively used by engineers in the nineteenth century but it is slow and expensive compared to mathematical analysis. These tests enabled the direction and magnitude of the principal stresses (see page 99 et seq) to be identified. The reinforcement was placed in a simplified pattern of the principal **tensile** stresses.

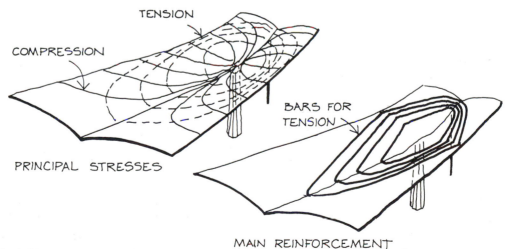

Fig.9.51

The internal forces that result in the principle tensile and compressive stresses provide the push/pull forces which resist the overall bending moments and shear forces. They are at a maximum at the column support where the overall moments and shear are at a maximum.

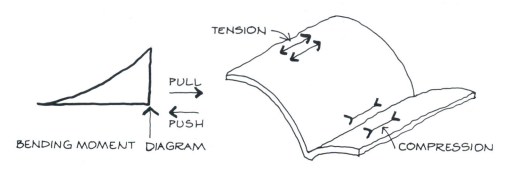

Fig.9.52

Unlike a beam (Fig.4.18) these forces are not vertically above one another, the tensile force is at the crown and the compressive force in the valley. The curved geometry of the shell roof provides the depth between these forces, that is the lever arm.

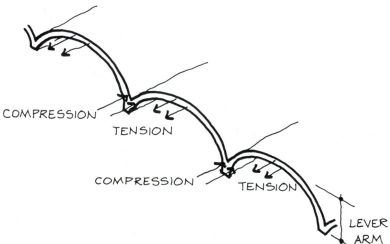

Fig.9.53

Although the shells act as cantilevers from the support columns the patterns of the principle stresses show that the structural action is two dimensional in the curved surface. The action of the roof causes up and down forces on the columns (Fig.9.49) and these become loads on the transverse frames (Fig.9.47). The other loads on the frames are from the reactions to the grandstand seating, the promenade floor and the staff gangway.

286   **Real Structures**

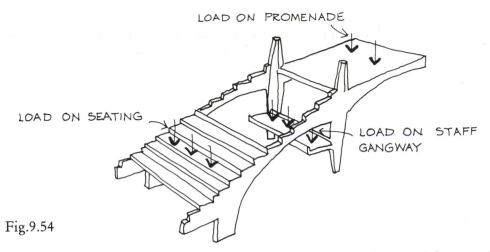

LOAD ON PROMENADE

LOAD ON SEATING

LOAD ON STAFF GANGWAY

Fig.9.54

The structural action of the transverse frames is similar to the portal frames of the Basic Structure and the arch frames of the Palm House. The frames resists the loads by internal forces which are bending moments, axial forces and shear forces. These can be represented by the appropriate diagrams. Only the bending moment diagram is shown.

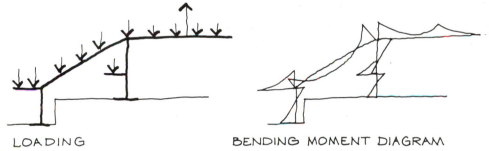

LOADING

BENDING MOMENT DIAGRAM

Fig.9.55

Frame action is dependent on 'stiff' joints and these joints are able to resist bending moments. This stiffness is readily achieved with in situ reinforced concrete by placing reinforcing bars **through** the joint for the push/pull forces.

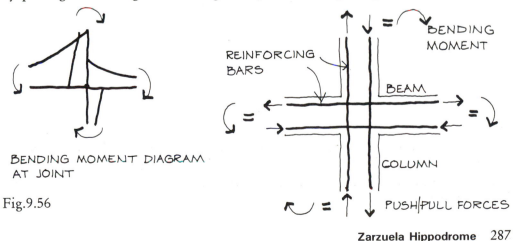

BENDING MOMENT DIAGRAM AT JOINT

REINFORCING BARS

BENDING MOMENT

BEAM

COLUMN

PUSH/PULL FORCES

Fig.9.56

Notice that the bending moment can change direction either side of a joint. This happens, for example, where the cantilever beam supporting the staff gangway connects to the column. If this was not a stiff joint the beam could not be a cantilever!

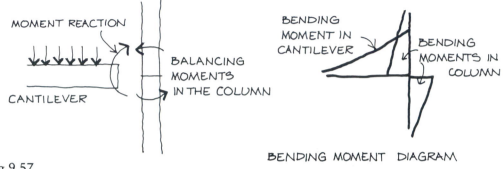

Fig.9.57

The arrangement between the roof and the promenade beam shows how the designer's understanding of structural behaviour means an effective structure is provided. The secret is the roof tie which provides the pull for the roof structure and the reduces the cantilever moment in the promenade beam. If the tie was removed large bending moments would be required to resist the roof load and the load on the promenade.

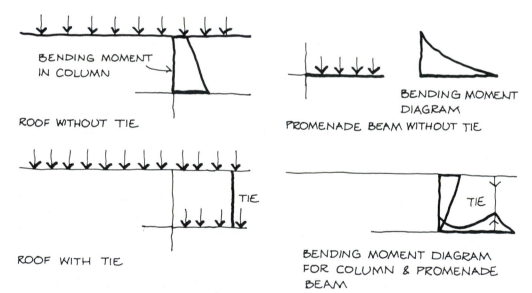

Fig.9.58

As the building is basically open the loads from the wind along the building are small, but all structures need some lateral strength or they could just fall over sideways! Here this lateral strength is again provided by frame action. This is achieved by using special longitudinal members, portal beams, which have stiff joints with the columns.

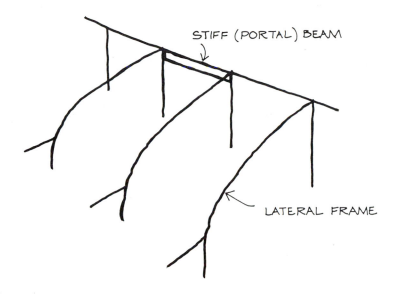

STIFF (PORTAL) BEAM

LATERAL FRAME

Fig.9.59

Rather like the Basic Structure (Fig.8.44) one bay is made stiff. This is done with the stiff joints forming a portal frame instead of using a diagonal bracing member.

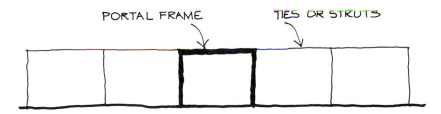

PORTAL FRAME   TIES OR STRUTS

Fig.9.60

Because concrete is a heavyweight material concrete structures rarely have problems of overall stability. Also stresses in concrete structures are usually quite low which means the elements have to be stocky to carry the loads, so they are rarely slender enough to initiate collapse by buckling.

This structure, unlike the Palm House, was designed by an engineer who was very conscious of the structural behaviour and took considerable trouble to investigate and quantify it. Where this was not possible by using analytical techniques scientific tests were carried out. An alternative would have been to redesign the roof so that analytical techniques available at the time could have been used.

9.4   CNIT Exposition Palace

In 1950 the Federation of Industries decided that a permanent exhibition centre should be built. This centre would provide space for temporary and permanent exhibitions for all types of French industrial equipment. It would be the 'Centres National des Industries et des Techniques'; hence CNIT. A site was chosen 7km from the centre of Paris at La Defense. The design for the centre was carried out by the architects Camelot, de Mailly and Zehrfuss. Their design was triangular in plan and had a roof that spanned between the apexes of the triangular plan without intermediate supports.

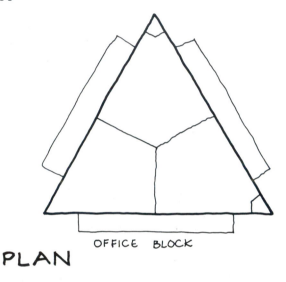

OFFICE   BLOCK

PLAN

Fig.9.61

The span of the roof is 218m on each face of the triangular plan. This was the longest roof span ever built using the final choice of construction, this was a concrete double shell.

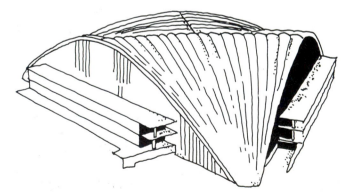

Fig.9.62

A four storey office block is built within each facade with the space between office block and the roof closed with a glazed facade. The structure of the offices blocks is separate from the roof structure. In the late 1980s the office blocks were removed and an hotel and a shopping complex were built under the original roof.

A number of leading engineering designers were asked to submit proposals for the roof structure. Seven proposals were submitted, three using steel as the structural material, three using reinforced concrete and one proposed a composite design using steel and concrete (page 131). The scheme chosen was of concrete and was submitted by Entreprises Boussion whose technical director was Nicholas Esquillan.

Their proposal was for a vaulted structure of reinforced concrete. To save weight the structure of the roof was of honeycomb construction, with thin top and bottom surfaces spaced apart by a two way arrangement of vertical webs. The whole roof is divided into three kite shaped sections by a three way joint.

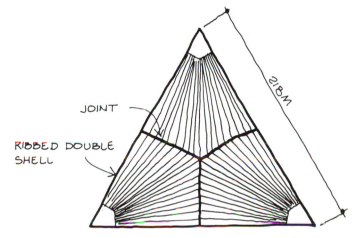

Fig.9.63

Because the roof is of concrete, as with the roof of the Hippodrome, self-weight is the dominant loading. Although the wind causes loads the building is so large that high wind pressures do not occur over the whole roof at any one time. For the effect of gravity load the bending moments are similar to those in a triangular slab supported at the corners.

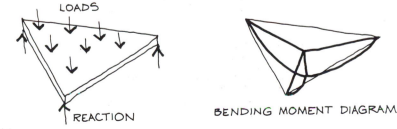

Fig.9.64

One kite shaped section of the slab roof could be regarded as acting as one half of a simple beam.

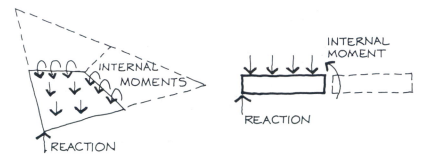

Fig.9.65

If the roof was a flat slab then these bending moments would be resisted by push/pull forces within the depth of the slab (Fig.3.40), but the roof is not flat but curved. The curve of the roof is the funicular shape for the self-weight, this shape is called a **catenary**. Because of this the bending moment and the shear forces are resisted by axial forces in the structure which follow the funicular line.

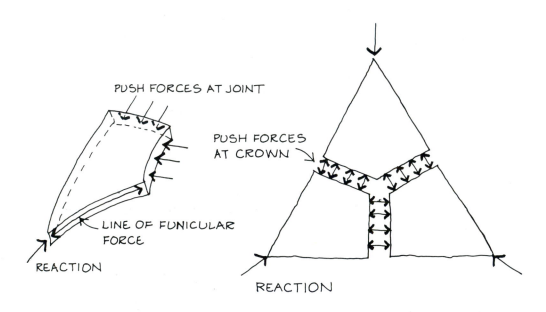

Fig.9.66

The top and bottom surfaces are also curved in section so that the surface is corrugated.

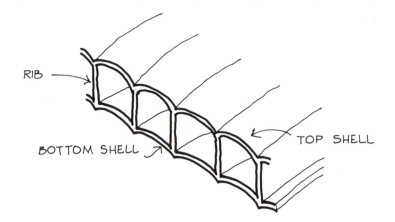

Fig.9.67

The plan dimensions of the structure reduce towards the supports but the axial force does not, this would mean that the stresses could increase as there is less structure to carry the forces. This is avoided by concentrating the longitudinal webs and by increasing the thickness of the top and bottom skins.

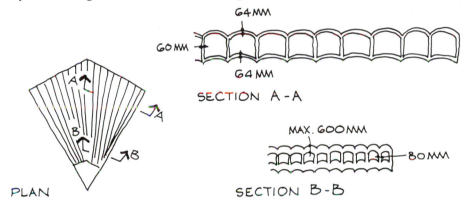

Fig.9.68

To prevent the centre of the roof being excessively high the curve of the roof is kept quite flat which reduces the overall lever arm.

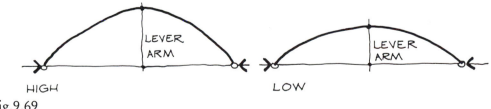

Fig.9.69

As the shape of the vault is a catenary the radius of the roof varies from point to point. At the crown the radius is 91m but at the supports it is 424m.

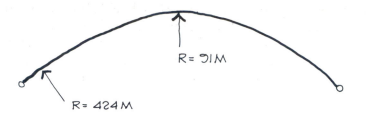

Fig.9.70

The radius at the supports is twice as large as the one used for the bridge at Sando in Sweden. When this bridge was built in 1943 it was the largest concrete arch in the world and also had the largest radius of curvature. As the curve is flat constructional inaccuracies could lead to the roof seriously deviating from the funicular line so great care was taken with the geometry during construction.

Concrete structures are rarely slender but this structure is slender locally and globally so the possibility of buckling initiated collapse was carefully checked. The whole roof can buckle in symmetric and asymmetric modes.

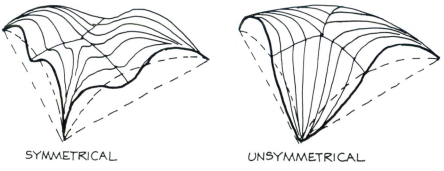

SYMMETRICAL   UNSYMMETRICAL

Fig.9.71

As the whole of the cross-section is in compression a collapse could be initiated by either the top or bottom surfaces buckling locally between the diaphragms.

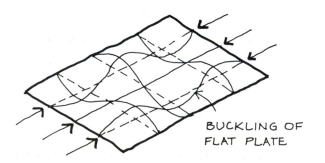

BUCKLING OF
FLAT PLATE

Fig.9.72

This buckling pattern requires alternate panels to buckle in opposite directions. This could happen if the panels were flat but this local buckling pattern is prevented by the local curvature of the panels. This curvature means that local buckling takes place at the local crowns (Fig.6.68) and this requires a much higher load than the alternate panel buckling. This was the reason that this local curvature between the diaphragms was introduced.

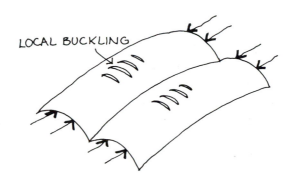

Fig.9.73

Not only are the main parts of the roof in compression due to the arch action but the triangular geometry and the rib arrangement cause compression across the shell at the crown joint. This is far from obvious.

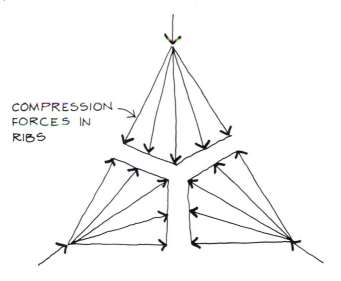

Fig.9.74

Because of the fan shaped pattern of the shells the axial forces at the joint meet at varying angles. At the facade they are in line but the angle varies towards the centre.

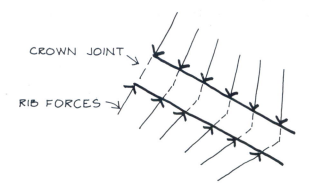

Fig.9.75

At the centre the third section balances the forces but elsewhere there is no balancing force as there are special rollers between the shells.

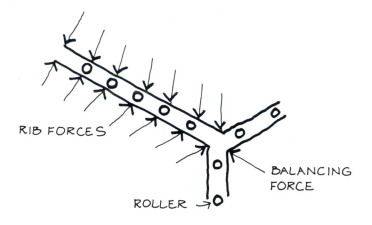

Fig.9.76

These angled forces cause a varying compression force in the top edge members of each shell section. These edge members, the crown walls, are strengthened to carry these forces.

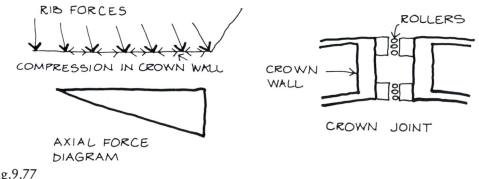

Fig.9.77

296   **Real Structures**

To maintain the overall compression in the shell the support points must provide horizontal as well as vertical reactions (Fig.7.19). These horizontal reactions form the pull forces which resist the overall bending moment.

Fig.9.78

If the shell was built between rigid abutments, natural rock for example, then the horizontal reactions could be provided by the foundations. Although the site of the building has natural rock near the surface site limitations and the construction of underground railways in the future prevented direct use of the foundation rock for horizontal reactions.

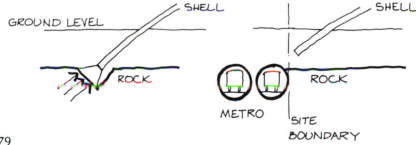

Fig.9.79

The horizontal reactions are provided by special tie members (Fig.8.53). These run along the lines of the facades.

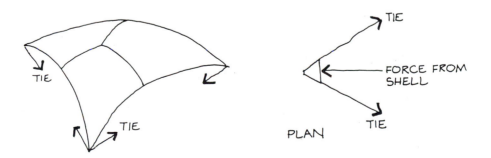

Fig.9.80

The level of the tie at the foundation was too high along the facades so it had to be diverted to a lower level.

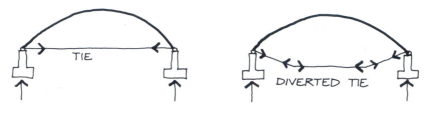

Fig.9.81

This diversion of the tie members requires an additional tie member at the point of change in direction. This is another example of a cable shape for a particular loading.

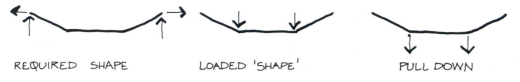

Fig.9.82

The pull down members are anchored in the underlying rock by excavating undercut holes so the concrete of the tie is wedged in the rock.

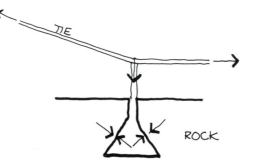

Fig.9.83

The sides of the shell are enclosed by the four storey office block and glazing.

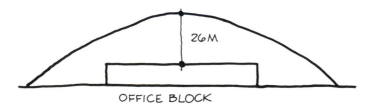

Fig.9.84

The facade supports are substantial steel structures as they have to span up to 26m from the roof of the office block to the shell roof.

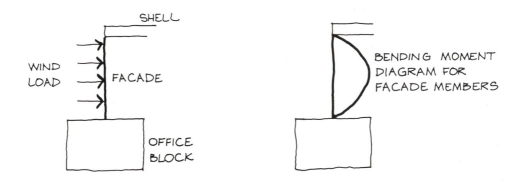

Fig.9.85

Because the top of the shell moves vertically under different loads there is a special joint between the shell and the facade structure to prevent the facade steelwork becoming part of the roof load path.

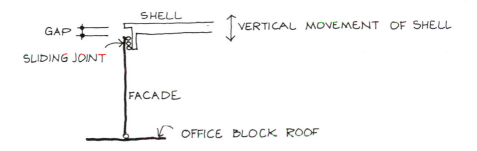

Fig.9.86

The CNIT Exposition Palace is an enormous building and the design and construction was a considerable undertaking. Using the six basic concepts listed on page 234 together with the necessary technical information the structural behaviour can be understood conceptually.

9.5   Federal Reserve Bank

Most office buildings are enclosures of cellular spaces (offices) and the building is usually planned on a rectangular grid with vertical columns at the grid intersections. The structure of the floors is an arrangement of beams and slabs carrying the loads to the columns by bending moments and shear forces.

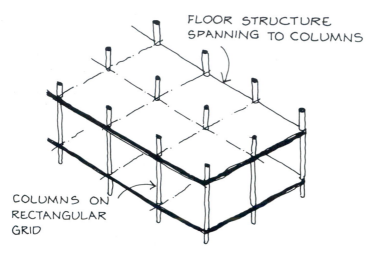

Fig.9.87

The vertical loads are carried directly to the ground by the columns. Horizontal wind loads, which are substantial for the taller office buildings, can be resisted by a variety of structural systems. For wind loads any building is essentially   a cantilever from the ground with lateral loads (wind) and axial loads (self-weight etc.).

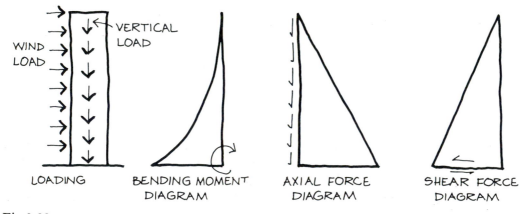

Fig.9.88

The structural system for resisting the bending moment and shear force from the lateral wind load can be beam-like, truss-like, frame-like or, in the case of guyed structures, almost funicular.

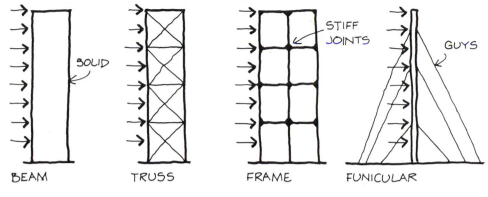

Fig.9.89

Where beam or truss structures are used they restrict circulation so they are placed near lift shafts or at the end of the building.

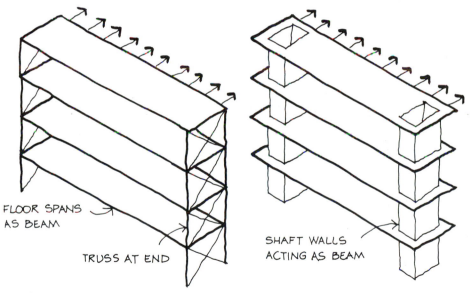

Fig.9.90

The Federal Reserve Bank, designed by architects Gunnar Birkets and Associates with engineers Skilling Helle Christiansen and Robertson was completed in 1973. It is a ten storey office building with underground car parking and bank vaults, quite a standard arrangement. But this building is far from standard as the whole of the office block spans across a three storey height space under the building!

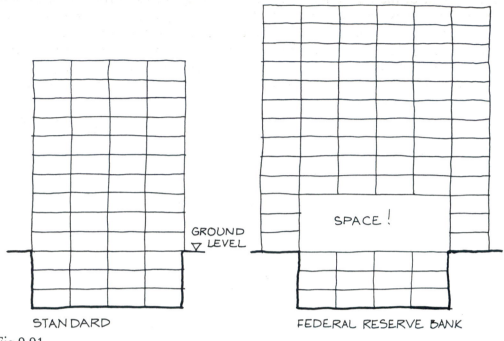

STANDARD   FEDERAL RESERVE BANK

Fig.9.91

Creating this space under a ten storey building means that the column loads which would normally be supported by the ground have to be transferred laterally. The building now has to span across the space.

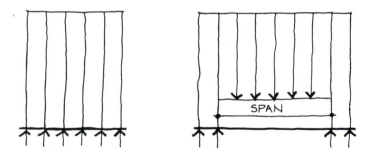

Fig.9.92

And the loads are transferred by internal forces of bending moments and shear forces.

LOADING   BENDING MOMENT   SHEAR FORCE
                   DIAGRAM   DIAGRAM

Fig.9.93

As the design of the building requires the building to span across the space the structural designers must choose a suitable structural system. There is no 'correct' system just the chosen one. The choices for spanning structures are the four types; beam-like, truss-like, frame-like or funicular. As the building that spans is ten storeys high even with one type, say truss-like, there are further choices. A roof level truss with hung floors or trusses at two levels supporting columns are examples of possible choices.

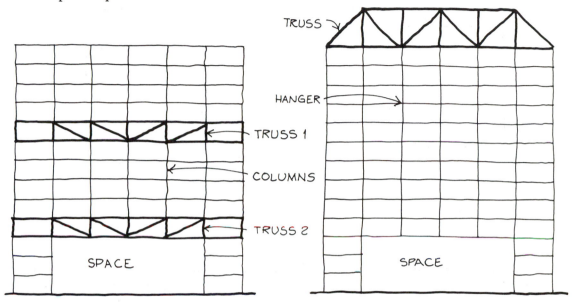

Fig.9.94

The choice for the structure was quite unusual as they chose a funicular structure — a hanging cable. The cable is the whole depth of the ten storey office building.

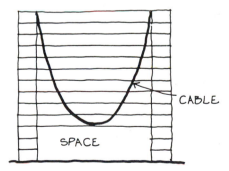

Fig.9.95

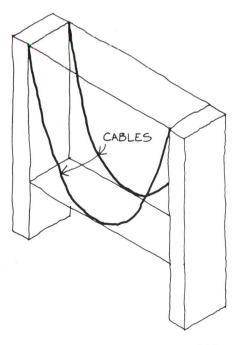

This choice means that a horizontal force must be provided at roof level so that the cable can resist the bending moment.

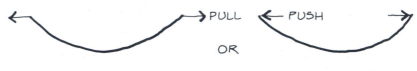

OR

Fig.9.96

In a suspension bridge the mid-air push force (Fig.7.13) is resisted by tensile forces in the back stays but this would be inconvenient for this building so a strut is used to provide the push force (Fig.7.15).

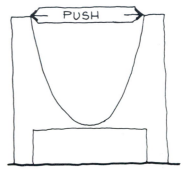

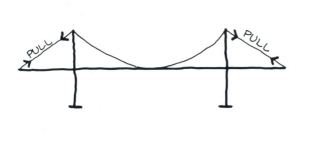

Fig.9.97

A truss-like structure has been chosen for the strut.

The floors trusses span across the building on to vertical members. These vertical members transfer the floor truss reactions to the cable. The vertical members above the cable are in compression whilst the members below are in tension.

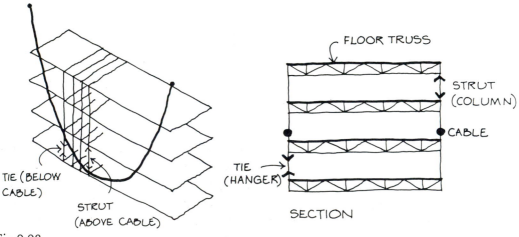

Fig.9.98

At each end of the cable/strut structure there are vertical reactions (Fig.7.15) which are resisted by thirteen storey high concrete towers. The complete spanning structure is the cable, the strut and these end towers. The construction of the facade visually emphasises the presence of the cable part of the spanning structure.

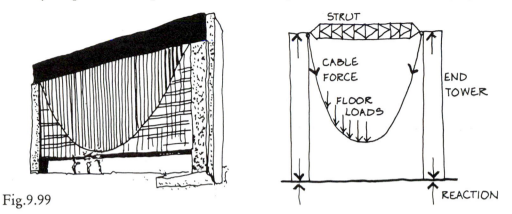

Fig.9.99

Not only does the structure have to resist vertical loads but it also has to act as a cantilever to resist wind loads. The cantilevering action is done by the concrete end towers. Because of the vertical load from the cable structure the forces at the base of the towers are always compressive. This is another example of combining axial and bending stresses (Fig.3.76).

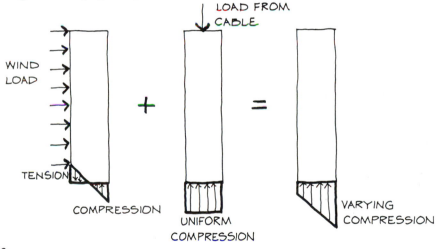

Fig.9.100

The wind load path starts at the cladding system and ends at the base of the cantilevering end towers. The cladding system spans vertically from floor to floor. The floors are loaded by the reactions of the cladding system and span as horizontal beams between the end towers. The end towers are loaded at each floor level by the reactions from the floors acting as horizontal beams. The end towers carry these loads by acting as cantilevers from the ground.

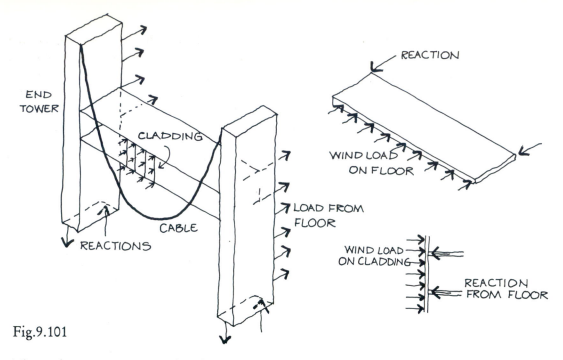

Fig.9.101

The end towers are considered to be concrete I-beams and is part of the planning of the accommodation of the end towers.

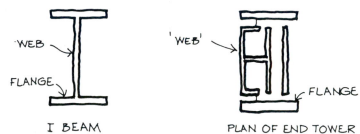

Fig.9.102   I BEAM   PLAN OF END TOWER

One of the main problems for the structural designer in using these core areas as vertical cantilevers is to ensure that the accommodation requirements allow horizontal shear forces to develop between the flanges and the web (Fig.4.32).

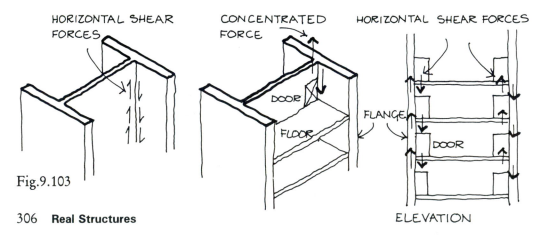

Fig.9.103

ELEVATION

For a cable to act as a funicular structure it must change shape with a change of load pattern (Figs.7.67 and 7.68). In this building the main load is the uniform vertical load from the building construction, but the pattern can vary when different layouts of furniture and equipment are adopted on each floor and of course the occupants tend to move about. For an ideally flexible cable each change would require a change in funicular shape and this would be difficult to achieve for a cable that is part of a building. The cables in this building can act as bending elements for the relatively small bending moments that are required to keep the cable in its basic shape. This is achieved but constructing a composite cable of a cable acting with a curved steel I-beam.

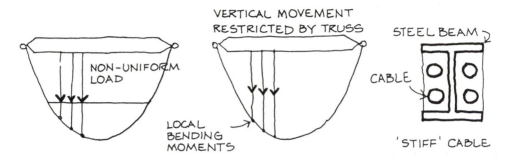

Fig.9.104

Whilst there is only small variations in the load of the completed building this is not the case during construction. Great care was taken by the builders to control the cable shape during construction as the cables were gradually loaded by the building elements. This was done by stressing the cable part of the 'cable' in stages as the load was applied.

There are a number of parts of the structure that must checked to ensure that buckling initiated collaps does not occur (see pages 183—195). The parts that are in compression are the roof level strut, the end towers and the columns.

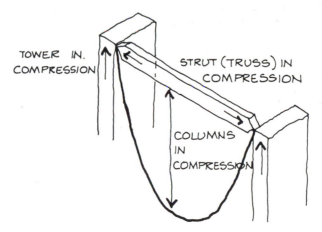

Fig.9.105

The roof level truss-like strut could buckle in a number of ways.

VERTICALLY   LATERALLY   LOCALLY

Fig.9.106

The towers could also buckle locally or as a complete structure.

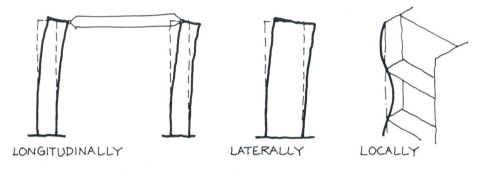

LONGITUDINALLY   LATERALLY   LOCALLY

Fig.9.107

It is unusual to be able to see all the parts of the structural system clearly when a building is complete, however, as can be seen, this photograph taken during construction clearly shows the structural system.

Fig.9.108 (Photographer: Balthazar Korab)

The Federal Reserve Bank is unusual as the major structural action is visually expressed by the completed building. The structure is extraordinary for an office block and it is difficult to understand why the designers went to such trouble and expense to span over a rather bleak plaza.

9.6   Bank of China

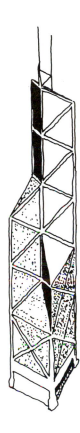

The headquarters building for the Bank of China was designed by the architect I.M.Pei and the structural designers were the engineers Leslie E.Robertson Associates of New York. When it was completed in 1990 it was the fifth tallest building in the world and the tallest building outside New York and Chicago. It is a massive building, 52m square on plan rising to a height, including the antennae, of 368m above road level. The gross area of the building is 133,000 sq.m and there are 70 storeys.

As buildings become taller the plan dimensions do not increase at the same rate. The reason for this is that although office workers rarely work by natural light there is a psychological need for windows, for 'outside awareness'. This means that everyone needs to be no further than about 18m from a window. This limitation on plan dimension causes taller buildings to be more slender than shorter ones.

The combination of increased height and increased slenderness has two effects on the structural design of tall buildings. The first is the fact that wind speeds increase with height with a consequent increase in wind loads on the faces of the building. All buildings act as cantilevers from the ground to carry wind loads (Fig.9.98). As the structure becomes more slender this cantilevering behaviour under wind load tends to dominate the choice of structural system.

Fig.9.109

Four structural systems are shown in Fig.9.89 for resisting lateral loading from wind and two of these systems are shown in Fig.9.90 for the 'slender' direction of a rectangular building. For a square building, like the Bank of China, there is no slender direction.

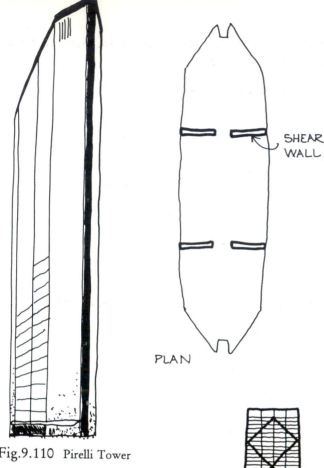

Early, very tall buildings, like the Chrysler and Empire State buildings were designed as framed structures (Fig.9.89). The lateral flexibility of these buildings was reduced by 'non-loadbearing' external and internal wall elements. The idea of using a vertical, beam-like structure — a **shear wall** — to carry the wind loads was first used by Pier Luigi Nervi in the structural design of the Pirelli tower in Turin in Italy.

Fig.9.110 Pirelli Tower

As the external cladding became lighter and commercial pressures demanded column free internal spaces the wind resisting structure was sometimes moved to the facade of the building. The pioneer of this structural system was Fazlur Khan who first used it for the DeWitt-Chestnut building in 1965. He also used this concept for the better known John Hancock Center built in Chicago in 1970.

Fig.9.111 John Hancock Center

Moving the wind resisting structure to the external facade meant that the floors could be structure free apart from the necessary stair/lift cores.

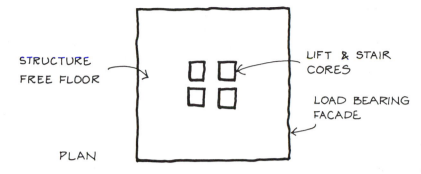

Fig.9.112

In the John Hancock Center the perimeter columns take the vertical loads directly to the ground.

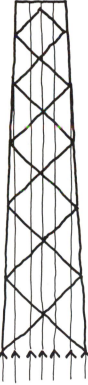

Fig.9.113

The Bank of China building uses the concept of the braced facade but with several important innovations. Before explaining the structural action it is helpful if the external shape of the building is understood. Essentially it is a cubical building with a pyramid roof but with each quadrant 'slid down' by different amounts.

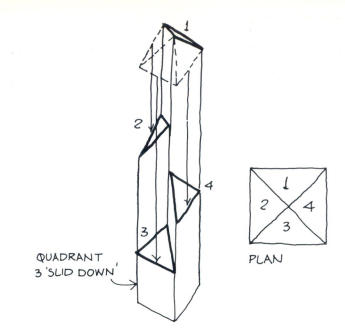

QUADRANT
3 'SLID DOWN'

PLAN

Fig.9.114

This sliding means that the floor plan varies with the height.

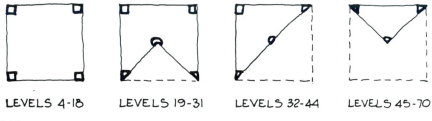

LEVELS 4-18   LEVELS 19-31   LEVELS 32-44   LEVELS 45-70

Fig.9.115

The John Hancock Center uses the whole facade for the windbracing structure but the Bank of China building uses a **megastructure** as the primary load path for both the wind loads **and** the vertical loads. This is really the same idea as the use of purlins and portal frames for the Basic Structure described in Chapter 8. The purlins are part of the secondary structure with the portals acting as a megastructure by carrying both the wind loads **and** the vertical loads.

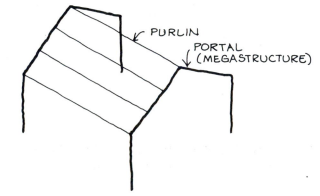

PURLIN

PORTAL
(MEGASTRUCTURE)

Fig.9.116

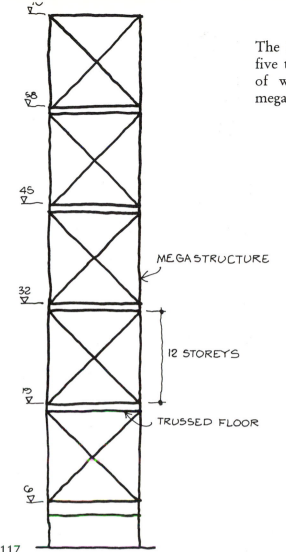

The Bank of China is a 'stack' of five twelve-storey 'buildings', each of which are supported by the megastructure.

Fig.9.117

There are four megacolumns, one at each corner, but due to the changing floor shape a fifth, central megacolumn is required at the higher levels.

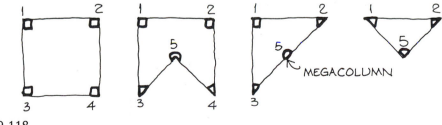

Fig.9.118

Amazingly, the central megacolumn stops at Level 25, its load being transferred to the corner megacolumns by a pyramid structure.

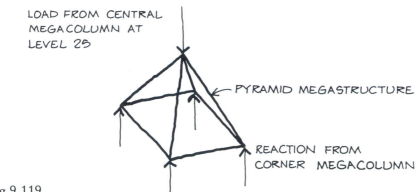

LOAD FROM CENTRAL MEGACOLUMN AT LEVEL 25

PYRAMID MEGASTRUCTURE

REACTION FROM CORNER MEGACOLUMN

Fig.9.119

At the bottom of each 12 storey building is a storey height trussed floor. This acts as the 'foundation' for the 12 storey building, transferring the load to the megacolumns.

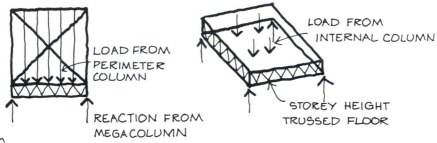

LOAD FROM PERIMETER COLUMN

REACTION FROM MEGACOLUMN

LOAD FROM INTERNAL COLUMN

STOREY HEIGHT TRUSSED FLOOR

Fig.9.120

The vertical loads in the perimeter columns are transferred directly into the facade megastructure at the points of structural intersection.

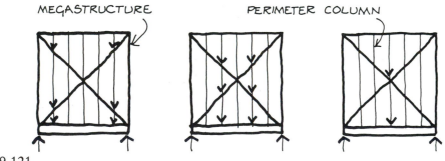

MEGASTRUCTURE

PERIMETER COLUMN

Fig.9.121

Hong Kong is in an area of very high winds — typhoons — and these cause wind loads that are approximately double the wind loads carried by the Chicago and New York skyscrapers. These loads are resisted by the truss action of the facade megastructures. The external facades have cross-braced trusses.

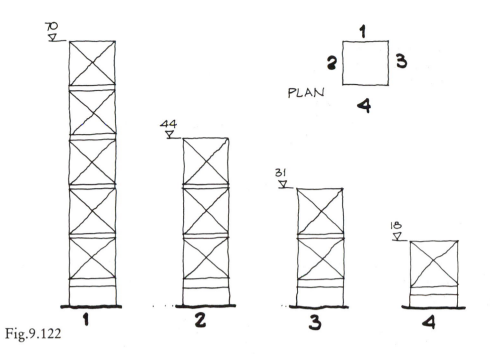

Fig.9.122

At the higher levels there are also external facades on the plan diagonals. These facades have diagonally braced trusses.

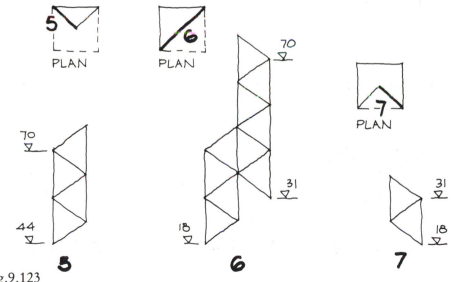

Fig.9.123

The vertical loads from the floors are transferred to the four corner megacolumns. These loads countcract the tension forces caused by the wind loads on the facade megatrusses. This maintains upward reactions at the base of the building under wind loading.

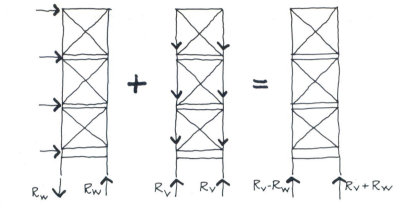

Fig.9.124

This is another example of the role of combined stresses (see pages 97—99). Although the external columns can carry tension forces it is difficult to provide substantial downward reactions at foundation level.

At the bottom of the tower the horizontal wind load as well as the vertical load has to be transferred to the ground. In the Bank of China this is done by providing horizontal and vertical structures to transfer these forces to concrete walls that are below ground. These are the perimeter walls of the basement. There are five elements in the load path for the horizontal wind forces. These are:

1   The facade megatrusses
2   A horizontal steel diaphragm structure at Level 4
3   A vertical steel/concrete core between Level 4 and the foundation
4   A horizontal concrete diaphragm structure at Level 0
5   Vertical concrete perimeter basement walls

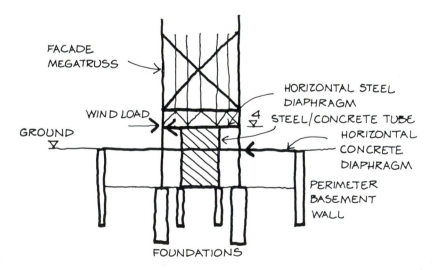

Fig.9.125

At Level 4 the horizontal wind loads from the facade megatrusses are transferred to the vertical steel/concrete core by forces in the plane of the steel diaphragm structure.

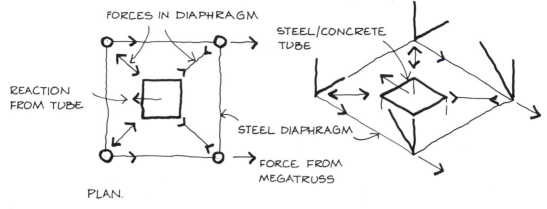

Fig.9.126

The core transfers these horizontal loads by shear forces in the core walls to the concrete diaphragm at Level 0.

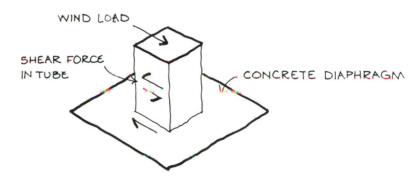

Fig.9.127

There are also vertical forces in the core caused by the push/pull forces from the bending moment. These are carried down to separate core foundations.

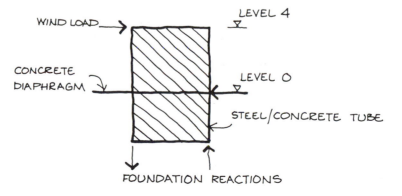

Fig.9.128

The horizontal forces in the Level 0 concrete diaphragm are transferred to the top of the vertical basement by forces in the plane of the diaphragm structure. The forces in the walls are transferred to the ground by friction forces on the faces and the base of the walls.

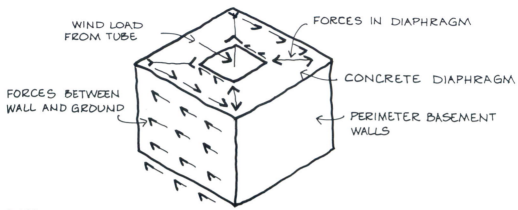

Fig.9.129

The weight of the structural steel required for the structure of the Bank of China building was far lower than that used for other tall buildings built in the Far East. This was partly achieved by the efficiency of the overall structural form but a significant contribution was made by the way the megastructure joints were constructed. At any joint in a structure the forces in the elements have to be transferred through the joint and the cost of these joints is often a substantial proportion of the total structural cost. This is particularly true for three dimensional structures due to the geometrical and structural complexities at the joints. This was overcome in the Bank of China building by using composite steel and concrete construction for the joints and members of the megastructure.

The facade megatrusses shown in Figs.9.122 and 9.123 were built as individual **plane** trusses with simple joints. Where they met at the corners to form the three dimensional megastructure they were connected by casting concrete around them to form the megacolumns and the joints of the megastructure.

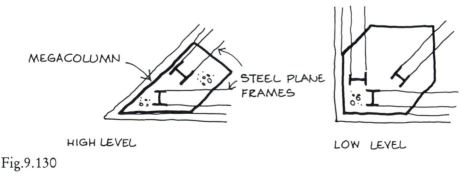

Fig.9.130

Both the structural concepts and the finished appearance of the Bank of China are clear and simple. However it should be appreciated that this was achieved by bold design decisions and a vast amount of complex detailed structural design.

CHAPTER 10 *Structural conception*

Having an understanding of how structural systems work, what structural materials are available and what loads structures must carry does not lead to an automatic method of how to design, or more accurately how to **conceive** a structure.

10.1 Structures in buildings

The structures of cranes' or bridges' only role is to carry the loads, whereas the structure of a building fulfils other roles. Frequently the designer of a building is more than one person so the structural designer is part of a team. Each member of the design team is primarily concerned with a different aspect of the overall design. A building is essentially a space that is protected from the natural environment and is constructed for a specific use. The structure of the building is part of the building construction and plays the role of giving the construction sufficient strength to withstand the loads to which the whole building is subjected. These loads are caused by natural phenomena such as wind and gravity and by the use of the building.

Structures are **part** of a building and cannot be conceived in isolation but must be conceived as part of the whole design. However they play a specific role, that of providing strength. Whilst the structure of a building is part of the construction the **concept** of the structure is not. Frequently design decisions are made before the structural concept is clear, often the physical size of structural members is considered without reference to an overall structure. The physical presence of the structure in a building is the concern of many members of the design team as it affects their design decisions. Often the role of structural design is seen as arriving at the physical size of structural elements rather than considering an overall design strategy.

So the structural designer of building structures is faced with a difficult task. Not only is the structural design part of a whole, over which he or she has no direct control, but the actual size and appearance of individual parts is often proscribed by others who have no concern for their structural action.

The structural designer must keep two principles firmly in mind, and these are:

- **There is no correct structure**
- **All loads must have a load path**

The first principle is often the cause of much difficulty to inexperienced designers because everyone likes to get the right answer, choose the correct structure, and it is conceptually important to realise that this is not possible. The obverse is that the chosen structure, provided that it satisfies all the requirements of the building design, is the **correct structure**. Before the structure is chosen alternatives may be considered but these rarely eliminate themselves so the designer must choose the correct structure.

The second principle is obvious as a principle but frequently non-structural requirements alter the chosen structural concept. This means that load paths may need to be altered locally or globally. It is essential that the consequences of any alterations are accepted. A simple example illustrates this point. Suppose part of a building has floors that span on to edge beams, and these beams span between columns that are spaced at regular centres.

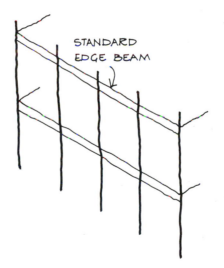

Fig.10.1

If for some non-structural reason a column at ground level has to be moved then the upper columns will have to be carried by a beam at first floor. The beam at first floor carrying the load from the columns above will have to be far stronger and therefore bigger than the other edge beams.

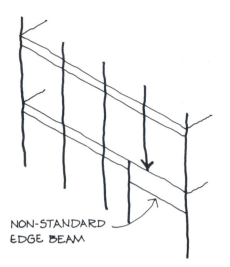

NON-STANDARD
EDGE BEAM

Fig.10.2

The two basic principles do not give any guidance on how to conceive a structure for a building however the building design does. The use of a building may determine the span of the floors or roof as the internal space requirements often determine the positions of vertical supports. An office space can have internal vertical supports but planning flexibility suggests these should be columns rather than walls. An auditorium, however large, can have no internal supports but does require, for sound isolation, heavy perimeter walls. A tall building needs vertical access so these can be grouped into stair and lift towers and these can be used by the structural designer to resist horizontal wind loads. These are simple examples that show how non-structural requirements for a building can guide a structural designer towards decisions about possible structural concepts.

10.2 Conceptual load paths

Before decisions are made about a particular structure the load paths for the different load cases must be identified. Because the load path for any loading **is** the structure it must be clear how each load path structure acts. Building structures provide the strength and stiffness for the building enclosure and this means that the load paths will carry loads that **span**, floors and roofs, load paths that transfer vertical **gravity** forces and load paths that resist **horizontal loads**. As buildings are three dimensional objects the structure also has to be three dimensional even though parts of the structure may be considered as two dimensional.

For gravity loads the load paths are conceived 'top down'. This is because each part of the building has to be supported by the structure below and also support the building above — just like a stack of bricks. To act as a load path the structure must be **complete** — that is no structural gaps.

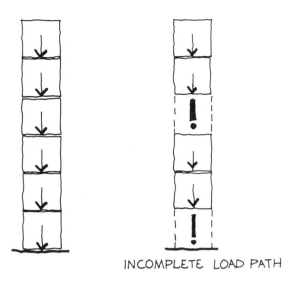

Fig.10.3

A solid brick column could support a statue but is not much use as a building structure however the idea of a complete load path can be applied to a stack of tables.

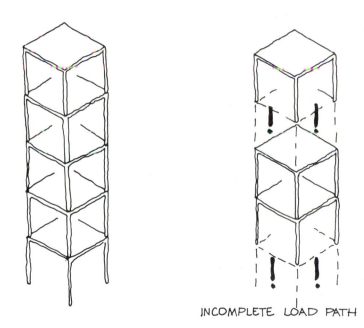

Fig.10.4

INCOMPLETE LOAD PATH

The idea of a complete gravity load path may seem obvious for stacks of bricks or tables but for complex buildings it may be far from clear. For example an hotel requires different types of space at different levels.

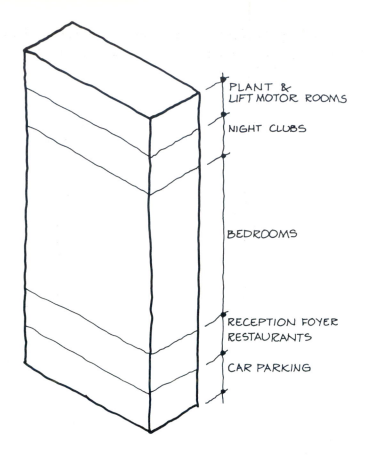

Fig.10.5

Each part has to support all the loads from above but each type of space suggests different types and spacing of vertical structure. Bedrooms have walls at close spacings whereas a car park needs widely spaced columns that allow an efficient car parking layout. It is rare that the position of vertical structure for differing uses coincides, this means that vertical loads will have to be diverted laterally by transfer structures or the position of the vertical structure will have to be a compromise.

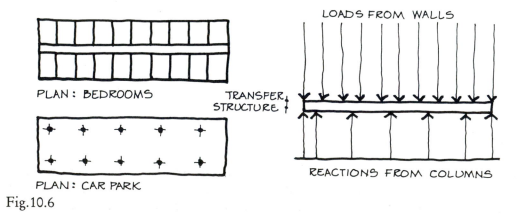

Fig.10.6

A similar principle applies for horizontal loads, usually caused by wind loading. For horizontal loading the building cantilevers from the ground and the cantilever structure must be complete from roof to foundation.

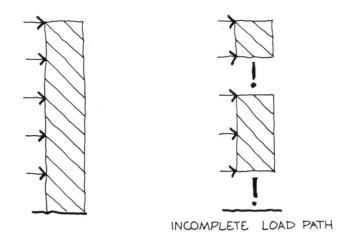

INCOMPLETE LOAD PATH

Fig.10.7

As the wind can blow from any direction the wind load paths must be complete in three dimensions.

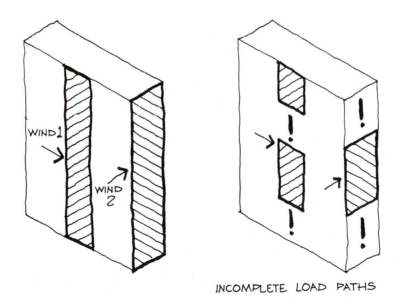

INCOMPLETE LOAD PATHS

Fig.10.8

For wind loads there are also horizontal structural elements which transfer wind loads to the vertical cantilever structure. These may be glazing, walls, floors or roofs acting as structural elements, and again these must act as complete load paths.

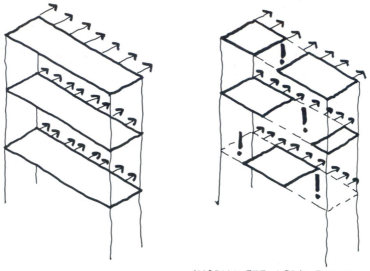

INCOMPLETE LOAD PATHS

Fig.10.9

During the design development of a building or as part of alterations to an existing building, part of a load path may need to be removed.

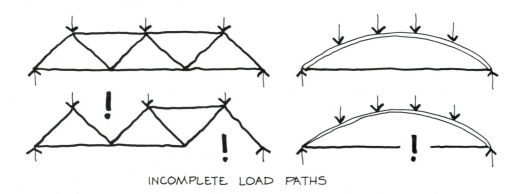

INCOMPLETE LOAD PATHS

Fig.10.10

It is clear for the structures shown in Fig.10.10 which part has been removed but when a structure is part of a building it may be far from clear. For example the St. Pancras station in London has a large curved roof. The structure of this roof is an arch and the horizontal thrust at the spring points is provided by a tie across the building at the level of the platforms. Access may be required through the platforms to the lower level by stairs or ramps and these will cut the tie. It is not obvious without investigation that the platform structure acts as a tie or whether the roof is an arch or a curved beam (Fig.7.73)! If an access is required, then the tie forces must be provided with a new load path in the region of the opening.

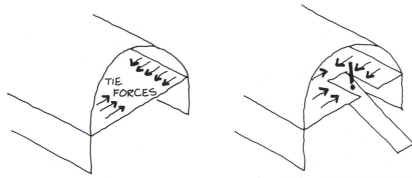

Fig.10.11   LOCALLY INCOMPLETE LOAD PATH

It must be clear to the structural designer that the completeness of **all** load paths is achieved and that non-structural requirements do not interrupt them.

10.3 Load path geometry

The idea of conceptual load paths is to establish a path of structure through a building for every load case, but conceptual load paths give no information about the actual geometry of the load paths. The geometry of the load path will determine the type of structural behaviour of the load path, that is beam, frame, truss or funicular behaviour. The conceptual load path has to act structurally and its geometry gives guidance to its behaviour.

The choice of load path geometry is dependent on many aspects of building design — use, economics, aesthetics, local skills or planning laws are examples. The structural designer must be aware what type of structural behaviour will result from a choice of load path geometry and what effect this will have on the structural details. As there is no correct load path there is no correct load path geometry, just the chosen one. However if the load path geometry is chosen on the basis of a particular type of structural action then alteration to the load path geometry, either locally or globally, will have structural consequences. Problems on particular projects can often be traced to misconceptions of the structural action of a chosen geometry. This can be illustrated by a simple example. Suppose a building is to have, for non-structural reasons, a pitched roof with overhanging eaves.

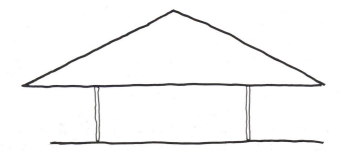

Fig.10.12

For vertical loads, the conceptual load path for the roof is a central span with two side cantilevers. The conceptual structural behaviour is characterised by the bending moment diagram.

LOADING   BENDING MOMENT DIAGRAM

Fig.10.13

Because of the overall form it would seem sensible to choose a load path geometry that gave truss-like structural behaviour — that is use a roof truss.

AXIAL FORCES

Fig.10.14

A truss like structure carries the bending moments and shear forces from the conceptual load path by axial forces, tensile and compressive, in the members of the truss. This leads to choices of structural elements that are suitable for axial forces. If during the design process it is decided, for non-structural reasons, to have a sloping rather than horizontal ceiling line then this will affect the structural geometry.

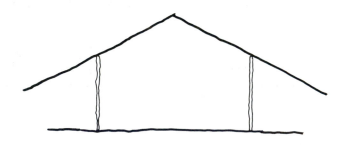

Fig.10.15

The conceptual load path (Fig.10.13) is unaltered but the chosen load path geometry is no longer suitable. A new load path geometry has to be chosen which can act as a beam-like structure.

BENDING MOMENT DIAGRAM

Fig.10.16

Beam-like behaviour needs elements that can resist internal forces that are bending moments and shear forces rather than axial forces. These beam-like elements will have a different geometrical shape to those chosen for the truss. Provided it is realised that this is a change in load path geometry as well as a change in building geometry then it is just part of the design process.

This simple example illustrates how important it is to understand that an alteration in load path geometry, whilst not affecting the efficacy of the conceptual load path, may have a profound effect on the type of structural behaviour.

10.4 Overall structural behaviour

Building structures are always subjected to a number of different loads and these can act in different combinations and in different directions. These loads act vertically and horizontally. The structure must provide load paths for all these loads from the point of application to the reaction from the ground. How these loads are 'chased' has been a recurrent theme of this book first introduced in Section 1.6. For a simple building the various load paths are examined in detail in Chapter 8. The load paths for a number of real structures are given in Chapter 9. The load path for each load case **is** the structure and, depending on the load path geometry, it will have a particular type of structural action.

Essentially there are four types of structural action for spanning members. These are beam-like, truss-like, frame-like and funicular, Chapter 7 explains how these different types act.

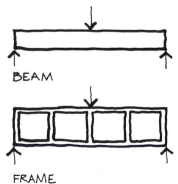 

Fig.10.17   FRAME   FUNICULAR

The structures shown in Fig.10.17 can only be a part of an overall structure as this has to enclose space. To do this a vertical element, a column, must be added.

Fig.10.18

The columns carry the vertical loads for the gravity load case but they must also provide the overall lateral stability and in doing so act as spanning structures themselves (Fig.6.23). This can be done by making the structure a portal frame or by cantilevering the columns from the ground, or both.

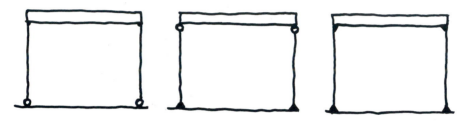

Fig.10.19

These structures enclose space, are stable and can carry vertical and horizontal loads.

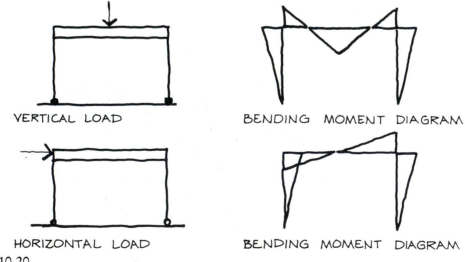

VERTICAL LOAD   BENDING MOMENT DIAGRAM

HORIZONTAL LOAD   BENDING MOMENT DIAGRAM

Fig.10.20

The beam-like spanning structure has become a portal frame. For both vertical and horizontal loads there is a bending moment in the 'column' which means it acts as a spanning structure.

The structural designer, when conceiving a structure has to be aware how the whole structure acts under each load case and how the choice of structural geometry causes the structure to act in different ways. This can be illustrated by briefly examining the structure for a single storey space.

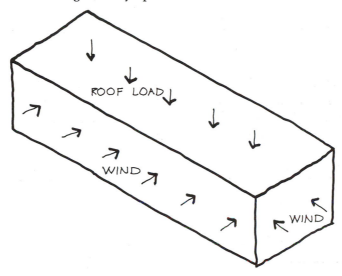

Fig.10.21

The structure will have to carry vertical loads applied to the roof and wind loads which can act in any horizontal direction. As this building is just a flat-roofed version of the building considered in detail in Chapter 8, the structure already chosen (Fig.8.7), would be one choice.

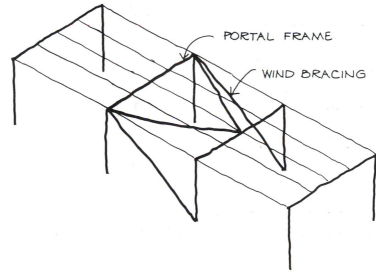

Fig.10.22

But other choices can be made. The roof structure could be a three-dimensional space frame (Fig.7.75B), supported on perimeter columns.

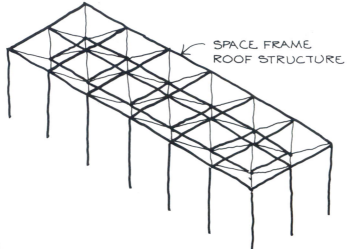

Fig.10.23

The columns, as with the portal frame, have to provide stability against overall collapse and also be part of the load path for horizontal loads.

Fig.10.24

Because the space frame is triangulated in the horizontal plane it can act as a 'wind girder', in any direction.

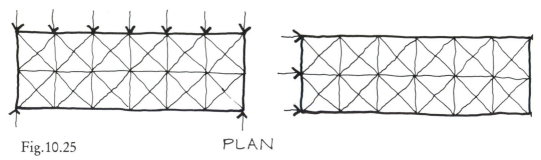

Fig.10.25   PLAN

Some columns could be chosen just to carry vertical loads whilst others, say the corner columns, could also provide stability and carry the horizontal loads.

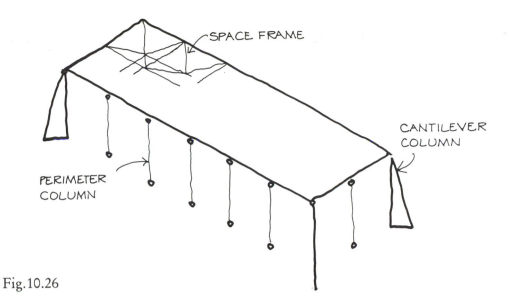

SPACE FRAME

CANTILEVER
COLUMN

PERIMETER
COLUMN

Fig.10.26

The corner columns act as cantilevers from the ground so they are spanning structures.

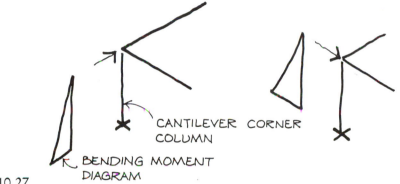

CANTILEVER CORNER
COLUMN

 BENDING MOMENT
DIAGRAM

Fig.10.27

To carry the bending moments in these corner columns, which act in more than one direction, a three-dimensional, truss-like structure could be chosen. The columns that only carry vertical loads could be simple tubular struts.

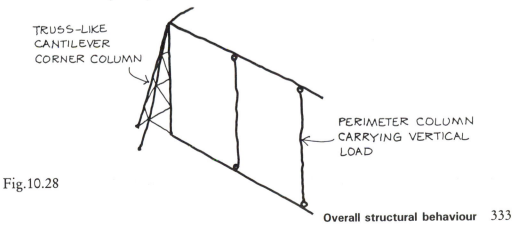

TRUSS-LIKE
CANTILEVER
CORNER COLUMN

PERIMETER COLUMN
CARRYING VERTICAL
LOAD

Fig.10.28

Overall structural behaviour 333

Two quite different structures have been chosen for this simple building and **both are correct** as they have been conceived by using an understanding of the overall structural behaviour.

Many other structures could be chosen to support the enclosure of this simple space. All these structures would be correct provided the choice of geometry was based on an understanding of the overall structural behaviour.

10.5 Choice of materials and elements

In Chapter 5 four basic materials were identified as being suitable for building structures, these were steel, timber, concrete and masonry. The reason that the choice is limited is that the materials have to be cheap. They also have to be durable, easily altered or repaired and to be constantly available. This is because buildings are expected to last a long time, be relatively maintenance free and to be altered without recourse to specialist suppliers or technology. The situation is quite different for non-building structures. For instance aircraft structures are very expensive, have a specific life and are regularly maintained by specialists who have ready access to the latest technology.

Fortunately this lack of choice of suitable materials has not resulted in a lack of variety either in building structures or in the buildings they hold up, after all building structures have rarely been built of anything else. The structural designer has to be aware which material is suitable for any chosen structure. Ideally the structural form and the structural material are conceived simultaneously. As each of the four materials are more suitable for different structural types the material choice is often implicit. Timber and steel are strong compared to their weight so are suitable where tensile forces are large. Where loads are compressive, masonry or mass concrete are suitable. These materials can be used for spanning structures if they are used compositely with a tensile material, steel, or are prestressed (see Section 4.5). Non-structural characteristics such as combustibility or susceptibility to chemical attack may influence choice (see Section 4.5). It is also necessary to know how the material can be joined (see Section 10.6).

With so many caveats the inexperienced designer can feel there are more problems than solutions so some broad guidance is needed. The main guidance is from structures that exist but each time and place favours different solutions. These will depend on material availability and the presence of suitable expertise in the chosen material. Concrete is made by mixing cement, aggregate and clean water so difficulty in obtaining any of these at an affordable price will preclude the use of concrete. The use of reinforced concrete also needs suitable steel reinforcement, expertise and technology to cut and bend the bars and material to make the formwork. These are usually readily available in industrialised areas but will not be available in remote rural areas. The choice will then be between local materials or the cost of transporting non-local materials, technology and expertise.

In the description of the action of structural systems (see Sections 7.2 to 7.5) no mention was made of materials. The chapter on real structures (Chapter 9) describes both structural systems and the use of various structural materials such as stone, wrought iron, reinforced concrete and steel.

As most parts of a structural system are required to span under some load case (see Section 10.4) the structural designer must be aware how the chosen structural material caters for the resulting internal forces. The beam-like, truss-like and frame-like spanning structures all require tensile strength in some part of the structure so masonry or mass concrete cannot be used. Beams and trusses of steel or timber are commonplace.

Fig.10.29

Frames also require tensile strength and simple frames such as portal frames (see pages 49—56) are made from both steel and timber. Multistorey frame (see Fig.9.89) and spanning frames (see Fig.7.50) are often made of steel.

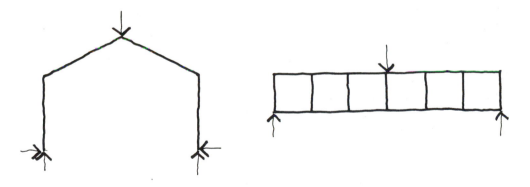

Fig.10.30

There are two types of funicular structures (see Section 7.4), hanging and arching. The hanging funicular structures are in tension so timber or steel are suitable but due to jointing problems timber is rarely used. For arches mass concrete or masonry are very suitable and this form of tension-free, spanning structure was the major form until the end of the eighteenth century.

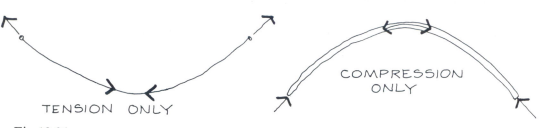

TENSION ONLY

COMPRESSION ONLY

Fig.10.31

Although structural materials are commonly used on their own they are also frequently combined to form composite materials or structures (see Section 4.5). Since the 1920s concrete reinforced with steel rods, usually called **rebar**, has become, together with steel, a widely used structural 'material' for building structures. Although heavy compared with its strength reinforced concrete is used for beams, slabs, frames, shells and even trusses. Great care has to be taken to ensure there is rebar in all areas of tension. This means that the structural designer has to decide the size and position of every bar!

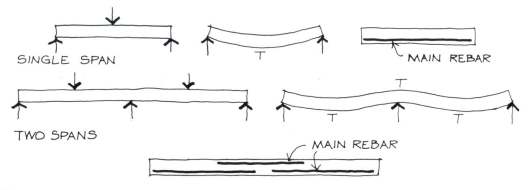

SINGLE SPAN

MAIN REBAR

TWO SPANS

MAIN REBAR

Fig.10.32

An alternative to rebar is **prestress** (see pages 129–133). Here the tensile stress caused by the structural actions are reduced to zero by using internal steel tendons to apply compressive stresses.

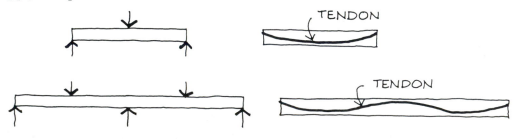

TENDON

TENDON

Fig.10.33

Reinforced and prestressed concrete are often regarded as structural materials but there are other ways of making composite structures. Two examples have already been given, that of steel beams with concrete slabs (see pages 128—129) and the use of reinforced concrete with masonry (see page 133). A further example is the composite behaviour of structural steelwork and concrete used in the Bank of China (see page 309) to form mega reinforced concrete.

Two different materials or two forms of the same material can be combined to form composite elements. A steel plate can be used with timber to form a flitch beam. Timber I or box beams can be made using ordinary timber sections with plywood sheeting.

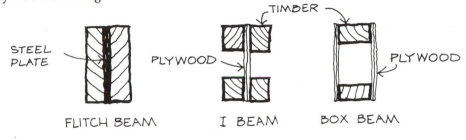

Fig.10.34

There is also a choice for the shape of the structural element. Element's section shape should be stress effective (see pages 86—88), the effect of cross-section shape is explained in Section 4.3. Section shape also has an effect on axial stability (see Section 6.4). Elements can also be shaped over their length (see page 89).

Each of the four, or five if reinforced concrete is classed as a structural material, can be shaped in different ways. Mass and reinforced concrete can be made into almost any shape, limited by the skill of the makers of the formwork and the patience of the designers and the fixers of the rebar.

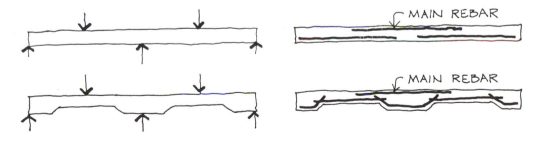

Fig.10.35

In shaping reinforced concrete for structural efficiency the benefit must be available to the client in the form of lower cost — this is often difficult to judge as building costs vary continuously.

Structural steelwork is available in simple bars, rods and plates of different sizes. In industrial areas **standard sections** are available. They are made by rolling hot steel into a variety of cross-sectional shapes — hence **hot rolled sections**. The size and shape may vary by producer or may comply with a national standard. In areas where a national standard applies the choice is easy for the structural designer but where the sections are obtained from various sources the exact size and shape may only be known as construction begins. The usual range of hot rolled sections are angles, channels, I sections, tees, round and square tubes. Sizes vary from 50 to 1000mm.

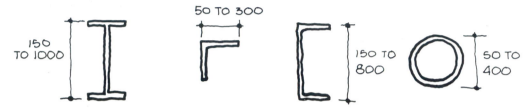

Fig.10.36

With the use of cutting and welding equipment these sections can be altered to form structurally efficient structures. This is commonly done at the knee joint of portal frames.

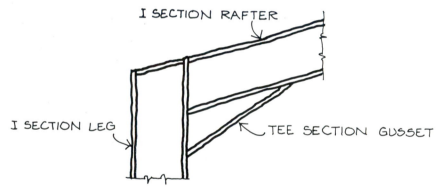

Fig.10.37

Steelwork fabricators cut and weld steel as part of normal operations but, as with complex reinforced concrete structures, the cost of complexity must be outweighed by an overall saving.

Timber is normally cut, converted to use the correct term, into lengths with a rectangular cross section. In some areas the sizes are standard which is an advantage to the structural designer. The structural performance of timber varies greatly with species of which there are two basic types — hardwood and softwood. In the Northern hemisphere structural timber is predominately softwood but in the tropics and the Southern hemisphere structural timber is usually hardwood. Timber sheet materials are also available in many parts of the world as plywood, chipboard and hardboard, and these can be used structurally. Structural timber is most often used as simple beams with a rectangular cross-section or made into simple trusses. These can be on a large scale, for instance timber structures have been used for the construction of airship hangers.

Masonry, in the form of mud dried bricks, is one of the oldest building materials. The strength and size of blocks and bricks varies widely. The strength of masonry, rather than the units themselves, is usually limited by the strength of the mortar in which the bricks or blocks are laid. Sizes of the basic units vary but tend to be standard in an area and this will determine the overall sizes of masonry structures as it is far better to use whole units rather than cut them.

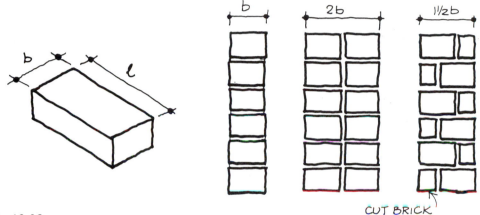

Fig.10.38

The key to a sensible choice for a structural material is local availability and expertise. This often dictates the range of structural forms which can be used economically in any area at a particular time. This requires the structural designer to be aware of the cost and availability of materials before structural decisions are made.

Structural designers sometimes tire of the usual materials and yearn for 'new materials'. The new materials are usually sought from more high-tech industries such as aerospace. Although this pursuit of new materials is clothed in acceptable notions such as progress or innovation often the purpose is to gain attention for the user of the 'new' material. Sometimes these new materials make their appearance in new forms of construction such as tent structures or structural glass facades.

Tent buildings date from pre-history but from the 1970s stressed tents have been promoted by a number of designers. These require durable, strong fabrics which are now available as teflon coated glass fibre. This material is not cheap and has no application in ordinary building.

Another new material is toughened laminated glass used as a structural element in a glass facade. This type of glass, originally developed for the windows of cars and aeroplanes, is now used as 'fins' for strengthening glass only facades.

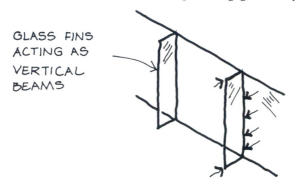

GLASS FINS
ACTING AS
VERTICAL
BEAMS

Fig.10.39

These uses of new materials produce expensive structures for clients who want attention seeking designs. Of course there are proper innovations, new materials and processes. In the past the introduction of iron, steel, welding and prestressing were all innovations that made significant differences to the way building structures were conceived and constructed. At present the choice of structural material for most building structures is still between steel, timber, masonry or concrete, mass or reinforced.

10.6 Element connection

The load path for each load case has to be complete — there can be no gaps (see pages 323—328). It is rare that this can be achieved without having to join parts of the structure together. They may be joints between similar of different structural materials, or they may be joints between major structural elements.

A structure transfers load by internal forces and at points of support the internal forces are balanced by reaction forces.

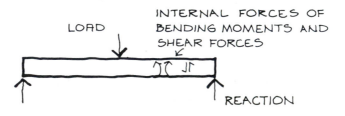

LOAD

INTERNAL FORCES OF
BENDING MOMENTS AND
SHEAR FORCES

REACTION

Fig.10.40

The reactions may balance axial or shear forces or bending moments. For a cantilever beam with vertical and horizontal loads the reactions provide vertical and horizontal forces and a moment reaction.

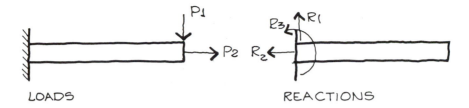

Fig.10.41

Like points of support, joints have to transfer the internal forces to the adjacent part of the structure. Suppose, for the cantilever shown in Fig.10.41, there is a joint in the beam.

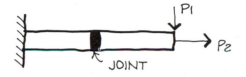

Fig.10.42

At the joint the forces are the same as the forces at the 'cuts' in a beam (see pages 43—46), except now the joint is a cut!

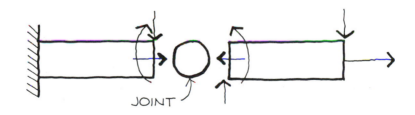

Fig.10.43

The joint in the cantilever beam has to transfer axial and shear forces and a bending moment. For a simple spanning beam, a joint at the end only has to transfer shear forces.

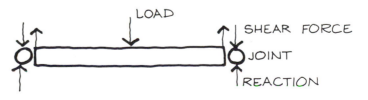

Fig.10.44

Whilst a joint is the connection between two, or more, parts of a structure it is still part of the load path, so calling it a joint is arbitrary from the conceptual point of view. But how the elements are joined together may affect the structural behaviour. For example a two span beam may be continuous over the central support. At this support there is a bending moment as well as shear forces.

LOAD   BENDING MOMENT   SHEAR FORCE
              DIAGRAM   DIAGRAM

Fig.10.45

If a joint is made between the two spans that can only carry shear forces then the structural behaviour will be altered. The structure now acts as two, adjacent, simply supported beams

LOAD   BENDING MOMENT   SHEAR FORCE
              DIAGRAM   DIAGRAM

Fig.10.46

The differences between an arch and a curved beam (Fig.7.73) is dependent on the structural designer's choice of joint at the support points. If the designer chooses joints that can transfer vertical and horizontal forces then the curved structure will act as an arch. If the joints can only transfer vertical forces then it will act as a curved beam.

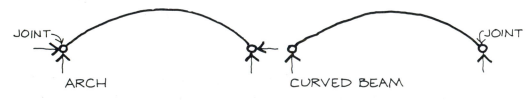

JOINT   JOINT

ARCH   CURVED BEAM

Fig.10.47

To aid the process of using structural concepts structural designers have evolved standard names and symbols for the different types of structural joints. Joints that can transfer all forces are called **fixed** or **encastre** joints, joints that transfer forces but no bending moments are called **pin** joints and joints that only transfer a force in a specific direction are called **sliding** joints. These joints are drawn on structural diagrams in a standard way.

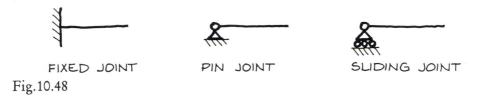

FIXED JOINT   PIN JOINT   SLIDING JOINT

Fig.10.48

This allows structural designers to draw diagrams of structures that make their structural behaviour clear. The familiar simple structures of a cantilever beam and a simply supported beam can now be drawn as **structural diagrams**.

CANTILEVER   SIMPLY SUPPORTED BEAM

Fig.10.49

Using these symbols, the structural diagrams of the curved structure make it obvious which is the arch and which is the curved beam.

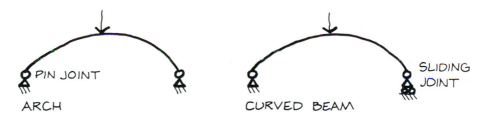

PIN JOINT   SLIDING JOINT

ARCH   CURVED BEAM

Fig.10.50

Choosing the position and types of joints is part of the process of conceiving structures. The structural designer has to introduce joints to allow the transport and erection of the different structural elements. What structural behaviour these joints need is determined by how the structure is expected to behave at the joint positions and the practical considerations of the joint details.

How are the symbolic joints in the structural diagrams to become real joints in real structures? This largely depends on the structural material being used at the joint. Structural masonry is constructed by jointing the individual bricks or blocks to each other by introducing a bed of mortar between them.

Element connection 343

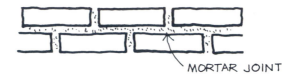

Fig.10.51

MORTAR JOINT

Steel can be joined by welding, by heating the metal at the joint and introducing molten steel the steel is joined so that the material becomes continuous at the joint.

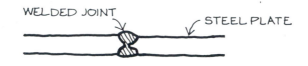

WELDED JOINT   STEEL PLATE

Fig.10.52

Welding is best carried out under workshop conditions so welded joints in steel structures are used to make steelwork elements that are transported to the site.

When reinforced concrete is constructed in its final position, that is built in situ, joints are made simply by casting new concrete around reinforcing bars that have been left projecting from the part to be joined.

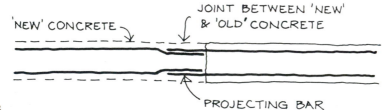

JOINT BETWEEN 'NEW'
'NEW' CONCRETE   & 'OLD' CONCRETE

Fig.10.53

PROJECTING BAR

The ease with which joints can be made in this way is one of the main reasons for the widespread use of reinforced concrete.

As trees grow they form joints, branch to trunk, as part of the growing process. There is currently no way of growing cut pieces of timber into timber structures so it has to be joined by other means.

When different materials are to be joined mechanical fixings have to be used. These are of two basic types — a specific strong object or glue. Examples of specific strong objects are bolts, screws and nails whilst the range of glue types is enormous. Nowadays there is a strong glue which will bond together almost any combination of materials.

344   **Structural conception**

To be able to design joints the structural action must be clear to the designer. Like structures in general, there is no correct joint but a number of choices. There is a load path through a joint and these can often be complex. The choices and load paths is illustrated by considering a joint between two steel I sections that are part of a beam.

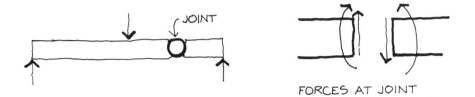

FORCES AT JOINT

Fig.10.54

The forces that are to be transferred through the joint are a shear force and a bending moment. The bending, push/pull forces, are mainly transferred by horizontal tensile and compressive stresses in the flanges (see pages 86—87) and the shear forces by vertical shear stresses in the web (see page 113).

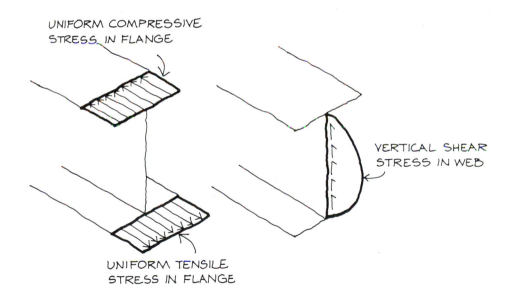

UNIFORM COMPRESSIVE STRESS IN FLANGE

UNIFORM TENSILE STRESS IN FLANGE

VERTICAL SHEAR STRESS IN WEB

Fig.10.55

Conceptually the joint is made by joining the flanges to take the tension and compression and the webs to take the vertical shear.

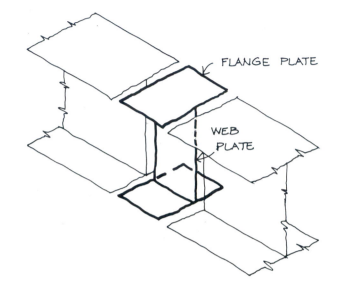

FLANGE PLATE

WEB PLATE

Fig.10.56

One choice would be to weld the whole section together.

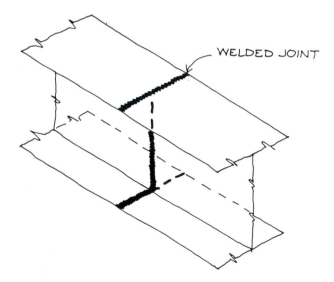

WELDED JOINT

Fig.10.57

For making joints on site bolted connections are usually preferred. For this a number option are available. Loose flange and web plates can be used to 'splice' the beams together.

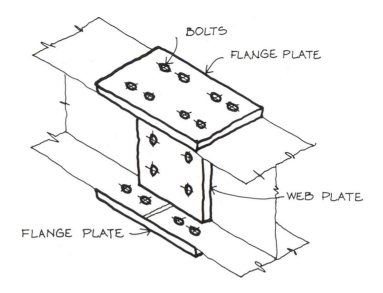

Fig.10.58

As a example of a joint load path consider the bottom flange plate. The tensile load in the flanges are transferred to the flange plates by shear forces in the shafts of the bolts.

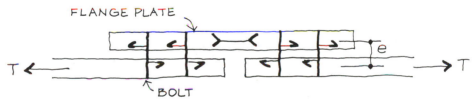

Fig.10.59

There is an eccentricity in the load path which may cause some local bending in the plate.

Fig.10.60

The uniform tensile stress in the flange is transferred into the flange plate at the specific positions of the bolts.

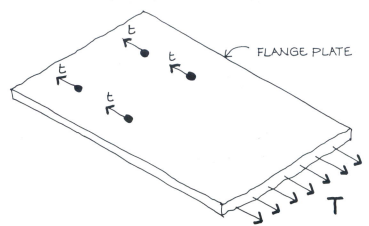

Fig.10.61

For horizontal equilibrium $4t = T$, but at the bolt positions the tensile stress is altered from a uniform distribution to a non-uniform stress distribution.

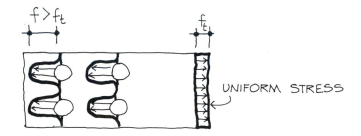

Fig.10.62

As the area near the bolts is smaller than the whole flange the stresses are higher than the uniform stress. There is a maximum allowable stress for the steel (see pages 87—89) and the high stresses concentrated at the bolts must not exceed this. This indicates that it is better to make the joint in a part of the beam where the stresses are less than maximum.

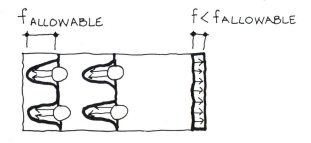

Fig.10.63

A similar joint could be made by welding the plates to one of the beams in the fabrication shop and bolting them to the other beam on site.

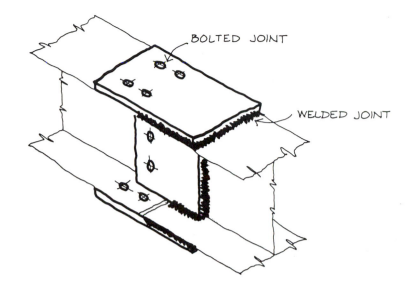

Fig.10.64

Another type of bolted joint can be made by welding plates across the ends of both beams then bolting the plates face to face on site.

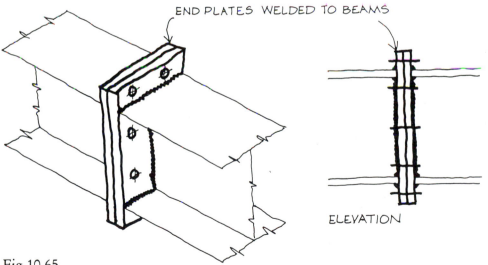

Fig.10.65

For this joint the load path is quite different to the load path in the plated joint. In this joint the load transfer causes bending moments in the end plates and the bolts carry shear and tension.

There are many 'standard' ways of joining elements and these are given in technical guides. The positioning and behaviour of joints in structures can affect the overall behaviour of the structure so the structural designer should consider them as part of the structural concept rather than an additional requirement.

10.7 Structures and building construction

The structure of a building, whilst fulfilling the specific role of giving strength and stiffness to the building enclosure, is not physically a separate part of the building construction. The structural elements form part of building elements and the structural designer needs to know how 'the structure' will relate physically to the other elements, often designed by other members of the design team. During the design process the structural designer often has to modify the structural design to accommodate design developments carried out by other members of the design team.

Any object that is hard is subjected to gravity forces which cause internal forces in the object. In this sense all parts of the building are structures but the structural designer is usually concerned with the **primary** structure. This is a rather nebulous concept as all the load paths have to be complete from the point of load application. For instance when the wind blows on a building causing wind loads these are often applied to the window panes. Except for unusually large panes the structural designer is not concerned with the pane as a structure. What constitutes the primary structure usually becomes clear during the design process.

Sometimes parts of the structure fulfil a dual purpose, as part of the enclosure and part of the primary structure. This is particularly true for masonry walls which are part of the enclosure as well as acting as part of the primary vertical load path. This can cause difficulties as more than one member of the design team may be concerned with their design and each member may not be aware of the dual role. For example the inner leaf of a cavity wall may carry floor loads and thus require a specific strength. Other members of the design team are concerned with the thermal insulation that the inner leaf provides. To obtain the required thermal insulation the strength may be reduced. Or in domestic buildings some internal walls may be loadbearing whilst others are only space enclosing elements. As the construction may be similar for both walls this can lead to confusion.

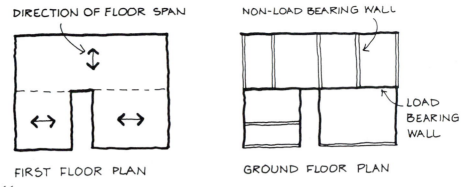

Fig. 10.66

Even with specific structural elements such as reinforced concrete columns in an office building, the building construction can influence their shape and position. This is specially true for the columns that support the floor perimeter.

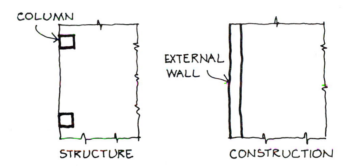

Fig. 10.67

There are various options, not always chosen by the structural designer. The columns can relate to the external enclosure in a number of ways.

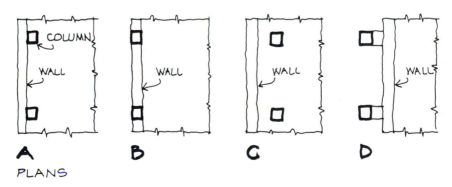

Fig. 10.68

In A the columns are positioned just inside the external wall which means the inner face is not flush. This will affect the layout of furniture, loose or built-in. In B the columns are within the wall and the wall may need extra width to accommodate the column.

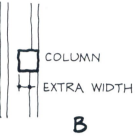

Fig.10.69

To reduce this width the column size needs to be the minimum possible which may make the column slender (see pages 192–193).

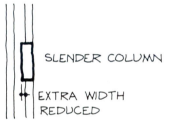

Fig.10.70

In C the columns are placed within the building which means that the floor has to cantilever past the columns thus locally altering the structural behaviour.

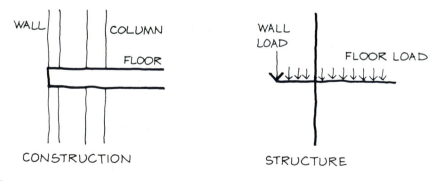

Fig.10.71

In D the column is placed outside the building so it has to be connected to the floor it is supporting by a beam that penetrates the external wall.

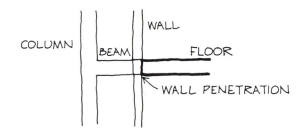

Fig.10.72

This beam needs a 'hole' in the wall which is a potential source of rain penetration. To combat this, complicated waterproofing details have to be devised and built correctly. The beam can also create a 'cold bridge' conducting heat from the building or cold into the building. This can cause local condensation with consequent deterioration of materials. As with structural design in general there is no correct position for the column and many buildings have been constructed with columns in all the positions shown in Fig.10.68.

Another aspect of building construction that frequently affects the structure is the installation of environmental services. These range from small wires for telecommunications to large ducts for air handling and all these will need openings somewhere in the primary structure. Many services are run at ceiling level.

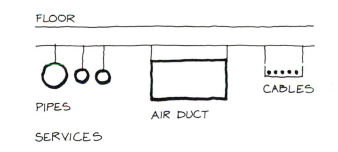

Fig.10.73

These services are often concealed from the general building user by installing a suspended ceiling below the services.

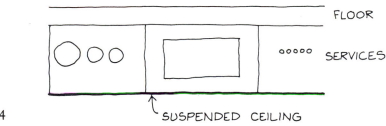

Fig.10.74

These diagrams appear simple but services run in all directions. If there are downstand beams or trusses for large spans, the services may have to run through them to keep the construction depth to a minimum.

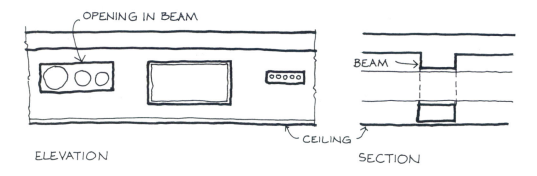

ELEVATION

SECTION

Fig.10.75

Depending on the size and position of these openings the beam may turn into a frame (see Fig.7.64)! Where trusses are used the diagonals may need to be removed locally which affects the structural behaviour (see Fig.7.64 again).

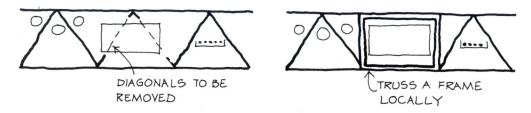

DIAGONALS TO BE REMOVED

TRUSS A FRAME LOCALLY

Fig.10.76

Often ducts for small pipes have to run in reinforced concrete floors to supply perimeter radiators.

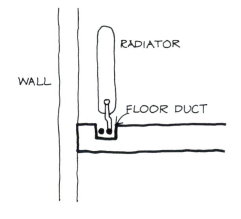

Fig.10.77

These ducts cause considerable complexity for the reinforcement as well as weakening the structure locally.

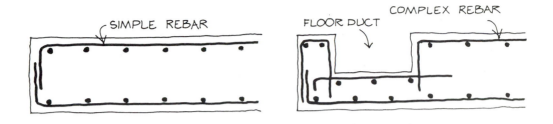

Fig.10.78

With these local alterations to the primary structure the structural designer must ensure that the conceptual load paths are complete and the structure at the positions of the local alterations are still strong enough to transfer the internal forces.

These examples show how the designer of building structures needs a knowledge of building construction to anticipate the relationship of the primary structure to the whole construction and to be able to discuss this relationship with other members of the design team. This knowledge is not easy to acquire, especially as the structural designer rarely designs the building construction. The successful designer sees the primary structure as part of the whole design and expects that the design process will require alteration to the initial structural design. These alterations will often be made by members of the design team who do not understand the structural concepts so will be unaware of their effect. Local alterations can usually be made with some added local complexity but if an alteration in structural concept is required then it has to be made and its consequences accepted. Because of the inevitable alterations needed during the design process it is unwise to size the structural elements so tightly that small alterations cause major structural problems. This is not being uneconomic — just sensible.

FURTHER READING

There is a vast literature on structural engineering that fills whole specialist libraries. The majority of these books deal with technical aspects involving mathematical idealisations and numerical calculations. Most of the books and articles listed below are descriptive rather than technical and should be accessible to readers of this book. The more general introductory books apply equally to the first three chapters. Because of the more advanced nature of the topics dealt with in chapter 4 and 6 there are no introductory texts - the texts listed are technically difficult!

CHAPTER 1 *Loads and load paths*
CHAPTER 2 *Internal forces*
CHAPTER 3 *Structural element behaviour*

AJ MacDonald - **Structure & architecture** - Butterworth 1994
BN Sandaker & AP Eggen - **The structural basis of architecture** - Phaidon 1993
M Salvadori etc. - **Why buildings fall down** - Norton 1992
AJ Francis - **Introducing structures** - Macmillan 1994
JB Gauld - **Structures for architects** - Longman 1995
JE Gordon - **Structures or why things don't fall down** - Penguin 1978
M Salvadori - **Why buildings stand up** - WW Norton 1980 - ISBN 0 393 30676 3
HS Howard - **Structure an architect's approach** - McGraw Hill 1966 (out of print)

CHAPTER 4 *More advanced concepts of stress*

J Heyman - **Elements of stress analysis** - OUP 1982 - ISBN 0 521 245230
JT Oden - **Mechanics of elastic structures** - McGraw-Hill 1967 (out of print)
D Johnson - **Advanced structural mechanics** - Collins 1986 - ISBN 0-00-383165-5

CHAPTER 5 *Structural materials*

JE Gordon - **The science of strong materials** - Penguin 1968
G Weidmann et al - **Structural materials** - Open University 1990 - ISBN 0 7506 1901 5
J Atkinson - **The mechanics of soils and foundations** - McGraw-Hill 1993 - ISBN 0-07-707713-X

CHAPTER 6 *Safe structures and failure*

CIRA - **Rationalisation of safety and serviceability factors in structural codes** - CIRA report 63 - Jul77

PA Kirby & DA Nethercote - **Design for structural stability** -Granada 1979 - ISBN 0 258 970634
G Ballio & FW Mazzolani - **Theory & design of steel structures** - Chapman Hall 1983 - ISBN 0 412 23660 5
RM Francis - **Quebec bridge** - Conf. Canad. Soc. Civil Eng. Vol II p655-677 1981

CHAPTER 7 *Structural geometry and behaviour*

RJ Mainstone - **Development of structural form** - Penguin 1975 - ISBN 0 14 00 65032 (out of print)
E Torraja - **Philosophy of structures** - Univ. of California Press 1958 (out of print)

CHAPTER 8 *Behaviour of a simple building*

LJ Morris & DR Plum - **Structural steelwork design (Chapter 12)** - Longman 1988 -ISBN 0-582-023357-2

CHAPTER 9 *Real structures*

G Cook - **Portrait of Durham cathedral** - Phoenix House 1948 (out of print)
J Fitchen - **The construction of Gothic cathedrals** - Univ. of Chicago Press 1961 - ISBN 0 226 252203 06102-3
S Minter - **The greatest glass house** - HMSO 1990 - ISBN 0 11 250035 8
JL Guthrie et al - **Restoration of the Palm House** - Proc. ICE Dec88 p1145-1191
E Diestelkamp - **The design & building of the Palm House** - Jnl. of Garden History No. 3 1982 p233-272
E Torroja - **The structures of Eduardo Torroja** - Dodge Corp 1958 (out of print)
N Esquillan - **Shell vault of the exposition palace Paris** - Jnl. of Struct. Div. ASCE Jan60
Structure of the Federal Reserve Bank - Architectural Record Oct 1971 p106-109
LE Robertson et al - **Structural Systems for the Bank of China** - Proceedings of the Fourth Conference on Tall Buildings - Vol 1 - 1988

CHAPTER 10 *Structural conception*

W Addis - **The art of the structural engineer** - Artemis 1994
A Holgate - **The art of structural design** - OUP - ISBN 0 19 356 177 6
D Billington - **The tower and the bridge** - Princeton 1983 - ISBN 0 691 02393 x (out of print)
A Hodgkinson - **AJ handbook of building structure** - Architectural Press 1974 - (out of print)
S Brand - **How buildings learn** - Viking 1994 - ISBN 0 670 83515 3
A Orton - **The way we build now** - Chapman Hall 1988 - ISBN 0 419 15780 8